VALUE
BASED
MANAGEMENT

Financial Management Association Survey and Synthesis Series

The Search for Value: Measuring the Company's Cost of Capital
Michael C. Ehrhardt

Lease or Buy? Principles for Sound Decision Making
James S. Schallheim

Derivatives: A Comprehensive Resource for Options, Futures, Interest Rate Swaps, and Mortgage Securities
Fred D. Arditti

Managing Pension Plans: A Comprehensive Guide to Improving Plan Performance
Dennis E. Logue and Jack S. Rader

Efficient Asset Management: A Practical Guide to Stock Portfolio Optimization and Asset Allocation
Richard O. Michaud

Real Options: Managing Strategic Investment in an Uncertain World
Martha Amram and Nalin Kulatilaka

Beyond Greed and Fear: Understanding Behavioral Finance and the Psychology of Investing
Hersh Shefrin

Dividend Policy: Its Impact on Firm Value
Ronald C. Lease, Kose John, Avner Kalay, Uri Loewenstein, and Oded H. Sarig

Value Based Management: The Corporate Response to the Shareholder Revolution
John D. Martin and J. William Petty

VALUE BASED MANAGEMENT

The Corporate Response to the Shareholder Revolution

John D. Martin
J. William Petty

Harvard Business School Press
Boston, Massachusetts

Library of Congress Cataloging-in-Publication Data

Martin, John D., 1945–
    Value based management : the corporate response to the shareholder
revolution / John D. Martin, J. William Petty.
        p. cm.—(Financial Management Association survey and synthesis
series)
    Includes bibliographical references and index.
    ISBN 1-57851-800-1 (alk. paper)
        1. Value analysis (Cost control) 2. Industrial management. I. Petty,
J. William, 1942–   II. Title. III. Series

    HD47.3.M37 2000
    658--dc21   00-031910

The paper used in this publication meets the requirements of the American
National Standard for Permanence of Paper for Publications and Documents
in Libraries and Archives Z39.48-1992.

Text design by Wilson Graphics & Design (Kenneth J. Wilson)

Dedication

As we contemplated the dedication of this book, we considered a number of possibilities. Frequently, authors dedicate their work to family members, which is easily justified given how important they are to us. However, in the process of our investigation of value based management, we came to know and admire a number of executives and managers who have suffered through the pains of adopting, implementing, and managing value based management systems. For us, these individuals are unrecognized heroes. They are after all making a meaningful difference in the lives of individual investors who place their financial future in the hands of these managers. So here's to the men and women whose efforts in implementing value based management programs have created wealth for untold millions of investors—which we confess includes our own 401(k) retirement plans.

Contents

Preface

The Financial Management Association in conjunction with the Harvard Business School Press cosponsors the publication of the Survey and Synthesis Series in an effort to bridge the gap between financial research and the practice of finance. The subject of this book is value based management (VBM), which is the generic term for a set of management tools used to facilitate managing a firm's operations in a way that enhances shareholder value. VBM is a relatively recent innovation in financial practice that has only recently begun affecting financial research. The purpose of this book is to provide a survey of the tools and practices of VBM in a way that will be useful to academics and business practitioners alike.

In a sense VBM is itself a synthesis of multiple business disciplines and subjects. From finance VBM has adopted the goal of shareholder value creation along with the acceptance of the discounted cash flow valuation paradigm. From business strategy VBM has accepted the notion that value creation is a result of investing in market niches or opportunities where the firm has some comparative advantage over current and potential competitors. From accounting VBM has adopted the basic structure of the firm's accounting statements and modified them for its own purposes. And finally, from organizational behavior VBM has adopted the notion that "what you measure and reward gets done." Thus, the VBM system constitutes a measurement and reward system designed to encourage employees to focus their activities on the creation of shareholder value.

The development of VBM actually hinges upon some fundamental principles that have long been a part of the world of academic finance. First, VBM adopts as a given that value creation depends on discounted cash flow valuation concepts. Second, VBM is built upon the belief that a firm's actions are of great interest to the investing public. Thus, the manager should assume the perspective of the firm's investors when deciding how best to run the business.

Business practice has evolved along two avenues. Capital budgeting practice adopted the notion of discounted future cash flow valuation. However, performance evaluation of ongoing operations for most firms continues to be based on annual accounting measures such as earnings and earnings growth. The inconsistency between these performance measures and shareholder value creation has long been recognized, but applying forward-looking valuation approaches presents some very difficult problems. VBM systems purport to resolve these problems and have gained widespread following, for instance, a special issue of *Fortune* magazine every year ranks the greatest U.S. wealth creators, and the *Wall Street Journal* provides rankings based on total shareholder returns.

Three principal methods are being used in value based management, corresponding for the most part to the particular managerial consulting firm that serves as its proponent:

1. The free cash flow method as proposed in one form or another by such firms as McKinsey & Co. and LEK/Alcar

2. The economic value added/market value added (EVA/MVA) method espoused by Stern Stewart & Co.

3. The cash flow return on investment (CFROI) approach used by the Boston Consulting Group and HOLT Value Associates

Although frequently promoted as new developments, all three of these techniques rely on the basic theory that underlies the use of traditional discounted cash flow methods for evaluating new investment opportunities. This is not to say that VBM does not bring something new—and needed—to the table. VBM is a way to assess the success or failure of *ongoing operations;* that is, it provides management with a method for evaluating the performance of the firm's existing assets or assets-in-place, using the same standard that is used to evaluate new asset acquisitions (i.e., the anticipated contribution to share value). This distinction is important because up to 40 percent of a firm's assets are not subjected to any discounted cash flow evaluation before being acquired. Consequently, managers of these assets have never been held accountable in terms of value creation or lack of it. In addition, VBM provides a structure for connecting performance with compensation— a matter of primary importance if we want managers to have the incentive to act in the shareholders' interest.

The growing interest in VBM can be largely attributed to the rising prominence of shareholder interests in the management and control of U.S. corporations. This increasing concern for shareholder interests can be directly traced to the dramatic rise in institutional share holdings of U.S. corporations over the last two decades. The increase in ownership concentration of common shares in the hands of institutional investors has set the stage for increasing pressure on corporate management to focus on shareholder concerns. Thus, this book and others like it arise out of the need for managers of all firms—large or small, public or private—to be better prepared to respond to the growing pressure they face to create shareholder value.

Recognition of the need for a Survey and Synthesis book on VBM also ensued from our work in an extensive benchmarking study on shareholder value based management. In that study, we had the opportunity to interact with a number of firms that actively manage for shareholder value. There we observed that firms sponsoring the research had an intensive desire to become effective at managing for shareholder value but were struggling with how best to do it. A final catalyst for the book came from corporate recruiters, especially consulting firms that seek graduates who are familiar with VBM.

We divide the book into three parts, beginning with a discussion of the imperative for change that has produced the VBM revolution. Part II surveys the tools of VBM and includes a chapter that reviews incentive compensation systems that constitute a critical element of any VBM system. Part III takes a critical look at the theoretical and empirical underpinnings of VBM. Our objective there is to provide a summary of what is known or not known about the use of VBM and its effect on the creation of shareholder wealth. We also discuss the lessons learned by a wide variety of VBM adopters, which provide invaluable guidelines to potential VBM adopters based on the successes and failures experienced by others.

Acknowledgments

We want to express our sincere appreciation to the many individuals whose encouragement and cooperation were essential to the completion of this book. Their willingness to be open and helpful speaks to their conviction that managing for shareholder value should be a matter of primary importance to every company. Specifically, we thank the following executives:

James Breen and Judith V. Whipple, Briggs & Stratton Corporation
Steven L. Werkheiser, Northrop Grumman Corporation
Terry Pardue, Procter & Gamble Company
Don Macleod, National Semiconductor Corporation
Matthew J. Devine and Denis J. Voisard, CSX Transportation
James C. Benjamin, Harnischfeger Industries, Inc.
Bob Dettmer, PepsiCo, Inc.

H. Virgil Stephens, Eastman Chemical Company
Phil Goulding, Shell Oil Corporation

In addition, we were very fortunate to receive the guidance of a number of value based management consultants, including John McCormack (Stern Stewart & Co.), Steve O'Byrne (Shareholder Value Advisors), and Rawley Thomas (Boston Consulting Group).

We also acknowledge the work of the American Productivity and Quality Center (APQC) who sponsored a benchmarking study on *value based management*. As participants in this study, this experience served to stimulate our interest in this intriguing and truly significant subject area. Specifically, we acknowledge the help of Michelle Hurd, Peggy Newton, and Pegi Panfely at the APQC International Benchmarking Clearinghouse. Also, associated with the APQC benchmarking study we acknowledge the sponsoring companies, which included Bell Canada, Chevron Corporation, ENI SPA, KPMG Peat Marwick LLP, Lagoven S.A., Northrop Grumman Corporation, Petro Canada, and Weyerhaeuser Company.

We also express our appreciation to the individuals who worked with us in the editorial and production process. At the Harvard Business School Press, we thank Kirsten Sandberg, whose advice and counsel and a lot of persistence helped bring this book to fruition. (We only hope she never tells why we lost the manuscript in the DFW airport.) Also, we thank Lindsay Whitman and Erin Beth Korey for their frequent assistance in keeping the process moving forward and making those "little" things happen that otherwise become "big" things. And finally, to Nancy Benjamin and Carol Keller at Books By Design, Inc., we say thank you for all your hard work at getting the book through production and keeping us on schedule, which was no easy task—and you did it with class.

VALUE
BASED
MANAGEMENT

PART *I*

INTRODUCTION TO VALUE *B*ASED *M*ANAGEMENT AND THE *I*MPERATIVE FOR *C*HANGE

The last two decades of the twentieth century witnessed dramatic change in the way that corporations are being run. The source of that change has been the resurgence of shareholder power and the consequent refocusing of managerial energy on creating shareholder value. While many may decry the "greediness" of this, few are anxious to give up the tremendous increases they have experienced in the value of their pension plan assets.

In Part I we describe the nature and origins of value based management (VBM). In addition, we review the accounting-based system that relied on earnings and revenues as the principal value drivers and that is being replaced by the new VBM metrics.

Chapter 1

What Is Value Based Management?

> Every individual endeavors to employ his capital so that its produce may be of greatest value. He generally neither intends to promote the public interest, nor knows how much he is promoting it. He intends only his own security, only his own gain. And he is in this led by an invisible hand to promote an end, which has no part of his intention. By pursuing his own interest he frequently promotes that of society more effectually than when he really intends to promote it.
>
> **—Adam Smith,** *The Wealth of Nations* **(1776)**

Why do individuals buy common stock? Danny DeVito, playing the role of Larry the Liquidator in the movie *Other People's Money*, put it this way when he addressed the annual shareholders meeting of the New England Wire and Cable Co.: "Lest we forget, the reason you became a stockholder in the first place was to make money." Thus, to a stockholder an investment is successful when the value of the investor's funds grows.

Managers create shareholder value by identifying and undertaking investments that earn returns greater than the firm's cost of raising money. When they do this, there is an added benefit to society. Competition among firms for funds to finance their investments attracts capital to the best projects, and the entire economy benefits. This is Adam Smith's invisible hand at work in the capital markets. Resources get directed to their most productive use. In this way, the productivity of those resources is optimized, which results in more goods, services, and jobs. The key insight behind Smith's notion of an invisible hand is captured in the opening quotation from his *Wealth of Nations* treatise: In seeking private gain the individual investor produces the maximum public good.

The notion that a firm's management should make decisions that lead to increased shareholder value is far from controversial. After all, the common shareholders do "own" the firm. In fact, it is not uncommon to see corporate mission statements that endorse shareholder value maximization as the firm's primary goal. For example, the 1995 annual report of the Olin Corporation states, "The primary goal of any company is to manage its operations to create long-term value for shareholders and employees alike." Unfortunately, the goals of a firm's management are not always aligned with those of the firm's stockholders. As a consequence, many (perhaps even most) large corporations are not run on a day-to-day basis so as to maximize shareholder wealth.[1] In fact, many proceed to diminish shareholder value year after year.

Table 1.1 lists the top five and the bottom five shareholder wealth creators among the 1,000 largest U.S. corporations as of year-end 1998. The ranking is based on market value added (MVA), which was devised by Stern Stewart & Co. to measure how much wealth a firm has created at a particular moment in time.[2] MVA is equal to the difference between the market value of a firm (debt plus equity) and the amount of capital that has been invested in the firm. For example, in 1998 investors had invested roughly $11 billion in the assets of top-ranked Microsoft, and the market value of this investment at the end of 1998 was over $328 billion. On the other end of the spectrum, investors had invested over $85 billion in General Motors, and this investment was worth nearly $18 billion less at the end of 1998. Table 1.1 also provides information concerning the rates of return earned on each firm's invested capital as well as the market's assessment of the firm's cost of capital. These two pieces of information highlight a fundamental paradigm of value based management, that is, firms that earn higher rates of return than their capital costs create shareholder wealth but those that fail this simple test destroy it.

How is it that some firms can create so much value for their shareholders while others do not?[3] Value creation, very simply, results from the marriage of opportunity and execution. Opportunities must be recognized and in some cases created, and this is the stuff of which

Table 1.1 Top Five and Bottom Five Creators of Shareholder Wealth Among U.S. Companies, 1998 ($ millions)

Company	Market Value Added (MVA)	Invested Capital	Return on Invested Capital (%)	Cost of Capital (WACC) (%)
Top Five Wealth Creators				
Microsoft	$328,257	$10,954	56.16	12.64
General Electric	285,320	65,298	19.29	11.92
Intel	166,902	23,626	35.44	12.92
Wal-Mart Stores	159,444	36,188	13.24	9.82
Coca-Cola	157,536	13,311	31.22	11.24
Bottom Five Wealth Creators				
Union Pacific	(5,286)	30,191	2.42	7.26
Loews Corporation	(11,425)	22,486	2.13	9.94
Nabisco	(12,171)	35,041	3.42	7.52
CNA Financial Corporation	(12,948)	20,349	−0.28	10.24
General Motors	(17,943)	85,173	1.99	9.36

Source: Stern Stewart & Co., 1999.

business strategy is made. However, opportunity is not enough. Firms must have employees who are ready, willing, and able to take advantage of business opportunities, and it is this side of the value creation equation upon which this book focuses. Specifically, how can we design a system of incentives that will encourage employees to think and act like business owners?

Financial economists beginning with Berle and Means (1932) have addressed the fundamental problems that arise where ownership and control of the modern corporation are separated. When a firm's owners (stockholders) are different from its management, an agency problem arises. Fundamentally, managers control the firm and can make decisions that benefit themselves at the expense of the firm's stockholders. The various proponents of value based management (VBM) systems think they have the answer to this problem. They propose that the contributions of individuals and groups toward the creation of shareholder value be measured using their proprietary performance measures and that rewards be structured accordingly.[4]

Figure 1.1 Constructing a Sustainable Cycle of Value Creation

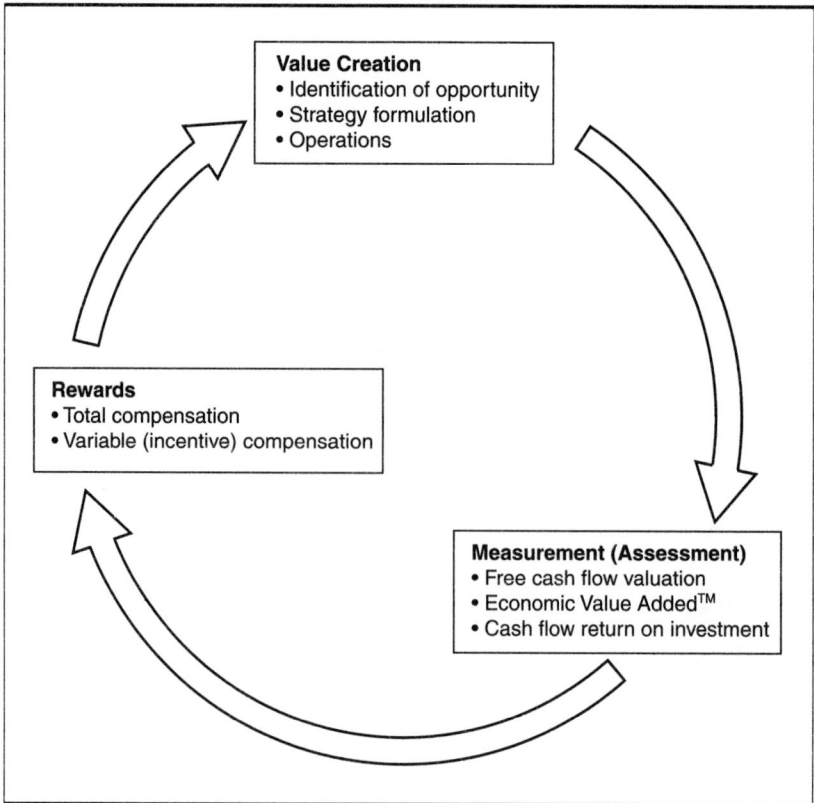

Figure 1.1 captures the key elements of a VBM system designed to build and support a sustainable cycle of value creation. We emphasize the notion of sustainability because value is created over time as a result of a continuing cycle of strategic and operating decisions. The fundamental premise upon which VBM systems are based is that to sustain the wealth creation process, managerial performance must be measured and rewarded using metrics that can be linked directly to the creation of shareholder value. Thus, the marriage of value based performance metrics and incentive compensation is the very heart of the VBM programs we review in this book.

A key consideration in VBM is that the measurement and reward system be *capital market focused*. That is, the key to successfully transforming an employee who thinks like an employee into an employee who thinks like an owner is to measure and reward the employee using methods that parallel the rewards earned by owners. This requires that the firm's internal measurement and reward system mirror the external (capital market) system as closely as possible. Designing and implementing such a system is the challenge of VBM.

Alternative Valuation Paradigms: Accounting Model versus Discounted Cash Flow

Two competing paradigms have been used to measure the creation of shareholder value: the accounting model and the discounted cash flow model. Table 1.2 captures the essential elements of both. Although both these models can in theory be used in a consistent manner, they generally are not. If management uses the accounting model to think about the value of its equity, then it will focus on reported earnings in conjunction with the market's valuation of those earnings as reflected in the price/earnings ratio. For example, if the price/earnings ratio is 20, then a one-dollar increase in earnings per share will create $20 in additional equity value per share. Similarly, a one-dollar loss in earnings per share will lead to a drop of $20 in share value. To see what's wrong with this assessment of equity value, consider the following scenario. The firm sacrifices one dollar in current period earnings per share by investing in R&D that is expected to create valuable investment opportunities for the firm in the future. In this circumstance, investors may not penalize the firm's share price and may even drive it to a higher level following the announced investment in R&D—despite the lower earnings per share.[5]

The discounted cash flow model of equity value incorporates investor expectations of future cash flows into the indefinite future as well as the opportunity cost of funds when determining the value of

Table 1.2 Competing Models of Equity Valuation

	Accounting (Earnings) Model	Discounted Cash Flow Model
Equity value	Price/earnings ratio × Earnings per share	Present value of future cash flows
Value drivers	Determinants of accounting earnings and the price/earnings ratio	Determinants of firm future cash flows and the opportunity cost of capital

the firm's equity. In this model, the R&D investment in the previous example would lead to a reduction in cash flow during the periods in which the investment is being made, but would correspondingly increase future cash flows when the anticipated rewards of the investment are being reaped.

New capital investment or capital budgeting analyses in virtually all firms are now based upon a discounted cash flow model, which is consistent with the basic notion that a firm's stock value at any moment in time is equal to the discounted value of expected future cash flows accruing to the shareholders. However, these same firms often use earnings as the primary value driver to evaluate the performance of the capital that is already in place within the firm. The problem with using earnings in this case, as we have just seen, relates to the fact that maximizing earnings and earnings growth does not necessarily maximize share value, because share value reflects the present value of all future cash flows (not just current earnings). VBM models seek to redress this problem by using performance metrics that are based on discounted future cash flows.

Connecting Business Strategies with the Creation of Shareholder Wealth

How can we know whether a strategy will create shareholder value? In an uncertain world the answer to this question can only be known after the strategy has been implemented and run its course. However, the manager of operations must assess the success or failure of the strategy at finite intervals along the way so that those responsible can be rewarded for their success or punished for their shortcomings. The typical metrics used to measure a firm's periodic performance are based on historical accounting information that is readily available. Examples include firm earnings, earnings growth, or financial ratios such as the firm's profit margin or return on invested capital. These are almost always single-period accounting-based measures of performance that suffer from two important limitations. First, since these performance measures are based solely on one historical period of operations, there is no reason to believe that they are good indicators of value to be created over the entire life of the venture. Second, accounting information systems do not incorporate an opportunity cost of the owner's capital. VBM systems attempt to overcome both of these limitations.

The Tools of VBM

Although the tools of VBM go by a number of names, three principal subgroups of methods are in use: (1) the free cash flow method as proposed in one form or another by McKinsey & Co. and LEK/Alcar;[6] (2) the economic value added/market value added (EVA/MVA) method espoused by Stern Stewart & Co.; and (3) the cash flow return on investment/total shareholder return (CFROI/TSR) method used by the Boston Consulting Group.[7] In subsequent chapters we develop each method in detail and discuss their similarities and differences.

What Makes a VBM Program Successful?

We believe that three primary elements are essential to the success of a VBM program. First, the VBM program must have the full and complete support of the top executives of the company. Very simply, successful VBM systems are top-down directives that, in many cases, completely transform the operating culture of the firm. Although the impetus for the adoption of the VBM system may have come from a planning group, financial officer, or someone else in the firm's corporate hierarchy, it is essential that the program gain support from the CEO if it is to have a reasonable chance of success. Second, for the VBM program to affect individual managers' behavior there must be some link between behavior and compensation. This is a straightforward restatement of the old adage, "What gets measured and rewarded, gets done." Finally, employees must understand the VBM system if it is to be effective in transforming behavior. This frequently means that simplicity is preferred to finely tuned measurement.[8] VBM systems work best where the firm's employees understand and accept the basic premise of the VBM system so that they are able to implement it in their day-to-day work. Thus, education and training are absolutely essential to the success of any VBM program. VBM is about transforming behavior, and for any VBM program to be successful it is essential that employees understand what they are being asked to do, why it is important, and how their own personal well-being will be affected.

Origins and Objectives of This Book

This book arose from the collective teaching and research of the authors applying the fundamental principles of business valuation to the management of the business enterprise over a quarter of a century.

It was also inspired by the results of a study carried out by the International Benchmarking Clearinghouse of the American Productivity and Quality Center (APQC) in 1996 in which the authors were co-researchers.[9] This study was a large-scale research effort designed to document the practices of a broad sample of firms that had successfully implemented a VBM system. Thus, the objectives of this book are twofold: first, to synthesize the competing VBM models, and second, to report the lessons learned by several companies that have implemented VBM programs.

The book is organized into three parts. Part I discusses the growing role of institutional investors in influencing corporations to manage their affairs in such a way as to maximize shareholder interests. Part II provides an overview of three principal tools of VBM. Here we synthesize the various methodologies in the context of discounted cash flow valuation, which constitutes a common theoretical thread running through all VBM metrics. We also highlight some conceptual difficulties that are encountered in implementing the tools of VBM. The principal issue revolves around the notion that a firm's stock price is equal to the present value of expected future cash flows. That is, does the discounted cash flow valuation paradigm provide a reasonably accurate representation of the valuation of a firm's equity in the marketplace? Part III describes the experiences of a sample of firms that have implemented VBM systems. The focus in this part is on identifying "lessons learned" so that a potential adopter might benefit from the experiences of others.

References

Berle, Adolph, and Gardner Means. *The Modern Corporation and Private Property.* New York: Macmillan, 1932.

Chan, Su Han, John Kensinger, and John Martin. "Corporate Research and Development Expenditures and Share Value." *Journal of Financial Economics,* Vol. 26, no. 2 (August 1990): 255–276.

Copeland, Tom, Tim Koller, and Jack Murrin. *Valuation: Measuring and Managing the Value of Companies,* 2d ed. New York: Wiley, 1994.

McTaggart, James M., Peter W. Kontes, and Michael C. Mankins. *The Value Imperative: Managing for Superior Shareholder Returns.* New York: The Free Press, 1994.

Rappaport, Alfred. "New Thinking on How to Link Executive Pay with Performance." *Harvard Business Review* (March–April 1999): 91–101.

Stewart, G. Bennett III. *The Quest for Value.* New York: HarperBusiness, 1991.

Wise, Richard, and Peter Baumgartner. "Go Downstream: The New Profit Imperative in Manufacturing." *Harvard Business Review* (September–October 1999): 133–141.

Chapter **2**

The Shareholder Revolution and a Call for Change

The stockholder is therefore left as a matter of law with little more than the loose expectation that a group of men, under a nominal duty to run the enterprise for his benefit and that of others like him, will actually observe this obligation. In almost no particular is he in a position to demand that they do or refrain from doing any given thing. . . . The legal doctrine that the judgement of the directors must prevail as to the best interests of the enterprise is in fact tantamount to saying that in any given instance the interests of the individual may be sacrificed to the economic exigencies of the enterprise as a whole.

—Adolph Berle and Gardner Means,
The Modern Corporation and Private Property **(1932)**

*I*n 1993 Joseph Grundfest, a former member of the Securities and Exchange Commission (SEC), declared, "The takeover wars are over. Management won" (1993, p. 858). With the demise of the hostile take-over went a primary source of market discipline for corporate man-agers. In this chapter we recognize another source of market discipline in the actions of activist institutional investors who refuse to "vote with their feet" but instead seek to open a dialogue with the management and directors of their poorest performing companies. There is evidence that the process works, too. Activist institutional investors provide a voice for shareholder interests that is heard by the CEOs of the very largest corporations. Just ask the leaders at Eastman Kodak, Sears, and Westinghouse, to name a few.

In this chapter we investigate the nature of the shareholder-manager relationship by documenting the ownership and control of the common stock of publicly traded companies. Specifically, we consider the role of equity ownership in influencing managers to create value for the firm's stockholders. The broader issue here relates to corporate governance and the problem of motivating and controlling nonowner managers so that they seek to maximize share value.[1] We focus on two sources of managerial discipline: the market for corporate control during the 1980s (as exemplified by the bust-up leveraged buyout) and institutional shareholder activism that grew into a significant source of influence on corporate managers during the 1990s. We believe that these forces have been the primary drivers of shareholder interests over the last two decades and have permanently changed the reality of corporate governance. Very simply, we have witnessed a revival of managerial concern for shareholder interests. This has been a direct result of pressure brought to bear on corporate managers to improve the firm's performance or face the consequences.

The Market for Corporate Control in the 1980s

The market for corporate control in the United States during the 1980s has been dubbed the era of the bust-up LBO (leveraged buyout). LBO firms like Kolberg Kravis Roberts engaged in acquisitions of unprecedented size and proceeded to sell off divisions, lay off employees, and then bring back the smaller and leaner (more competitive) firms to the public through initial public offerings. Proponents of the bust-up LBO argued that the changes were long overdue and that LBOs led to changes that a recalcitrant and entrenched management was unwilling or unable to carry out. Opponents bemoaned the transfer of wealth from virtually all other stakeholder groups to the firm's common shareholders.

The net benefits of the takeover market of the 1980s will probably be debated for decades to come. However, one thing is certain: The takeovers that took place put corporate CEOs of even the largest firms on notice. They either had to improve their firms' performance in the hopes of raising their stock price or face the prospect of a hostile takeover. As a result, the active market for corporate control that characterized the 1980s provided an unprecedented source of discipline for corporate managers.

Alas, the takeover market of the 1980s came to an end when the junk bond market collapsed. Junk bonds were the brainchild of

Michael Milken and fanned the flames of the takeover market by providing huge sums of capital to would-be takeover artists. When Milken and his firm, Drexel Burnham Lambert, became mired in legal problems, the junk bond market collapsed and took with it the engine of the corporate takeover market. The collapse of the takeover market is illustrated in *Mergerstat Review* (1993) which reported that acquisitions of publicly traded companies peaked at 462 in 1988 and fell to only 148 in 1991 (tender offers declined from 217 to 20 over the same period).

Beginning in 1987, just as the corporate takeover market began to wind down, several public employee pension funds, led by the California Public Employees Retirement System (CalPERS) and the State of Wisconsin Investment Board, began campaigns of active involvement with their portfolio companies. Their involvement marked a significant change in the pattern of investment behavior for these institutions. They had traditionally been passive investors who evidenced their displeasure with a firm's performance by selling its stock if they owned it or not buying it if they didn't. The new activist investment strategy sought to improve the performance of portfolio companies through a program of active intervention by their institutional owners.

Laying the Groundwork for Institutional Investor Activism

The growth in institutional activism can be traced to two factors: the growth in institutional holdings of common stock that occurred over the period 1970–1990, and changes in the SEC rules related to communication among shareholders.

Institutional Ownership of U.S. Financial Assets

A major factor leading to increased institutional activism lies in the economic clout they now hold. Institutions control (hold in trust) over half of all publicly traded shares and more than 20 percent of all financial assets in the United States. Figure 2.1 illustrates the rapid growth in institutional holdings of U.S. financial assets since 1970, when the total dollar value of their holdings was only $672 billion. By 1980 their holdings had tripled, to $1.9 trillion, and by 1998 this total had grown to more than $15 trillion.

The rise in institutionally controlled assets can be traced in large part to the passage of the Employee Retirement Income Security Act (ERISA) in 1974. Among other things, this act resulted in the funding of private and public pension obligations. The administration of the

Figure 2.1 Institutional Ownership of U.S. Financial Assets, 1970–1998 ($ trillions)

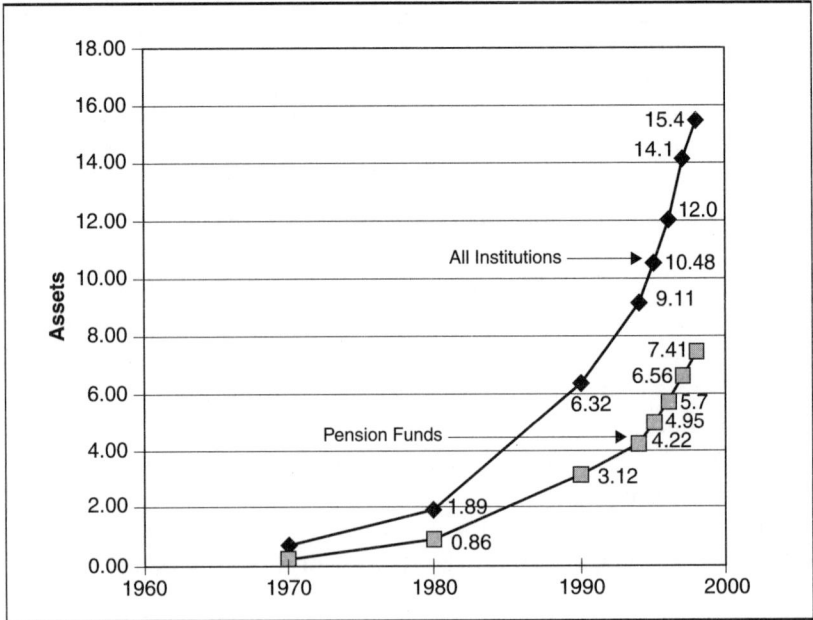

Source: Institutional Investment Report: Financial Assets & Equity Holdings, The Conference Board, August 1999.

pension assets set aside to satisfy the promised pension benefits came under the jurisdiction of the U.S. Labor Department, and these funds had to be managed in the best interests of the pension beneficiaries.[2] This latter requirement effectively removed control over pension plan assets from the corporation offering the pension plan.

Table 2.1 details, by type of institution, the growth in institutional and pension fund asset holdings between 1970 and 1998. The total assets held by institutions grew at an annual compound rate of over 20 percent. Pension funds, the largest single group of institutional investors, saw their asset holdings grow at a rate of 21.79 percent per year, a rate second only to that of the investment company category. Furthermore, within the pension fund group the state and local holdings grew the fastest over this period. This latter observation is particularly important because the state and local pension funds have been the most vocal of the new generation of activist institutional investors.

Figure 2.2 illustrates the mix of securities held by all financial institutions. Pension fund assets made up 48 percent of all institutional

Table 2.1 Growth in Assets Held by Institutions, 1970–1998 ($ billions)

	1970		1998		Compound Annual Growth Rate (%)
Private trusteed	$112.00		$4,060.00		22.08
Private insured	40.80		1,004.60		19.48
State and local	60.30		2,344.00		22.55
All pension funds		$213.10		$ 7,408.60	21.79
Investment companies		47.60		3,396.30	26.76
Insurance companies		225.10		2,537.40	14.41
Bank and trust companies		186.80		1,799.50	13.41
Foundations		n/a		290.40	n/a
All institutions		$672.60		$15,432.20	19.01

Source: Institutional Investment Report: Financial Assets & Equity Holdings, Volume 3, no. 1, The Conference Board, August 1999.

Figure 2.2 Assets Held by Types of Institutions, 1998

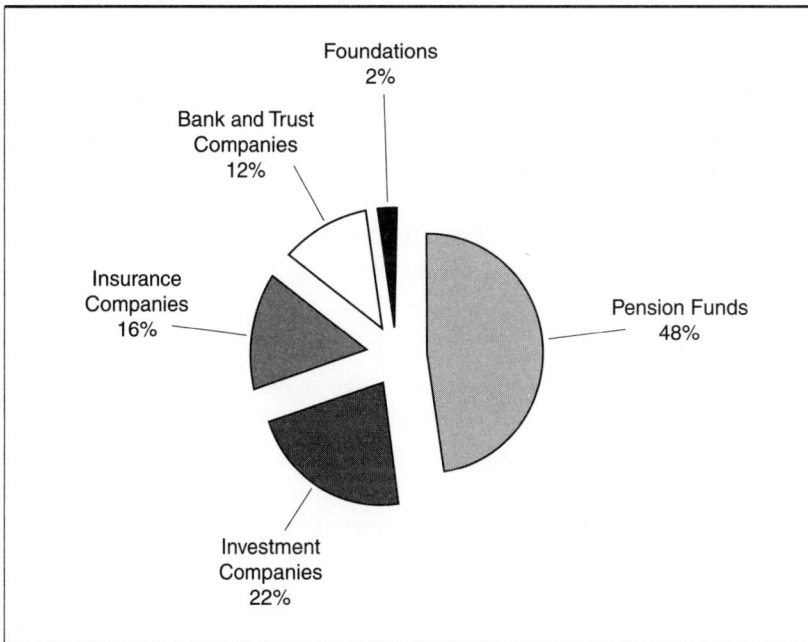

Source: Institutional Investment Report: Financial Assets & Equity Holdings, Volume 3, no. 1, The Conference Board, August 1999.

holdings in 1998, compared to only 32 percent in 1970. Clearly, pension funds, both public and private, are a growing segment of assets controlled by institutional investors.

The growth in investment by institutions was felt initially by the largest public corporations, whose stocks and bonds became the mainstays of pension fund portfolios. Institutional holdings of securities of the 1,000 largest U.S. companies rose from 46.6 percent in 1987 to an average of 57.6 percent for the third quarter of 1999.[3] In this same period institutional holdings of small cap stocks rose from 38 percent to more than 52 percent. In some industries institutions control an even higher proportion of member firms' shares. For example, by the third quarter of 1999 institutions owned 73 percent of the shares of firms in the paper industry, and there were fifty-five instances (up from four in 1987) in which institutions controlled more than 90 percent of a firm's shares. Clearly, institutions, and in particular pension funds, have gained prominence in the ownership of shares of U.S. corporations.

Still another factor that has contributed to the activism of state and local pension fund investors is that a large part of their equity portfolios is managed using an indexing strategy designed to minimize trading costs and mimic the return of a particular index. Since indexing limits the fund manager's ability to engage in trading to improve portfolio returns, it seems natural that these institutions would turn to active involvement with poor performers in their portfolios as a method for enhancing their portfolio returns. Panel A of table 2.2 documents the prevalence of indexing among the various types of institutional investors and shows that public pension funds are by far the most frequent indexers. In panel B of this table we get some idea of the extent to which the index strategy is used by some of the largest public pension funds.

Changes in the SEC Proxy Rules

The second key factor underlying the growing activism of institutional investors was the SEC revision of its rules regarding communication among stockholders. Prior to October 1992 the ability of investors to communicate with one another during a proxy contest was severely limited. Under the old rules any communication with anyone (another shareholder or the general public) that could be reasonably calculated to affect proxy-voting decisions was considered a solicitation of a proxy under SEC Rule 14a-1(1).[4] Choi (1997) notes that as a proxy solicitation such communication falls under Rule 14a-9's antifraud provisions as well as the mandatory disclosure requirements

Table 2.2 Indexing by Institutional Investors, 1998

Panel A. Indexing by Type of Institutional Investor	
Type of Institutional Investor	% Indexed Only
Corporate Pensions	15.2
Public Pension Funds	63.0
Mutual Fund Managers	10.1
Money Managers	11.8
Insurance Companies	4.8
Banks	36.6

Panel B. The Extent of the Use of Indexing by Individual Entities		
Pension Fund	% Equity Portfolio	% Total Assets
CalPERS	78.1	48.2
NY State Teachers	81.9	57.8
California State Teachers	79.2	49.2
Texas Teachers	93.7	55.4
New York Common	64.5	35.1
Federal Retirement Thrift Board	100.0	53.5
Florida State Board	58.2	39.2
Total Top 25 Indexers	60.6	36.5

Source: Institutional Investment Report: Turnover, Investment Strategies, and Ownership Patterns, Volume 3, no. 1, The Conference Board, January 2000.

of Rule 14a-3. Under the latter rule, solicitations are not allowed until a formal proxy statement containing information specified and approved by the SEC has been delivered to the solicited shareholder. What this all means is that under the pre-1992 rules it was very difficult for independent institutional investors to communicate with one another on how to respond to a proxy contest. They would potentially have to file a preliminary proxy statement with the SEC, wait for SEC approval, mail the formal proxy statement to all those with access to the communications, and then face Rule 14a-9's antifraud provisions.

On October 22, 1992, the rules of communication among stockholders changed in a significant way. The SEC announced a reform of its proxy solicitation rules that had the effect of exempting communications by a shareholder who is not seeking the power to vote the proxy directly. Very simply, Rule 14a-2(b) provides that most independent shareholders may freely engage in communications with one another over proxy contest issues.

With this freedom to communicate their ideas regarding proxy issues, combined with their substantial share ownership, institutional investors became a force to be reckoned with. Activist institutions moved quickly to take advantage of their newfound clout. One forum that has become very important in this regard is the Council of Institutional Investors (CII).[5] CII meets twice annually in Washington, D.C., and San Francisco to discuss issues of common concern to the member firms. Attendees are mostly institutional investors, particularly public employee pension funds such as the prominent California Public Employees Retirement System (CalPERS).

Pressure from Activist Institutional Investors

The focus of activist investors has always been on improving shareholder returns, but their strategies have changed over the years. For example, from 1987 until 1989 the primary focus of these investors was on hostile takeovers and antitakeover provisions. Beginning in 1990 the focus turned to corporate performance, specifically targeting companies that had failed to provide competitive long-term returns to their shareholders.

A Closer Look at Activist Institutional Investing

Kensinger and Martin (1996) interviewed executives from companies that had been targeted by activist institutional investors as well as representatives of the most active pension funds.[6] Their findings provide perspective concerning the role being played by these institutions in the markets of the new millennium.

Few Institutional Investors Engage in Activist or Relationship Investing

Relationship investing, whereby investors develop an active relationship with the firms in which they make investments, has a long history. Examples include investments by a single wealthy individual (or a small group) in start-up or turnaround situations. In a sense, relationship investing is similar in concept to venture capital investing, in which the investor brings personal expertise into the relationship, the difference being that the object of the investment is a large publicly traded corporation.[7]

The number of institutional investors engaging in relationship investing or institutional activism is currently very limited.[8] The leading activist institutions include CalPERS (sometimes allied with the California State Teachers Retirement System), the State of Wisconsin Investment Board, the Teachers Insurance and Annuity Association/College Retirement Equities Fund, the New York City Employee Retirement System, the New York State Employee Retirement System, and a private fund, LENS, Inc. Although the methods used by each of these investors may differ, the result is the same. Basically, they initiate contact with the CEOs of poorly performing companies in their portfolios and seek change in ways they believe will improve future performance.

Private funds espousing active ownership (such as the LENS fund) have had some success in attracting investments from public and corporate pension funds. For example, CalPERS invested approximately $500 million in Relational Investors between 1995 and 1999, a fund that employs corporate governance activism to turn around underperforming U.S. publicly traded companies.[9] In 1999 CalPERS invested $200 million in the UK Focus Fund, a joint venture of Hermes and shareholder activist Lens Investment Management.[10] UK Active Value has amassed a staggering $800 million, largely from North American institutional investors, to invest in underperforming companies across northern Europe. The fund has garnered a reputation as an aggressive fund manager in the UK by seeking to change boards and get companies taken over where it believes greater value can be realized.[11]

CII Is the Focal Point of Institutional Activism

The Council of Institutional Investors grew out of the turmoil of the 1980s as a defensive response to the corporate practice of paying greenmail and quickly expanded to include other common interests of its predominantly public pension fund members. Their concerns have included corporate governance and executive compensation, primarily in cases of companies with sustained below-average returns to shareholders. We include CII's Shareholder Bill of Rights in appendix 2A because it summarizes the concerns of many activist institutional investors. The primary concern is corporate governance, which determines how and for whom the firm is being run. CII's Bill of Rights makes it very clear that shareholder interests are preeminent.

CII has published a list of focus firms based on their poor historical performance since 1991. The CII list is published on its Web page and distributed to its membership "for educational purposes." The coordination of the screening process serves to spread the cost over the entire membership and reduces the free-rider problem associated with individual institutions' undertaking the process and publishing the list for all to use. Table 2.3 shows the council's 1999 focus list along with a description of the selection procedure and the list's location on the Web.

Table 2.3 Council of Institutional Investors Focus List, 1999

Advanced Micro Devices	Kmart
Archer Daniels Midland	Louisiana-Pacific
Autodesk	Milacron
Bethlehem Steel	Parametric Technology
Cabletron Systems	Reebok International
Foster Wheeler	Seagate Technology
Fruit of the Loom	Sears Roebuck
Great Lakes Chemical	Tenneco
Hilton Hotels	Thermo Electron
Humana	Toys "R" Us

Source: http://www.cii.org/focus99.htm

Note: The 1999 Focus List companies were identified by Standard & Poor's Compustat service. The methodology was to identify all companies in the S&P 500 index whose total stock returns (stock price appreciation plus dividends) had underperformed the industry group medians for the one-, three-, and five-year periods ending July 30, 1999. Companies were removed from the list if they outperformed the S&P 500 index for the five-year period.

The remaining companies were ranked based on the difference between the industry group's median five-year total return and the company's five-year total return (the returns deficit). The twenty companies with the highest returns deficit were selected for the 1999 Focus List.

Investor Communication Is Paramount

Generally, advocates of relationship investing recommend regular, long-term communication between boards or managers and owners. This involves more than management's passing on information to otherwise passive investors; it also involves accepting guidance from the owners and reform of executive compensation so that top executives' pay is linked to the returns on common stock, with compensation policy set by board members who are not part of management.

Managers who engage in "stonewalling" are displaying clear evidence of their reluctance to be accountable. Similarly, executives who display reluctance to communicate with investors are avoiding accountability. Listening to investors may not be enough, however, especially if the objective of communication with investors is to "educate" them (as though they were incapable of perceiving the true situation, even with adequate information). Investors seeking to be involved owners may want to roll up their sleeves and get down to serious discussion about the future direction of the company.

Executives who have experienced active ownership involvement by institutional investors suggest that CEOs become personally involved and that CFOs attend important meetings with investors to answer any financial questions that may arise. It is important, too, that top executives in operations, marketing, and other functional areas are available to answer questions in their areas—investor relations should extend beyond the investor relations staff. Also, it is fundamentally important to keep the dialogue moving—Dial Corporation's Gene Lemon says, "After the first reply, I would not again allow two months to go by without further contact. I would be more proactive. After, say, three weeks, I would call Richard Koppes [formerly general council with CalPERS] to follow up."

Institutional Investors Use Similar Targeting Procedures

Knowledge of activist institutions' screening process is obviously helpful to a management team trying to address apparent problems before investors feel compelled to act. The targeting procedures used by individual institutional investors are very similar (see appendix 2B for an example). Initially, researchers search for companies in the investor's portfolio whose stock returns have been below industry average (and below the market index) for a sustained period (generally three to five years). Usually there are also some executive compensation concerns or corporate governance concerns (such as board composition). A search of newspaper and magazine reports to gain information about the general reputation of the company may be made. Finally, the investing institution must believe that there is hope for a turnaround and that its involvement will speed the process. If the investor holds a substantial interest in the firm and there are other supportive institutional investors, then the investing institution approaches management and suggests changes.

Firms That Focus on Share Value Creation Are Not Likely to Be Targeted

From this description of the performance-screening process, it can be seen that management teams who are focused on share value creation, who are pursuing all avenues suggested by respected analysts, and who have obtained above-average results compared to their industry or the market index are not likely to be targeted.

The history of activist investing has seen an evolution from confrontational encounters with a firm's management to a "behind the scenes" cooperative approach. Recently, the leading practitioners of

institutional activism have increasingly relied upon private approaches, exercising more care in making potentially embarrassing
statements in press releases or interviews with officials of the fund.

Neither public nor private pension funds have sufficient staff,
expertise, or desire to micromanage the ailing firms in their portfolios,
so they restrict their influence to broad strategic issues rather than day-
to-day operational details. Even the most outspoken activists confine
their involvement to a few companies at a time (CalPERS, for instance,
focuses on twelve companies for intense involvement).

For example, the size of CalPERS's focus list basically reflects the
limits of its ability to give close attention to underperformers. To gain
sharper focus, it tries to avoid situations in which it has limited clout. It
tends *not* to target companies with significant stock holdings by company management or other insiders, because its influence would be
limited; and it is more apt to target companies with large holdings by
other institutional investors who take active roles.

Activist investors frequently focus on matters where the interests
of the officers and the stockholders may be in conflict. These include
the compensation of officers, expansion of the business (particularly
when it involves new areas), divestment from underperforming activities, and in a few cases, payment of dividends. Other areas of involvement include corporate governance, policy, strategy, financial structure, accountability, and disclosure. The investors press management
to focus on core competencies and to shed business units that allegedly
lack sustainable competitive advantage or pay out cash to investors (as
in several cases of leveraged recapitalization). They seek to make managers more accountable to the board of directors and to make the board
more responsive to stockholders. Factors that may be perceived as evidence of poor accountability include one or more of the following:

- Questionable disclosure practices
- Excessive executive compensation
- "Stonewalling": reluctance to respond to investor questions or to
  listen to investor concerns
- Insider (management)-dominated board of directors
- Lopsided board (i.e., lack of diversity)

Often, poor performance, questionable disclosure, excessive compensation, or other serious maladies have been found in combination
with an insider board or a lopsided board that by its composition tends

to be friendly toward current management. In those cases, the reform agenda has included proposed changes in board composition. The primary question is whether the board controls management, or vice versa. A reasonable first criterion is that independent members rather than manager-directors have the majority of seats. Obviously, in the case of insider boards, the chairman and CEO would not be effectively challenged on matters such as CEO compensation. Also, it is important that independent board members have suitable backgrounds and skills.

One of the foremost items on the reform agenda for activist institutional investors is to have key committees become completely independent, with membership entirely composed of independent directors. These key committees include the audit, nominating, and compensation committees.

Institutional Investors Often Follow Private-Sector Activists

Institutional investors frequently play the role of follower and supporter of private-sector activists. Although activist pension funds do their own screening and analysis to determine target firms, they frequently find themselves siding with private-sector investors who seek to alter the direction of poorly performing firms. Thus, if corporate managers have anything to fear from aroused shareholders, their greatest concern should be the propensity of institutional investors to follow leaders who arise spontaneously, attracted by the potential for realizing substantial value through active ownership involvement. The best defense of management is to do the things that increase shareholder wealth and maintain sound ongoing relationships with major investors. Then there will be little motivation for anyone to arouse the "sleeping giant." Viewed in this light, relationship investing is preventive medicine for all concerned.

Institutional Investors May Provide a Direct-Line Source of Capital

Institutional investors may provide a direct-line source of capital. Besides routine private placements, CalPERS has initiated so-called private equity arrangements involving a joint venture with a portfolio company. The first of these was a partnership with Enron Corporation to develop natural gas storage and transmission facilities. Capital for the $2 billion joint venture has come from Enron common stock contributed by Enron plus cash from CalPERS and a consortium of lenders. When the debt is repaid and CalPERS has received an agreed-upon return, the assets of the joint venture will transfer to Enron.

CalPERS also has private equity arrangements in cable communications and medical supplies.

Does Institutional Activism Improve the Performance of Targeted Firms?

A number of studies have documented that some recent activism has indeed improved targeted firms' performance. Nesbitt (1994) documents the excess returns (stock return less the market return adjusted to reflect the stock's risk) for the forty-two different firms targeted by CalPERS over the period November 24, 1987, through September 15, 1992. Returns are calculated for the five years prior to targeting and the five years after the initial targeting. He finds that during the pre-targeting period the cumulative return deficit (after adjusting for differences in risk) is 78.1 percent. In fact, only four of the forty-two firms actually outperformed the S&P 500 over the pre-targeting five-year period. The cumulative excess return over the post-targeting five-year period averages 29.1 percent for each firm. The return differences were even more dramatic where the set of forty-two targeted firms was divided into those that occurred during 1987–1989 and those that occurred during 1990–1992. As we noted earlier, the early targets were based on corporate governance issues (antitakeover provisions, greenmail) whereas the latter sample focused on poor performers. The eighteen early targets (1987–1989) exhibited the same negative excess returns during the pre-target period but continued to underperform during the post-targeting period. To the contrary, the poor performance targets (1990–1992) rebounded dramatically after targeting. These twenty-four firms recorded a five-year cumulative excess return of 99 percent.

Opler and Sokobin (1995) provide additional evidence that institutional activism improves the performance of targeted firms. They studied the post-targeting performance of the Council of Institutional Investors focus lists for 1991, 1992, and 1993 relative to a number of control groups. A total of ninety-six firms were targeted by CII during this period. In the year after being listed on a focus list the targeted firms experienced an average share price increase of 11.6 percent above the S&P 500.

Huson (1997) took a different approach to evaluating the impact of CalPERS activism on firms' performance. He studied changes in the targeted firms' real activities and documented significant changes in the frequency of divestitures, acquisitions, and joint ventures following targeting. He also examined how the stock market reacts to such announced real activities and finds that on average prices respond in a significantly more positive manner following targeting. This suggests that investors view the decisions made by management once they have been targeted as being more beneficial to shareholders than decisions made prior to targeting. Del Guercio and Hawkins (1999) make similar observations, noting that shareholder proposals have a significant impact on company policies. Similarly, Gillan, Kensinger, and Martin (2000) give indirect evidence that institutional pressure was involved in Sears' decisions to restructure itself during the late 1980s. Specifically, of the nineteen restructuring announcements made prior to the breakup of the firm in 1991, thirteen came after September 11, 1989, the date that CalPERS expressed concerns to Sears' management about the firm's performance.

The Dark Side of Institutional Activism

Public pension funds have been the primary source of corporate discipline through institutional activism. However, Romano (1993) argues that it is not so clear that these funds are free to provide the necessary disciplinary force. The problem is that public fund managers face considerable political pressure to temper investment policies with local considerations, such as fostering in-state employment, which are not aimed at maximizing the value of their portfolios. This results from the fact that public pension funds are regulated by the states and are exempt from ERISA.[12]

Romano (1993) provides evidence that pension funds with more politicized trustees (i.e., boards with a lower proportion of appointed and ex officio board members) perform worse than those with a less politicized board membership. To test this proposition Romano studied fund performance for fifty state pension plans over the five-year period 1985–1989. She found that earnings are indeed positively related to board independence. She estimates the wealth loss to pension beneficiaries resulting from political interference with fund investment policies at $28 billion (absence of an independent board, $15 billion; social investment and South African investment restrictions $5.6 billion and $7.6 billion, respectively).

Based upon her findings Romano offers five recommendations aimed at reducing the problem of politicization in the management of public employee pension funds.

Reform Public Pension Fund Boards to Include a Less Politicized Membership

Board members elected by beneficiaries (compared to appointed board members) are less likely to be influenced by political pressures to act in ways that are not in the best interests of beneficiaries.

Apply ERISA's Fiduciary Standards to Public Funds

This should eliminate social investing pressures, and states could individually impose ERISA standards on their pension funds. These standards would eliminate pressures to invest in socially desirable investments but would not eliminate political pressure on voting decisions.

Mandate Passive Investment Strategies

Increased use of passive (indexed) investment strategies would reduce the opportunities for state officials to pressure public pension fund managers to engage in social investing or non-value-maximizing share voting. Passive investment management eliminates the ability of public funds to engage in economically targeted or socially targeted investments.

Constitutionalize Fund Board Independence

To prevent raids on fund assets by fiscally distressed state governments, some states have mandated the independence of fund boards. For example, following the 1992 legislative attack on CalPERS an initiative called the California Pension Protection Act was put on the ballot to amend the state constitution and vest fiduciary power and obligation, including investment management and system administration, in the retirement fund board exclusively. Another provision was to state that the board's fiduciary duty to its participants and beneficiaries has precedence over any other duty, such as a duty to employers and tax-payers to minimize administration costs.

Switch to Defined Contribution Plans

This would effectively transfer control over investments from pension fund boards to individual employees. With decision power diffused across numerous plan beneficiaries, the likelihood that political pressure would push substantial pension fund assets into high-risk, low-return projects would be minimized.

Clearly, institutional activism is not a perfect mechanism for encouraging corporate managers to focus their energies on shareholder concerns. There are instances in which political pressures on public funds from state legislatures might be used to protect local interests at the expense of pension beneficiaries. However, even with these limitations the fact remains that pension beneficiaries and stockholder interests are closely aligned, and this should serve to ameliorate the political pressures on value-creating investments. Only the future will reveal if institutional activism will continue to be a force for improving shareholder returns.

Implications for Corporate Managers

Very clearly, the relationship between shareholders and managers has changed over the last twenty years. Common shareholders are no longer a disjointed group of individuals who "vote with their feet" when firm performance begins to lag. What does this mean for the corporate executive? We think there are three fundamental points that should be gleaned from the changes we have outlined in this chapter. First, the world of common stock ownership has changed in an important way since the passage of ERISA in 1974. The increased concentration of control over common shares by institutions and their subsequent shareholder activism have heightened managerial concern about firms' performance, and this added pressure is not likely to go away. Second, institutional investors and their clients are primarily interested in performance from the perspective of the common shareholder. This means that the best way for management to avoid being the object of concern by institutional investors is to focus on shareholder returns and stock performance. Finally, if a firm should become the object of shareholder activism, management would be advised to "sit back and recall who owns the shop."[13]

Summary

Professional managers control large, publicly held firms and as such are the agents of the firms' owners (the common stockholders). When a manager's personal interests come into conflict with those of the shareholders, an agency problem exists. That is, managers can (unless otherwise restricted or enticed from doing so) make choices that are consistent with their own personal preferences rather than serve shareholder interests. Managers make crucial decisions regarding the markets in which the firm competes, the products and services it offers, how the firm's output is priced and sold, and how the firm will respond to competitive forces. Therefore, from the owners' perspective the success of the firm is in significant measure a result of the managers' abilities and their willingness to make decisions that are consistent with shareholder interests.

In this chapter we investigated the nature of the shareholder-manager relationship by documenting the ownership and control of the common stock of publicly traded companies. Our perspective has been to consider the role of equity ownership in influencing managers to create value for the firm's stockholders. We limited our discussion to the 1980s and 1990s because it is during this short period that we have witnessed a revival of shareholder interests with pressure being brought to bear on corporate managers to improve the performance of their firms or face the consequences. The key factor characterizing shareholder interests during the 1990s has been the growth of institutional investor activism, which began with the close of the LBO merger wave of the 1980s and continues today. We described the practices of some of the key activist institutions and reviewed the evidence related to their effectiveness in motivating improved company performance.

But the future is not certain and it is not known whether institutional activism will continue to make shareholder interests paramount. An important class of financial institutions—public employee pension funds—is subject to political pressure from state legislatures and other elected officials to heed goals unrelated to shareholder value. To the extent that these goals lead these pension funds to put pressure on firms to accomplish social ends, performance is likely to suffer. To date the evidence suggests that on the whole activist institutions have stuck to their performance goal. Only the future will tell whether this situation will continue.

One thing is certain. The rise of institutional ownership has given new voice to shareholder interests. The 1990s have seen shareholder concerns raised to new heights, and this phenomenon is likely to continue because every worker who is covered by a pension plan that invests in common stock has a stake in the outcome. Institutional capitalism has given rise to greater concern for share value, and value based management has become the tool of choice for trying to satisfy these concerns.

Appendix 2A

The Council of Institutional Investors Shareholder Bill of Rights

*I*n 1986 the Council of Institutional Investors distributed its Shareholder Bill of Rights, which reads as follows.

Preamble

American corporations are the cornerstones of the free enterprise system, and as such must be governed by the principles of accountability and fairness inherent in our democratic system. The shareholders of American corporations are the owners of such corporations, and the directors elected by the shareholders are accountable to the shareholders. Furthermore, the shareholders of American corporations are entitled to participate in the fundamental financial decisions which could affect corporate performance and growth and the long range viability and competitiveness of corporations. This Shareholder Bill of Rights insures such participation and provides protection against any disenfranchisement of American shareholders.

I. One Share–One Vote

Each share of common stock, regardless of its class, shall be entitled to vote in proportion to its relative share in the total common stock equity of the corporation. The right to vote is inviolate and may not be abridged by any circumstance or by any action of any person.

II. Equal and Fair Treatment for All Shareholders

Each share of common stock, regardless of its class, shall be treated equally in proportion to its relative share in the total common stock equity of the corporation with respect to any dividend, distribution, redemption, tender, or exchange offer. In matters reserved for shareholder action, procedural fairness and full disclosure is required.

III. Shareholder Approval of Certain Corporate Decisions

A vote of the holders of a majority of the outstanding shares of common stock, regardless of class, shall be required to approve any corporate decision related to the finances of a company which will have a material effect upon the financial position of the company and the position of the company's shareholders; specifically, decisions which would:

A. Result in the acquisition of 5 percent or more of the shares of common stock by the corporation at a price in excess of the prevailing market price of such stock, other than pursuant to a tender offer made to all shareholders;

B. Result in, or is contingent upon, an acquisition other than by the corporation of shares of stock of the corporation having, on a pro-forma basis, 20 percent or more of the combined voting power of the outstanding common shares or a change in the ownership of 20 percent or more of the assets of the corporation;

C. Abridge or limit the rights of the holders of common shares to:
   1. Consider and vote on the election or removal of directors or the timing or length of their term of office; or
   2. Make nominations for directors or propose other action to be voted upon by shareholders; or
   3. Call special meetings of shareholders to take action by written consent;

D. Permit any executive officer or employee of the corporation to receive, upon termination of employment, any amount in excess of two times that person's average annual compensation for the previous three years, if such payment is contingent upon an acquisition of shares of stock of the corporation or a change in the ownership of the assets of the corporation;

E. Permit the sale or pledge of corporate assets which would have a material effect on shareholder values;

F. Result in the issuance of debt to a degree which would leverage a company and imperil the long-term viability of the corporation.

IV. Independent Approval of Executive Compensation and Auditors

The approval of at least a majority of independent directors (or if there are fewer than three such directors, the unanimous approval of all such outside directors) shall be required to approve, on an annual basis:

A. The compensation to be provided to each executive officer of the corporation, including the right to receive any bonus, severance or other extraordinary payment to be received by such executive officer; and

B. The selection of independent auditors.

Appendix 2B

The CalPERS System for Identifying Target Firms

CalPERS's system of institutional activism has been widely discussed in the financial press and provides an interesting example of how a financial institution can exert pressure on a portfolio company to improve its performance (and consequently its stock price).[14] The CalPERS performance appraisal system begins with a mechanical stock return screening for all the companies in its 1,000-plus security portfolio. Portfolio companies are sorted from high to low based on their annual holding period returns (ending stock price plus dividend divided by beginning stock price) for the last five years. The stocks in the bottom quartile provide the basis for subsequent analyses. The next screening eliminates firms that might prove to be particularly difficult to influence through investor activism (e.g., firms that have high insider ownership, low institutional ownership) or that have made recent changes in management, corporate structure, or strategy that could lead to an improvement in their performance. This analysis reduces the set of firms to under 100 firms, which are then subjected to an in-depth economic analysis using annual reports, analysts' opinions, and other sources of public information. The set of firms is then reduced to 50 firms, which make up CalPERS's "failing 50" list.

CalPERS further categorizes the "failing 50" firms into two tiers for purposes of corporate activism. First, it identifies the 10 of the "failing 50" that it thinks offer the greatest likelihood for a turnaround. These firms constitute its "focus 10" list for the year. The CEOs of each of these firms is contacted with a letter that outlines CalPERS's concerns about the firm's poor performance and requests a meeting with the firm's outside directors. If the firm does not respond in twenty to thirty days, it is sent a shareholder proposal designed to address factors that CalPERS feels contributed to poor performance. The proposal is withdrawn if the company takes action to address its performance problem. The second group of firms, tier II, consists of 21 companies that are also part of the "failing 50" but differ from the "focus 10" firms in that their problems are more difficult to diagnose and the potential for turnaround is thought to be less. These firms, like the "focus 10" firms, receive a letter detailing what CalPERS sees as specific problems. However, no shareholder proposals are submitted during the current proxy season.

CalPERS's arsenal of persuasive tools consists of the use of proxy proposals, "just vote no" for corporate directors as a protest, and public pressure via the press. With its substantial proxy-voting power and its ability to communicate freely with other institutional investors, CalPERS can bring significant pressure on an incumbent management to actively seek ways to improve the firm's performance. The "just vote no" strategy involves simply voting against management's slate of directors. This strategy has been strongly advocated by Joseph Grundfest (1993) a former member of the SEC and professor of law at Stanford University. CalPERS has also made frequent use of the popular press to bring pressure on the managers of its focus firms to redouble their efforts to improve performance. For example, CalPERS targeted Sears, Roebuck and Co. in 1989, noting its record of poor performance. Three years later Sears' management went through a major restructuring that was at least partially a result of the pressures brought by CalPERS and other institutional investors.

The key point here is that CalPERS as well as a number of other activist institutional investors have used poor past stock return performance as the lightning rod for bringing pressure on firms to improve their performance. Thus, institutional activism has served to increase the priority of stockholder interests in the eyes of both corporate managers and boards of directors.

Although we do not discuss their practices here, there are a number of other activist institutions (see Kensinger and Martin 1996). Some of the more prominent activists have been the State of Wisconsin Investment Board, the New York State and Local Retirement Systems, the New York City Retirement Systems (including city employees, teachers, fire fighters, and police), and the College Retirement Equity Fund.

References

Berle, Adolph, and Gardner Means. *The Modern Corporation and Private Property.* New York: Macmillan, 1932.

Choi, Stephen. "Proxy Issue Contests: Impact of the 1992 Proxy Reforms." Working paper, University of Chicago, 1997.

Del Guercio, Diane and Jennifer Hawkins. The Motivation and Impact of Pension Fund Activism. *Journal of Financial Economics* (1999): 293–340.

Gillan, Stuart L., John W. Kensinger, and John D. Martin. "Value Creation and Corporate Diversification: The Case of Sears, Roebuck & Co." *Journal of Financial Economics* 55, 1 (2000): 103–138.

Gillan, Stuart L., and Laura Starks. "Corporate Governance Proposals and Shareholder Activism: The Role of Institutional Investors." Working paper, Graduate School of Business, University of Texas, Austin, 1998a.

———. "A Survey of Shareholder Activism: Motivation and Empirical Evidence." *Contemporary Finance Digest* 2, 3 (1998b): 10–34.

Grundfest, Joseph A. "Just Vote No: A Minimalist Strategy for Dealing with Barbarians at the Gate." *Stanford Law Review* 45 (April 1993): 857–937.

Huson, Mark. "Does Governance Matter? Evidence from CalPERS Interventions." Working paper, University of Texas and the University of Alberta, 1997.

Jensen, Michael C., and William H. Meckling. "Theory of the Firm: Managerial Behavior, Agency Costs and Ownership Structure." *Journal of Financial Economics* 3 (1976): 305–360.

Kensinger, John, and John D. Martin. *Relationship Investing: What Active Institutional Investors Want from Management.* Morristown, N.J.: Financial Executives Research Foundation, 1996.

Monks, Robert, and Nell Minow. *Corporate Governance.* Cambridge, Mass.: Blackwell, 1995.

Nesbitt, Stephen L. "Long-Term Rewards from Corporate Governance." Working paper, Wilshire Associates, Santa Monica, Calif., 1994.

Opler, Tim C., and Jonathan Sokobin. "Does Coordinated Institutional Activism Work? An Analysis of the Activities of the Council of Institutional Investors." Working paper, Fisher College of Business, Ohio State University, Columbus, 1995.

Pound, John. "The Promise of the Governed Corporation." *Harvard Business Review* (March–April 1995): 89–98.

Romano, Roberta. "Public Pension Fund Activism in Corporate Governance Reconsidered." *Columbia Law Review* 93 (1993): 795–853.

Chapter 3

Why the Old Metrics Don't Work

> Performance measurement is an essential part of management control in that it validates whether the results anticipated from planned action are realized. Because what gets measured gets attention, the kind of performance an organization chooses to measure will motivate actions that improve the measure. Traditionally, bottom-line measures such as profit, revenue, and cost have been used to evaluate managers' performance. But in the face of competitive reality, new strategies with new action plans and new performance systems are needed.

—Kiran Verma, "Total Factor Productivity Management" (1992)

*J*ust reading the financial press, it is easy to get the impression that a firm's earnings per share are the principal driver of its stock price. For example, on July 16, 1996 at 3:59 P.M., Intel Corporation reported second-quarter earnings of $1.17 per share, eight cents higher than Wall Street estimates and eighteen cents above the previous year's earnings. On the day of the earnings announcement Intel's shares were the most actively traded on the Nasdaq market, with a total of 25 million shares changing hands before the close of the market. Intel's shares closed at $70 at the end of the day and rose $2 during after-hours trading. It would appear that share value is directly tied to earnings and earnings growth.

Does a firm that is managed for earnings and earnings growth maximize the value of the common stockholder's investment in the firm? Proponents of value based management (VBM) argue that a firm's earnings provide an insufficient indicator of value creation. Specifically, rewarding a firm's management for earnings and earnings growth can even lead to decisions that reduce shareholder value.

This chapter addresses the issue raised in chapter 1 as to whether the accounting or economic (discounted cash flow) model of the firm best describes the value creation process. We demonstrate the well-documented shortcomings of performance measures based on traditional accounting information when used as tools for managing for shareholder value. Specifically, accounting performance metrics can lead to managerial decisions that are inconsistent with shareholder interests.

Managing Earnings versus Managing Shareholder Value

Proponents of VBM make the case that accounting numbers prepared using generally accepted accounting principles (GAAP) are not designed to reflect value creation. Furthermore, earnings provide very noisy and sometimes misleading signals to the financial manager who seeks to maximize shareholder value. To show the limitations of the accounting earnings metric, we first review the fundamental tenets of the basic discounted cash flow (DCF) valuation model. The value of any earning asset using the DCF model is a function of the amount, timing, and risk of expected future cash flows. Consequently, if the manager is to run the business in such a way as to maximize shareholder value, the performance measurement system must capture all three of these fundamental determinants of value. In the discussion that follows we find that the GAAP earnings measure falls short in five important respects when used as the basis for managing for shareholder value.

Problem #1: Accounting Earnings Do Not Equal Cash Flow

This criticism is actually a bit misleading because we certainly can get to cash flow by making appropriate adjustments to reported accounting numbers. The point is, however, that reported earnings are not equal to cash, and cash is what we are concerned about when trying to manage for the creation of shareholder value.

Problem #2: Accounting Numbers Do Not Reflect Risk

Reported accounting earnings do not reflect the riskiness of those earnings. That is, a firm's accounting system reports "what happened," not "what might have happened." As a consequence, there is nothing in reported earnings that indicates anything about the riskiness of the firm's operations. Since risk is a principal determinant of the value of the firm's equity, this omission is critical.

The level of a firm's reported earnings and its variability from period to period are determined by a combination of influences that are outside the firm's control (e.g., business conditions in the overall economy and in the firm's industry) as well as by policy choices the firm's management has made (e.g., the firm's choice of operating and financial policies). To see the effect of a firm's policy choices on earnings variability, consider the effect of financial policy on the volatility of a firm's reported earnings for the two firms shown in table 3.1. The unlevered firm uses no financial leverage, whereas the levered firm has borrowed half its funds and pays 12 percent interest on its debt. Figure 3.1 demonstrates graphically the greater sensitivity of the levered firm's earnings per share (EPS) to changes in the level of operating income or earnings before interest and taxes (EBIT). Note that if EBIT were to increase from $100 to $200 (a 100 percent increase), EPS for the unlevered firm would increase by 100 percent from $0.65 to $1.35, whereas the levered firm's EPS would increase by 350 percent from $0.52 to $1.82. Financial leverage has the effect of increasing the sensitivity of a firm's EPS to changes in EBIT, thus leading to a more volatile stream of earnings. This added volatility in EPS is not apparent in a single year's reported earnings.

Problem #3: Accounting Numbers Do Not Include an Opportunity Cost of Equity

The relation between changes in economic value and earnings is further obscured by the fact that traditional earnings calculations do not incorporate the opportunity cost associated with the owners' investment in the firm. Interest expense and preferred stock dividends are considered when calculating accounting earnings. However, no required return on equity capital is considered in the calculation of accounting earnings. The absence of a cost for owner-supplied capital means that reported earnings overstate the value creation for the period from the firm's operations. For example, in 1997 Motorola reported operating earnings of more than $1.2 billion. Some investors might have seen this positive earnings performance as an indication that the firm was in good financial health. However, Motorola's total invested capital for the year was approximately $32 billion. If Motorola's investors require a 10 percent return on their capital, then

Table 3.1 Financial Leverage and Earnings Volatility

	Unlevered Firm	Levered Firm
Debt	—	$500
Equity	$1,000	$500
Interest rate	12%	12%
Tax rate	35%	35%
Number of shares	100	50

Unlevered Firm				Levered Firm			
EBIT	Interest	Net Income	EPS	EBIT	Interest	Net Income	EPS
—	—	—	—	—	$60.00	$ (39.00)	$(0.78)
$ 50.00	—	$32.50	$0.33	$ 50.00	60.00	(6.50)	(0.13)
100.00	—	65.00	0.65	100.00	60.00	26.00	0.52
150.00	—	97.50	0.98	150.00	60.00	58.50	1.17
200.00	—	130.00	1.30	200.00	60.00	91.00	1.82
250.00	—	162.50	1.63	250.00	60.00	$123.50	2.47
300.00	—	195.00	1.95	300.00	60.00	156.00	3.12
350.00	—	227.50	2.28	350.00	60.00	188.50	3.77
400.00	—	260.00	2.60	400.00	60.00	221.00	4.42
450.00	—	292.50	2.93	450.00	60.00	253.50	5.07

Figure 3.1 Earnings per Share and Financial Leverage

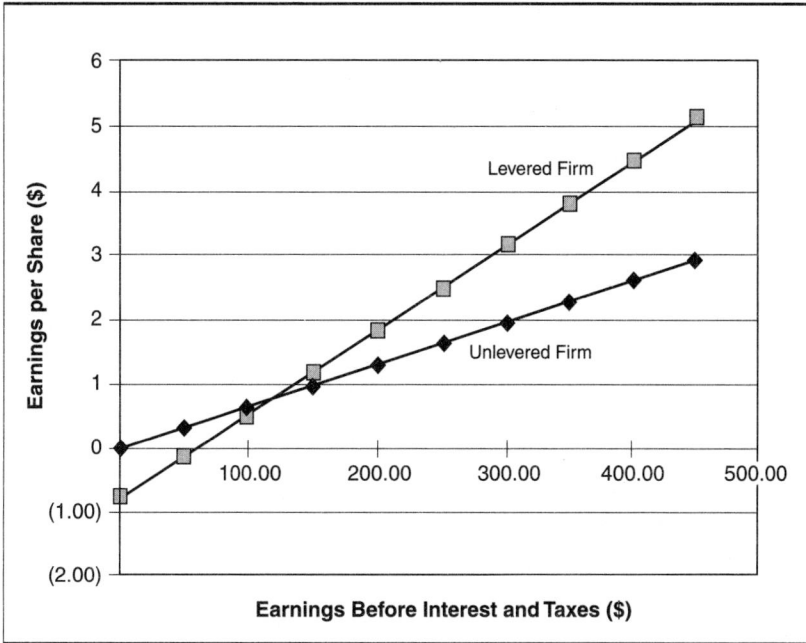

the firm needs roughly $3.2 billion just to provide them with their required return. Motorola fell short of this mark by a substantial amount.[1]

Problem #4: Accounting Practices Vary from Firm to Firm

Any student of financial statements is aware of the effect (sometimes material) that a change in accounting policy can make on a firm's reported earnings. Typical examples include the various methods that a firm can use to account for its inventories (e.g., last in/first out (LIFO) versus first in/first out (FIFO) inventory) or rules of the governing accounting bodies (e.g., the Financial Accounting Standards Board) regarding how a firm can account for R&D expenditures or foreign currency translation gains and losses. Except for the effect on cash flow (e.g., via the firm's current and future tax liabilities) these accounting practices are unimportant insofar as the performance of the firm is concerned. Nonetheless, accounting practices can and do have a material influence on the firm's reported earnings.

Problem #5: Accounting Numbers Do Not Consider the Time Value of Money

Reported earnings are not adjusted for the effects of the time value of money. Economic value, which underlies the economic model of the firm, considers the timing, amount, and riskiness of future cash flows. Specifically, the economic or intrinsic value of a firm is equal to the present value of its expected future cash flows discounted at a rate that properly reflects their risk. The rate of return that investors require will reflect both the riskiness of the future cash flows and the anticipated rate of inflation. Since accounting earnings calculations do not account for the time value of money, they do not provide reliable signals to the manager who seeks to maximize shareholder equity.

The Traditional Accounting Approach to Performance Evaluation

The seasoned financial analyst will quickly point out that many of the shortcomings of accounting earnings measures that we have discussed to this point can be overcome through combining income statement and balance sheet information into financial ratios. Specifically, the return on net assets (RONA) ratio has been widely used as a measure of financial performance. Although RONA represents an improvement over the earnings measure alone, we demonstrate here that it too is a flawed indicator of shareholder value creation.

Using RONA to Evaluate Capital Expenditure Proposals

We begin our discussion by defining RONA. There are at least two generally used definitions of RONA. The first uses net income in the numerator and the second uses net operating profit after taxes (NOPAT) in the numerator:

$$RONA_1 = \frac{\text{Net income}}{\text{Total assets}} \qquad (3.1)$$

$$RONA_2 = \frac{\text{Net income } + \text{ Interest} \times (1 - \text{Tax rate})}{\text{Total assets}}$$

$$= \frac{\text{Net operating income} \times (1 - \text{Tax rate})}{\text{Total assets}} \qquad (3.2)$$

$$= \frac{\text{NOPAT}}{\text{Total assets}}$$

The first measure, or RONA$_1$, is often criticized for inconsistently comparing after-interest income to the total asset base, and the second measure, RONA$_2$, seeks to rectify this shortcoming by including in the income figure the after-tax interest payment to the firm's creditors. The RONA$_2$ measure in eq. (3.2) is internally consistent in comparing total assets to total earnings, and for this reason we use this version of RONA in the discussion that follows. However, even this variant of RONA suffers from problems that make its use as a tool for evaluating strategies and performance at either the business unit or corporate level questionable.

The first difficulty that arises with the use of RONA as a performance measure is that it reflects accounting income, not cash flow. Since the value of a strategy or business unit depends on the amount, timing, and riskiness of future cash flows, the use of RONA can provide misleading signals for business decision making.[2]

To illustrate the shortcomings of the accounting-based RONA metric, we define a discounted cash flow (DCF) version of the RONA metric, RONA$_{DCF}$, that properly captures the economic return to a project over a specified interval of time (where PV represents the present value):

$$RONA_{DCF} = \frac{\text{Cash flow} + (\text{PV end of year} - \text{PV beginning of year})}{\text{PV beginning of year}}$$

(3.3)

$$= \frac{\text{Cash flow} + \text{Change in present value}}{\text{PV beginning of year}}$$

The DCF return (sometimes referred to as total shareholder return, or TSR) is the economic rate of return equivalent of RONA. Consider the following investment example: The Alpha Resale Company is considering an investment of $4,000 in a project that is expected to produce cash flows of $400, $800, $800, $1,600, and $2,500 over the next five years. Alpha estimates that its cost of capital is 12 percent such that the project's net present value (NPV) is zero:

$$NPV = \frac{\$400}{(1.12)^1} + \frac{\$800}{(1.12)^2} + \frac{\$800}{(1.12)^3} + \frac{\$1,600}{(1.12)^4} + \frac{\$2,500}{(1.12)^5} + (\$4,000) = 0$$

Table 3.2 shows the calculation of the traditional accounting-based RONA and the discounted cash flow variant, RONA$_{DCF}$, for each year of the project's five-year life. Panel A shows the RONA$_{DCF}$ calculations for each of the five years of the project's life. Since the project earns a

Table 3.2 Calculation of RONA$_{DCF}$ and Accounting RONA

	Year 1	Year 2	Year 3	Year 4	Year 5
Panel A. Calculation of RONA$_{DCF}$					
1. Cash flow	$ 400	$ 800	$ 800	$ 1,600	$ 2,500
2. PV beginning of year	4,000	4,080	3,770	3,422	2,233
3. PV end of year	4,080	3,770	3,422	2,233	0
4. Change in PV [(3) − (2)]	$ 80	$ (310)	$ (348)	$(1,189)	$(2,233)
5. Economic income [(1) + (4)]	$ 480	$ 490	$ 452	$ 411	$ 267
6. RONA$_{DCF}$ [(5) ÷ (2)]	12%	12%	12%	12%	12%
Panel B. Calculation of Accounting-Based RONA					
1. Cash flow	$ 400	$ 800	$ 800	$1,600	$2,500
2. Less: Depreciation	800	800	800	800	800
3. Net income	$ (400)	$ 0	$ 0	$ 800	$1,700
4. Book value beginning of year	$4,000	$3,200	$2,400	$1,600	$ 800
5. Less: Depreciation	800	800	800	800	800
6. Book value end of year	$3,200	$2,400	$1,600	$ 800	$ 0
7. Accounting (RONA) [(3) ÷ (4)]	−10%	0%	0%	50%	212.5%

zero NPV, it also earns an annual RONA$_{DCF}$ equal to the firm's cost of capital. Panel B shows the calculations for the accounting-based RONA, which rely entirely on accounting income and book value numbers. A quick comparison of the RONA$_{DCF}$ and RONA calculations reveals that RONA is not a very useful indicator of RONA$_{DCF}$. RONA ranges from −10 percent to 212 percent; it bears no apparent relationship to the DCF return earned by the project nor does it indicate that the project is a zero NPV project.

Unfortunately, the traditionally measured RONA cannot generally be used as a surrogate for RONA$_{DCF}$. Bierman (1988) notes two basic problems with using traditional RONA to measure performance.[3] First, it is frequently calculated incorrectly. Second, even if it is correctly computed, there is a tendency for RONA to distort decision making. Even in light of its shortcomings, some have argued that RONA can be used to evaluate a going concern or business unit's performance even though it fails as a measure of project performance. In the next section, we demonstrate that this is not the case.

Using ROS and RONA to Evaluate Business Unit Performance

The evaluation of divisional and business unit performance is a crucially important problem for which many measures have been used. We demonstrate here that two commonly used metrics, return on sales (ROS) and RONA, have serious shortcomings. Specifically, we identify the adverse incentive effects for a firm's divisional managers where ROS and RONA are used as the basis for performance measurement and incentive compensation.

Consider the hypothetical Roxy Manufacturing Company, whose three divisions are described in table 3.3. If we evaluate the performance of the three divisions using ROS—measured as after-tax net operating income divided by revenues—then division C with its ROS of 17.3 percent is the top performer, followed by divisions B and A. However, the ROS ratio is seriously flawed in that it only captures information from the firm's income statement and does not reflect the investment required to produce the reported sales and earnings. The RONA ratio addresses this shortcoming of ROS by incorporating the firm's assets into the performance measure.

To see how RONA incorporates both the firm's profit margins and the investment in assets required to produce sales, decompose the

Table 3.3 Analyzing Divisional Performance

	Division A	Division B	Division C
Revenues	$20,000	$22,000	$36,000
Less: Variable costs	10,000	8,250	10,080
Less: Fixed costs	5,600	8,820	17,000
Net operating income	$ 4,400	$ 4,930	$ 8,920
Less: Taxes (30%)	1,320	1,479	2,676
Net operating profit after tax (NOPAT)	$ 3,080	$ 3,451	$ 6,244
Total assets	$14,000	$21,000	$34,000
Performance Measures			
After-tax return on sales (ROS)	15.4%	15.7%	17.3%
Asset turnover (Sales ÷ Total Assets)	1.43	1.05	1.06
Return on net assets (RONA)	22.00%	16.43%	18.36%
Residual Income (10% required return)	$ 1,680	$ 1,351	$ 2,844

RONA ratio into two basic components. First, recall that RONA was defined in eq. (3.2) as:

$$\text{RONA} = \frac{\text{Net operating income} \times (1 - \text{Tax rate})}{\text{Total assets}}$$

Note, however, that RONA can be restated as the product of after-tax ROS and asset turnover:

$$\text{After-tax ROS} = \frac{\text{Net operating income} \times (1 - \text{Tax rate})}{\text{Sales}}$$

$$\text{Asset turnover} = \frac{\text{Sales}}{\text{Total assets}}$$

$$\text{RONA} = \frac{\text{Net operating income} \times (1 - \text{Tax rate})}{\text{Sales}} \times \frac{\text{Sales}}{\text{Total assets}}$$

This decomposition allows us to identify the sources of any differences in performance that we might observe across divisions.[4] For example, when we rank Roxy's three divisions based on their respective RONAs, we see that division A is the top performer, followed by divisions C and B—in contrast to the C, B, A order obtained with ROS. Looking at the asset turnover ratios, we can see the reason for this reshuffling. Division A's asset turnover ratio is dramatically higher than those of divisions B and C, and this is the reason for its increase in ranking. In other words, division A uses its assets more efficiently than division B or division C.

Although RONA is generally considered to be an improvement over ROS as a performance metric, its use as the basis for performance appraisal and incentive compensation can lead to decisions that are inconsistent with shareholder interests. Specifically, if division managers try to maximize the RONAs of their divisions, this can cause highly profitable divisions to reject good projects from the perspective of the firm as a whole. For example, consider what would happen to the RONA of division A if the division were to engage in an expansion that increased its after-tax operating income by $210 from $3,080 to $3,290 and its total assets by $2,000, representing a return of 10.5 percent on the incremental investment. Although the expansion may look good to the firm as a whole, where a 10 percent return is viewed as acceptable, the adoption of the project will lead to a decrease in division A's RONA from 22 percent to 20.56 percent, as follows:[5]

$$\text{Pre-expansion RONA} = \frac{\$3,080}{\$14,000} = 22.00\%$$

$$\text{Post-expansion RONA} = \frac{\$3,290}{\$16,000} = 20.56\%$$

By accepting the project, the manager of division A reduces the relative performance of his division and correspondingly his incentive compensation for the year.

Residual Income as a Measure of Divisional Performance

Residual income (RI) has been suggested in the managerial accounting literature as an improvement upon RONA as a measure of divisional performance:[6]

$$\begin{aligned} \text{RI} &= [\text{Net operating income} \times (1 - \text{Tax rate})] \\ &\quad - (\text{Required rate of return} \times \text{Total assets}) \qquad (3.4) \\ &= \text{NOPAT} - (\text{Required rate of return} \times \text{Total assets}) \end{aligned}$$

where NOPAT is net operating profit after taxes. Note that RI is a dollar-based performance measure that incorporates information from both the firm's income statement and balance sheet. In the bottom row of table 3.3, with a required rate of return of 10 percent, we see that division C actually made the largest dollar contribution to the firm although division A offered the highest rate of return on assets. Let's consider the effect of the proposed expansion on division A's RI:

Pre-expansion RI = $4,400(1 − 0.30) − 0.10($14,000) = $1,680

Post-expansion RI = $4,700(1 − 0.30) − 0.10($16,000) = $1,690

Consequently, where the division manager is rewarded based on the RI produced by the division, the proposed expansion will be undertaken.

Although RI solves an incentive problem associated with RONA, it is not a perfect measure. RI is a short-term historical measure that may penalize long-term investments. For example, consider the effects of R&D expenditures on RI. An expenditure is made today that it is hoped will lead to profitable investment opportunities in the future. Since R&D expense reduces NOPAT by an amount equal to the after-tax R&D, RI will decrease as a result of the expenditure. The division manager who is compensated based on RI then has an incentive to delay the

R&D expense, which can have an adverse effect on the overall value of the firm. We return to this discussion in several ensuing chapters. More will be said about residual income in chapter 6.

Summary

Accounting information is prepared in accordance with generally accepted accounting principles. These principles come from a number of sources, the most important being the Financial Accounting Standards Board and the Securities and Exchange Commission. Since accounting information is prepared largely for the purpose of assessing historical performance, it should not be surprising that performance measures based solely on historical accounting information have some limitations when used to assess future performance. Thus, the problems we have noted with the use of accounting-based measures are not problems with the accounting system itself or with the way accounting information is prepared but instead with the use of that information for purposes for which it was never intended.

In part II we review the new performance metrics referred to under the rubric of value based management. We argue that value based management is more than simply a performance tool designed to overcome the shortcomings of accounting-based measures. However, the reader should be forewarned that many of the limitations of the accounting measures highlighted in this chapter are also applicable to the measures of VBM.

References

Bierman, Harold. "Beyond Cash Flow ROI." *Midland Corporate Finance Journal* (Winter 1988), 36–39.

Blumenthal, Robin Goldwin. "'Tis the Gift to Be Simple." *CFO Magazine* (January 1998), 61–63.

Dearden, J. "The Case Against ROI Control." *Harvard Business Review* (May–June 1969), 124–134.

Horngren, Charles T., George Foster, and Srikant M. Datar. "Systems Choice: Performance Measurement, Compensation, and Multinational Considerations." Chap. 26 in *Cost Accounting: A Managerial Emphasis*, 9th ed. (Upper Saddle River, N.J.: Prentice Hall, 1997).

Seed, A. H. "Using Cash Flows to Measure Business Unit Performance." *Corporate Accounting* (Summer, 1983).

Verma, Kiran. "Total-Factor Productivity Measurement, Pertinent or Passé?" Chap. 10 in *Performance Measurement, Evaluation, and Incentives*, ed. William J. Bruns, Jr. (Boston: Harvard Business School Press, 1992).

PART **II**

VALUE BASED MANAGEMENT:

NEW TOOLS FOR MEASURING AND REWARDING CORPORATE PERFORMANCE

The founding principle underlying value based management is the discounted cash model of firm value. However, VBM is more than a performance measurement system. Proponents argue that if it is to be successful it must be used to tie performance to compensation. The guiding principle underlying the use of VBM, then, is that measuring and rewarding activities that create shareholder value will ultimately lead to greater shareholder value.

In this part, we survey the most widely used tools of VBM, including free cash flow, economic value added, cash value added, and cash flow return on investment. However, our objective is not only to define and synthesize but to critique. We highlight a fundamental source of difficulty for virtually all VBM systems arising out of their inherent single-period nature and the multi-period nature of the value creation process. This shortcoming becomes clear when we try to extend the use of the VBM metrics to capital budgeting decisions and when we discuss managerial incentive issues.

Chapter **4**

Free Cash Flow Valuation: The Foundation of Value Based Management

> The value of any stock, bond or business today is determined by the cash inflows or outflows—discounted at an appropriate discount rate—that can be expected to occur during the remaining life of an asset.

> **—Warren Buffett,** *Berkshire Hathaway Annual Report* **(1992)**

*A*ll the methods of value based management that we discuss in this book share a common theoretical heritage—they are without exception rooted in the concept of free cash flow valuation. Specifically, they are all built upon the underlying premise that the value of any company, or of its individual strategies and investments, is equal to the present value of the future free cash flows that the entity is expected to generate.

Free cash flow analysis became the measurement standard in the 1980s and continues to be the primary method for valuing a company or a strategic business unit. We particularly see free cash flow models being used more and more in evaluating strategic decisions, in such areas as acquisitions, joint ventures, divestitures, and new product development. In earlier decades we heard only about earnings as the primary driver of value. Today there is increasing interest—from Warren Buffett to the U.S. Postal Service—in the relevance of free cash flows for managing a firm to create shareholder value. While there has been an ongoing debate regarding the use of specific value based management techniques, free cash flow analysis as the core valuation concept has not been questioned.

The growing attention being given to free cash flows is no doubt linked to a changing philosophy. As emphasized in chapter 3, the traditional accounting measures of earnings per share or return on net assets, among others, are no longer viewed by many as being adequate benchmarks of value creation. More investors than ever think "investment accounting" (an alias for free cash flows) is the correct paradigm, which in their minds bears little relation to the historical accounting statements. In short, many have come to believe that it is free cash flows that matter.

As a result of this change in perspective, U.S. corporations have significantly altered their management of free cash flows. In 1960 free cash flows were at a negative ten cents per share, but by 1996 they were at an all-time high of $15 per share, or $76 billion in the aggregate. Firms simply are not allowing cash to sit around as they once did. Cash as a percentage of total assets for the S&P industrials has fallen from 10 percent in 1986 to 6 percent in 1999. Also, less cash is being invested in plants and equipment. Instead, much of the cash is being returned to investors by reducing debt levels and buying back stock. In 1996, $176 billion was used to repurchase stock, compared to $99 billion in 1995, the previous record year (Davies 1997). We even believe that the financial crisis that occurred in Asia in the late 1990s had something to say to investors regarding the importance of cash flows. Many corporations learned the hard way that it is easier to get cash into Asia than to get it out. All the concrete and steel that was used to create highways and airports were irreversible investments when the economy experienced a sharp downturn. Managers simply lost sight of the fact that in the final analysis only if cash is returned to the firm and ultimately to the investors will value be created.

In this chapter, we define and show how to measure free cash flows; we then explain how free cash flows are converted to their present value through the use of the discounted cash flow model. We describe and illustrate the use of the free cash flow valuation concept, and talk about the role of value drivers in management's efforts to increase shareholder value. Finally, we think about what the investor needs and wants when it comes to information about the firm, which includes free cash flows.

The Beginning for VBM: Free Cash Flows

We begin with the basic notion that

Firm value is the present value of a company's future free cash flows.

Then we restate the problem as

Firm value is the present value of the free cash flows from existing assets plus the present value of growth opportunities.

This revision allows us to assign shareholder value to new strategies, which LEK/Alcar (a consulting firm well known as an enthusiastic advocate of creating shareholder value) calls strategic value analysis (see Rappaport 1998). In chapter 5 we consider the passionate views of Stern Stewart & Co. on this subject, where they restate the free cash flow paradigm as

Firm value is equal to the present value of all future "economic value added" [or what they have popularized as EVA] plus invested capital.[1]

In chapter 6 we examine the idea, as argued by the Boston Consulting Group and the HOLT Value Associates—with no less fervor than that of Stern Stewart—that

Firm value is equal to the present value of all future "cash value added" plus invested capital.[2]

After this survey we see that everyone agrees that all these methods for finding firm value give identical results, at least in theory. But then comes the rest of the story: there is great disagreement as to which approach is "best" at providing management answers that lead to increased shareholder value. The intensity of the disagreement has brought about what the popular press has come to call the "metric wars."

What Is a Free Cash Flow?

To begin with the basics, what is a free cash flow? Most managers think a lot about cash flow. They forecast it, worry about it, discuss it with their bankers, and constantly search for ways to improve it. But the concept is not widely understood. Just ask someone to define cash flow, and you will get a wide variety of responses, ranging from the balance in the firm's checking account to some ill-defined cash amount provided by the firm's operations.

The appropriate definition and measurement of a firm's cash flow is driven by the reason for computing the cash flow. That is, how we intend to use the calculation matters. As one choice, we could use the conventional accountant's format, called a cash flow statement. In this statement, the accountant explains what caused the reported change in a firm's cash balance from one balance sheet to the next. Such knowledge, while meaningful for some purposes, has little relevance in managing the firm to create shareholder value. Instead we are interested in the investor's perspective as to why cash flows matter. While there is similarity in the computations, the difference in perspective between the accountant and the investor is not merely semantic. The investor wants to know the relevant cash flow in order to determine firm value, which is exactly what we want to know as well.

What is the cash flow that matters to the firm's investors? It is the cash that is free and available to provide a return on the investors' capital. Simply stated—after all, it is not a complex matter—free cash flow is the amount that is available for the firm's investors.

In addition, free cash flows are one and the same regardless of whether we view them from the firm's or the investor's perspective. There is an important equality that must be understood if we are to grasp the significance of free cash flows within a valuation context:

> The cash flows that are generated through a firm's operations and investments in assets equal the cash flows paid to—received by—the company's investors.

That is,

$$\text{Firm's free cash flows} = \text{Financing or investors' cash flows}$$

Let's look more closely at measuring free cash flows, first from the firm's perspective and then from the investor's perspective.

Calculating a Firm's Free Cash Flows

A company's free cash flows are equal to its after-tax cash flows from operations less any incremental investments made in the firm's operating assets. Specifically, free cash flows are calculated as follows:

operating income

+ depreciation and amortization

= earnings before interest, taxes, depreciation and amortization (EBITDA)

− cash tax payments

= after-tax cash flows from operations

− investment (increase) in net operating working capital, which is equal to current assets less non-interest-bearing current liabilities

− investment in fixed assets (capital expenditures) and other long-term assets

= free cash flow

In the foregoing calculation, we add back depreciation because it does not involve a cash payment. Also, the cash tax payments are the actual taxes paid, not the amount accrued in the income statement. Notice, too, that only the non-interest-bearing debt, such as accounts payable and accrued wages, are included in computing the increase in net working capital.[3]

To illustrate how to compute free cash flows, consider Johnson & Johnson's 1999 operations, a year in which the company produced $1.78 billion in free cash flow. The makeup of J & J's free cash flow was as follows (billions of dollars):[4]

Operating income		$5.391
Depreciation		1.444
Earnings before interest, taxes, depreciation, and amortization (EBITDA)		$6.835
Cash taxes		1.877
After-tax cash flows from operations		$4.958
Nonoperating income		.024
Investment in current assets	$1.714	
Increase in non-interest-bearing current liabilities	.108	
Investment in net working capital		$1.606
Investment in fixed assets and other long-term assets		1.601
Free cash flows		$1.775

Thus, in 1999, Johnson & Johnson generated $4.96 billion from operations plus $24 million from nonoperating activity. This amount, however, was reduced by the incremental investment in net working capital of $1.6 billion and by another $1.6 billion invested in fixed assets and other long-term assets.

What happened to the $1.78 billion in cash flow that Johnson & Johnson produced? Quite simply, this amount was "free" to be paid out to the firm's investors. Determining the amount of cash received by Johnson & Johnson's investors can validate this fact.

Calculating the Investors' Cash Flows

We can compute the cash flows received by a firm's investors, i.e., the financing cash flows, as follows:

> interest payments to creditors
> + repayment of debt principal
> − additional debt issued
> + dividends paid to stockholders
> + share repurchases
> − additional stock issued
> = financing cash flow

Thus, the financing cash flows are simply the net cash flows paid to the firm's investors, and if negative, the cash flows that are being invested in the firm by the investors. We already know that Johnson & Johnson had $1.78 billion in free cash flow in 1999. We should expect this amount to be equal to the cash flow received by the investors, which is confirmed as follows (billions of dollars):

Interest paid to creditors	$ .197
Reduction (repayment) in debt principal	.082
Dividend payments	1.479
Repurchase of stock	.017
Free cash flows	$1.775

As already suggested, the firm's free cash flows are *always* the same as the cash flows remitted to the firm's investors.

Free Cash Flows: That's What Matters

Even the infamous Motley Fool, a Web-based investment advisory service, recognizes that to some investors free cash flows drive a firm's value. According to *The Motley Fool:*

> Dell Computer continues to roll on, gaining $8⅝ to $118³⁄₁₆ this morning after reporting second-quarter results that again blew the rest of the industry off the face of the earth. The direct seller of computer systems reported its eighteenth consecutive quarter of record revenues and fourteenth consecutive quarter of 40 percent or more year-over-year growth in revenues. The company ended the quarter as the industry's leader in profitability, revenue, and unit growth, and in asset management. Indeed, the company's focus on economic returns on capital rather than EPS growth are part of the reason why the Dell model, conceptually and practically, continues to lead the industry and create value for shareholders.
>
> "People can point to a Dell as an example of a market mania or people can point to things that people say about Dell as another sign of a market top. I simply think Dell demonstrates the limitations of looking at accounting-based returns rather than looking at the economic returns," said Randy Befumo of Legg Mason Fund Adviser in Baltimore. "GAAP accounting for earnings does not capture the $1.5 billion in cash that Dell has generated from its negative working capital float over the past eleven quarters." Once again, free cash flow (earnings before depreciation minus capital investment and working capital investment) ran in excess of reported earnings at Dell—the eleventh quarter in a row for that to take place. At its highest point, free cash flow was running at 323 percent of reported earnings. [As a result,] the company generated a 217 percent return on invested capital and $641 million in cash from operations.

—Dale Wettlaufer
The Motley Fool
http://www.fool.com
August 19, 1998

To summarize, a company's free cash flow is equal to its cash flow from operations less any additional investments in working capital and long-term assets. Furthermore, a firm's free cash flow is equal to the amount distributed to its investors—thus, the name *free* cash flow.

We find it interesting that when we present this equality to executives, some do not find it as intriguing and significant as we do. A few will say, "What's the big deal? All we would have to do is change the amount or form of what is paid to the investors and thereby change the free cash flow." While this is true, they fail to understand that the amount and makeup of a firm's free cash flows are not the result of "playing with the numbers." Instead, free cash flows are the consequence of management policies and practices that have implications for the investors regarding the firm's value. We should recognize that a firm's free cash flows are the result of operating, investing, and financing decisions, not some ad hoc number that can be manipulated as we want.

Free Cash Flows and Firm Valuation

The makeup of a firm's cash flows and how they are distributed to investors is essential information in managing a firm's cash resources, particularly for a growth firm. But as already noted, there is another reason for computing a firm's cash flows—to ascertain firm value. One "true believer" stated the following about the importance of free cash flows:

> The value of a corporation is determined by the investors' perception of that firm's ability to generate cash over the long haul. Cash flow is always the preferred approach. Being focused on cash flow helps each manager see how his or her actions can result in an increase in the firm's stock price.

Let's return to the Johnson & Johnson example, where the firm's investors received $1.78 billion in cash flow during 1999. Assume that Johnson & Johnson's investors expected the firm to generate this same cash flow of $1.78 billion each and every year into the future. What does this suggest to us about the firm's value?

Within the context of a discounted cash flow model of firm value, we could think of Johnson & Johnson's value as equal to the present value of its expected future cash flow stream. In other words, the company's value is the present value of the future cash flow stream of $1.78 billion, discounted at the investors' required rate of return.

Valuing the Firm: Framing the Analysis

Using free cash flows for valuing a firm is relatively straightforward. Firm value is the present value of future cash flows for the entity as a whole. Specifically, a firm's economic or strategic value is equal to the present value of its free cash flows discounted at the company's cost of capital, plus the value of the firm's nonoperating assets:

$$\text{Firm value} = \frac{\text{Present value of}}{\text{free cash flows}} + \frac{\text{Value of}}{\text{nonoperating assets}}$$

Nonoperating assets here include such items as marketable securities, excess real estate, or overfunded pension plans. We then compute shareholder value as

$$\text{Shareholder value} = \text{Firm value} - \text{Future claims}$$

where future claims include interest-bearing debt (both short-term and long-term), capital lease obligations, underfunded pension plans, and even contingent liabilities. The value of each of these claims should be determined by asking the question, If this claim were to be settled today, what would have to be paid?

To this point, we have essentially stated the obvious: To value a firm, we project future free cash flows and then determine their present value. But the question is how to frame the analysis.

Free Cash Flows—But for How Long?

Projecting a company's cash flows for the life of the firm is no easy task. We could conceivably do as one Japanese firm reportedly has done and develop a strategic plan for 250 years, estimate the expected cash flows, and then calculate their present value. However, given the difficulties with forecasting distant cash flows, a more sensible approach is to divide the firm's cash flows into two parts: (1) cash flows to be received during a finite period that corresponds to the firm's strategic planning period, and (2) cash flows to be received after the strategic planning period. For example, Texas Instruments uses its long-range plan to project cash flows for ten years into the future. Then it computes the present value of the projected operating cash flows for the planning period and the present value of the "residual value" (the value beyond the ten-year projections) to estimate the value of the company. If the value is consistent with the current market price, then according to management, "Future plans are in line with what investors expect of our financial performance."

The length of the planning period should correspond to the duration of the competitive advantage that the firm enjoys. Only when a firm has a competitive advantage can management expect to earn returns in excess of its cost of capital. When the competitive advantage has dissipated, there is no incentive, at least not in terms of creating economic value, to continue to spur growth of the firm. Thus, growth duration is an important criterion for determining the length of the planning period.

To identify a firm's growth duration, we have to examine the company relative to its competition according to a number of factors. Consideration should be given to the presence of established distribution channels, any brand names the firm might own, and the firm's R & D efforts. The pharmaceutical industry, for instance, has a relatively long growth duration period because of patented products, proven processes, and R & D investment, which all raise the barriers of entry. In contrast, small companies in fragmented industries can have little if any sustainable competitive advantage and as such would have very short growth duration periods and very little, if any, economic value.

As to a method for estimating a firm's growth duration, we could make assumptions regarding the factors that affect a firm's free cash flows. We would hold these variables constant and then vary the length of the forecast until the present value of the cash flows less debt is equal to the market price of the firm's shares. Interestingly, most companies in a given industry fall within a relatively narrow range, signaling the market's perceptions about a firm's value growth duration.[5]

Forecasting Free Cash Flows

Once we have decided on an appropriate planning period, the task then becomes to estimate the firm's future cash flows. Doing so requires us to forecast the year-to-year sales for the planning period and an annual sales growth rate assumed to be constant in perpetuity after the planning period. We then project both the firm's future cash flows from operations and the asset investments to be made over time.

In asking what is important in managing shareholder value, we believe the answer is clear: free cash flows, not earnings, are the key determinant of value as determined in the capital markets. However, in forecasting a firm's free cash flows, we should not totally discount the informational content of earnings. It could very well be that past earnings provide a better basis for predicting future cash flows than the actual history of cash flows themselves. Earnings measure the results of operating cycles but involve judgment, which reduces their credibility. Cash flows, on the other hand, involve less judgment but do not measure the results of operating cycles. Thus, reported earnings can be helpful as a starting point for forecasting free cash flows.

The process of computing free cash flows can best be explained by an example. We recently valued a regional trucking firm, which we call here the Ashley Corporation (not the company's real name). To begin, we examined the firm's historical performance; we then studied the industry in which Ashley competes and its competitive position within the industry. The key issues of concern were the following:

• Sales for the most recent period

• Estimated sales growth rate for the planning period and a growth rate that could be maintained in perpetuity after the planning period—the latter typically approaching the inflation rate

• Expected operating profit margins: operating profits ÷ sales

• Projected ratio of operating assets to sales: net working capital, fixed assets, and other long-term assets relative to sales

• Cash tax rate

These variables have come to be known as *value drivers*, because they are the factors or drivers determining a firm's free cash flows, which in turn affect firm value.

Based on what we learned about the Ashley Corporation and its industry, we made some assumptions as a beginning point for estimating the firm's free cash flows (see table 4.1). These assumptions were based on the company's historical performance, adjusted for some

Table 4.1 Assumptions for Estimating Free Cash Flows, Ashley Corporation

Value Driver	Assumed Percentage		
	1–5 Years	6–10 Years	11 Years
Sales growth	8.0	5.0	2.6
Operating profit margin	7.0	7.0	7.0
Cash tax rate	27.0	27.0	27.0
Net working capital/sales	5.5	5.5	5.5
Fixed assets/sales	40.0	35.0	35.0
Other long-term assets/sales	2.0	2.0	2.0

anticipated changes. For instance, management had developed a strategy that it thought would allow the company to increase its sales ($240
million in the prior year) at about 8 percent for five years, declining to
5 percent the next five years, and then tracking the industry's inflation
rate of 2.6 percent thereafter. The sales projections were estimated by
considering unit sales growth, price increases, and the developing
trends within the trucking industry. Management further believed the
following:

- The firm's before-tax operating profit margins would remain relatively stable at 7 percent.

- Net working capital and other long-term assets had closely followed sales at 5.5 percent and 2 percent of sales, respectively.

- Fixed assets had increased disproportionately to sales in the past,
  and effort needed to be made to reduce fixed assets relative to
  sales. At the time, fixed assets were 45 percent of sales, but management aimed to reduce additional investments in fixed assets to
  40 percent of incremental sales over the next five years and 35 percent from that point forward.

Management also estimated that the firm was holding excess real estate worth $7.5 million that was not essential to the firm's operations.

Table 4.2 presents the results of the free cash flow calculations for
the Ashley Corporation across a ten-year planning period and also for
the eleventh year. The eleventh year is the first year of the residual period, when a constant growth rate in sales is assumed to begin and continue in perpetuity. For understanding the computations, several explanations might prove helpful:

- The annual sales for the first year are based on the beginning sales
  of the prior year of $240 million plus the projected 8 percent annual
  growth rate anticipated from the strategy being planned. For
  instance,

  Sales in year 1 = (1 + Sales growth rate) × Prior year sales
  $$= (1 + 0.08) \times \$240,000 = \$259,200$$

  This logic was used to determine sales in all ensuing years.

- Before-tax operating profits were assumed to be 7 percent of sales
  across all years.

- The cash taxes were projected to equal 27 percent of before-tax operating profits.

Table 4.2 Free Cash Flow Calculations, Ashley Corporation ($ thousands)

	\multicolumn{11}{c}{Years}										
	1	2	3	4	5	6	7	8	9	10	11
Value Drivers											
					Assumed Percentages						
Sales growth	8.0	8.0	8.0	8.0	8.0	5.0	5.0	5.0	5.0	5.0	2.6
Operating profit margin	7.0	7.0	7.0	7.0	7.0	7.0	7.0	7.0	7.0	7.0	7.0
Cash operating tax rate	27.0	27.0	27.0	27.0	27.0	27.0	27.0	27.0	27.0	27.0	27.0
Net working capital/sales	5.5	5.5	5.5	5.5	5.5	5.5	5.5	5.5	5.5	5.5	5.5
Fixed assets/sales	40.0	40.0	40.0	40.0	40.0	35.0	35.0	35.0	35.0	35.0	35.0
Other assets/sales	2.0	2.0	2.0	2.0	2.0	2.0	2.0	2.0	2.0	2.0	2.0
					Free Cash Flow Calculations						
Sales	$259,200	$279,936	$302,331	$326,517	$352,639	$370,271	$388,784	$408,223	$428,635	$450,066	$461,768
Operating profit	$ 18,144	$ 19,596	$ 21,163	$ 22,856	$ 24,685	$ 25,919	$ 27,215	$ 28,576	$ 30,004	$ 31,505	$ 32,324
Taxes	4,899	5,291	5,714	6,171	6,665	6,998	7,348	7,715	8,101	8,506	8,727
After-tax operating profits	$ 13,245	$ 14,305	$ 15,449	$ 16,685	$ 18,020	$ 18,921	$ 19,867	$ 20,860	$ 21,903	$ 22,998	$ 23,596
Incremental Investments											
Net working capital	$ 1,056	$ 1,140	$ 1,232	$ 1,330	$ 1,437	$ 970	$ 1,018	$ 1,069	$ 1,123	$ 1,179	$ 644
Fixed assets	7,680	8,294	8,958	9,675	10,449	6,171	6,480	6,804	7,144	7,501	4,096
Other assets	384	415	448	484	522	353	370	389	408	429	234
Total investment	$ 9,120	$ 9,850	$ 10,638	$ 11,489	$ 12,408	$ 7,494	$ 7,868	$ 8,262	$ 8,675	$ 9,108	$ 4,973
Free cash flow	$ 4,125	$ 4,455	$ 4,812	$ 5,196	$ 5,612	$ 11,427	$ 11,999	$ 12,599	$ 13,228	$ 13,890	$ 18,623
Present value	$ 3,619	$ 3,428	$ 3,248	$ 3,077	$ 2,915	$ 5,206	$ 4,795	$ 4,417	$ 4,068	$ 3,747	

Note: Sums may have insignificant rounding errors.

- The incremental investments for the different asset categories are based on the following calculation:

$$\begin{array}{c}\text{Incremental} \\ \text{asset investment} \\ \text{in year } t\end{array} = \left(\begin{array}{c}\text{Sales in year } t \\ -\text{Sales in year } t-1\end{array}\right) \times \text{Assets-to-sales percent}$$

Thus, for year 1 (thousands of dollars),

Net working capital = ($259,200 − $240,000) × 5.5% = $1,056

Fixed assets = ($259,200 − $240,000) × 40% = $7,680

Other long-term assets = ($259,200 − $240,000) × 2% = $384

Notice also that in computing the free cash flows, we did not add back depreciation expense as we did when computing Johnson & Johnson's free cash flows. In the Johnson & Johnson example, we were computing the firm's *historical* free cash flows. For the Ashley Corporation, we were estimating *future* free cash flows. In looking forward in time, it is common practice to assume that the depreciation expense is equal to the cost of replacing existing fixed assets. Depreciation is viewed as a proxy for reinvestment. Therefore, we do not add back any depreciation expense, but neither do we show a cash outflow for replacing already existing depreciable assets. The only addition to fixed assets occurs when sales increase and the firm needs additional fixed assets to support the increase in sales.

Computing a Firm's Economic (Strategic) Value

Having projected a firm's expected free cash flow stream, both for the planning period and for the first year of the post-planning or residual period, we discount these amounts back to their present value to determine the company's economic or strategic value. If we assume that a firm's strategic planning period is T years, the present value of the planning period free cash flows for years 1 through T would be computed as follows:

$$\begin{array}{c}\text{Planning period} \\ \text{present value}\end{array} = \frac{\text{Free cash flow in year 1}}{(1 + \text{Cost of capital})^1} + \frac{\text{Free cash flow in year 2}}{(1 + \text{Cost of capital})^2}$$

$$+ \ldots + \frac{\text{Free cash flow in year } T}{(1 + \text{Cost of capital})^T}$$

The value of the residual cash flows in year T (the end of the planning period), with cash flows beginning in year $T + 1$ and growing at a constant growth rate in perpetuity, would be calculated as follows:[6]

$$\frac{\text{Residual value}}{\text{in year } T} = \frac{\text{Free cash flow in year } T + 1}{\text{Cost of capital} - \text{Growth rate}}$$

Finally, a firm's economic value or strategic value is equal to the present value of the combined or total free cash flows:

$$\text{Economic value} = \frac{\text{Present value of all}}{\text{free cash flows}}$$

$$= \frac{\text{Present value of the}}{\text{planning period}} + \frac{\text{Present value of the}}{\text{residual period}}$$
$$\text{free cash flows} \qquad\qquad \text{free cash flows}$$

We can illustrate these present value computations by returning to the Ashley Corporation example. Relying on the forecasted free cash flows in table 4.2, we calculated the firm's economic value as follows (millions of dollars):

Present value of the cash flows for years 1–10	$38.52
Present value of the cash flows for the residual value	44.06
Firm's economic value	$82.58

The present value of the free cash flows for the first ten years, $38.52 million, is simply the sum of the individual present values for each of the ten years. In calculating the present value, we used a discount rate of 14 percent—our estimate of the firm's cost of capital. The present values of the cash flows for the first ten years are shown on the bottom row of table 4.2.[7]

Obtaining the present value of the residual cash flows requires two calculations:

1. Compute the residual value in year 10 based on the cash flows beginning in year 11 and continuing in perpetuity. This value is as follows (millions of dollars):

$$\frac{\text{Residual}}{\text{value in}} = \frac{\text{Free cash flow in year 11}}{\text{Cost of capital} - \text{Growth rate}} = \frac{\$18,623}{0.14 - 0.026} = \$163.36$$
$$\text{year 10}$$

2. Calculate the present value of the residual cash flow stream as follows (millions of dollars):

$$\begin{array}{c}\text{Present value} \\ \text{residual} \\ \text{cash flows}\end{array} = \frac{\text{Residual value in year 10}}{(1 + \text{Cost of capital})^{10}} = \frac{\$163.36}{(1 + 0.14)^{10}} = \$44.06$$

To continue, we added the excess real estate of $7.5 million to the firm's economic value to arrive at a total firm value of $90.08 million; we then subtracted the firm's outstanding interest-bearing debt of $42 million for a shareholder value of $48.08 million:

Firm's economic value	$82.58
Excess real estate	7.50
Firm value	$90.08
Debt	42.00
Shareholder value	$48.08

Determining the Discount Rate

To this point, we have assumed that we know the right discount rate, that is, the firm's cost of capital, to be used in present value calculations, which to be truthful we don't. Measuring a company's cost of capital is no easy task. Because estimates are likely to be inaccurate, we may even choose to compute a range of discount rates rather than a single point estimate of the cost. One *Fortune* 100 company, for instance, uses a band of 8 percent to 11 percent for its cost of capital. Nevertheless, we are left with no choice but to estimate the firm's cost of capital as best we can. In doing so, we rely on some basic ideas to guide our computations:

• A firm's cost of capital is an opportunity cost, not an out-of-pocket cost. The cost of capital is an economic concept, where the cost is based on the opportunity cost of the invested capital. As such, it is different from an accountant's concept of cost, which exists only if it is explicitly incurred. As far as the accountant is concerned, there is no cost for equity capital when computing a firm's income. But for the financial economist, the cost of equity is as real as the cost of debt and represents one of the more significant costs of doing business. In measuring the forgone return that could be earned elsewhere by the stockholder, the manager has to look to the capital markets to ascertain the opportunity cost as implied by the prevailing market price for the security.

• Since we measure a firm's free cash flows on an after-tax basis, the cost of capital should also be expressed after taxes.

• A firm's cost of capital, or more accurately its *weighted* cost of capital, should include the costs from all sources of capital, both debt and equity. There is a temptation to think of the interest rate on the firm's debt as its cost of capital, especially when the firm is financing an investment entirely by debt. This idea is not correct. We need to remember that increasing the firm's debt levels has implicit costs for the shareholders owing to the increase in the firm's risk. Thus, we should weight the costs of each and every source of capital by their relative contribution to the firm's overall financing. Specifically, the cost is computed as follows:

$$
\begin{aligned}
\text{Weighted cost} \atop \text{of capital} = & \left[\frac{\text{Cost of}}{\text{debt}} \times (1 - \text{Tax rate}) \times \frac{\text{Debt value}}{\text{Firm value}} \right] \\
& + \left[\frac{\text{Cost of}}{\text{equity}} \times \frac{\text{Equity value}}{\text{Firm value}} \right]
\end{aligned}
$$

where the debt and equity values relative to firm value are the percentages of the firm's total financing coming from debt and equity, respectively.

As already hinted, there are an almost unlimited number of issues to be resolved and procedures that could be used in computing a company's cost of capital that lie far beyond the scope of our study.[8] For our purposes, we limit our discussion to a relatively simple presentation.

To understand more about the cost of capital calculation, let's continue our example of the Ashley Corporation. At the time of the valuation, the management at the Ashley Corporation assumed that the firm's future financing would consist of 25 percent debt and 75 percent equity, with the equity coming from internally generated funds. The firm's before-tax cost of debt was 7.68 percent; thus, given a corporate tax rate of 27 percent, the firm's after-tax cost of debt was 5.61 percent: $7.68\% \times (1 - 0.27) = 5.61\%$.

The firm's cost of equity was estimated using the Capital Asset Pricing Model, which holds that

$$
\begin{aligned}
\text{Cost of equity} = & \text{ Risk-free rate} \\
& + (\text{Company beta} \times \text{Market risk premium})
\end{aligned}
$$

A risk-free rate of 6 percent was used based on the going interest rate for Treasury bills, along with a market risk premium of 8 percent.[9] The firm's beta was thought to be 1.35. Given this information, we estimated the firm's cost of equity to be 16.8 percent:

$$\text{Cost of equity} = 6\% + (1.35 \times 8\%) = 16.8\%$$

Using this information, the Ashley Corporation's weighted average cost of capital was estimated to be 14 percent:

	Percentage of Capital	After-Tax Cost	Weighted Cost
Debt	25%	5.61%	1.40%
Equity	75%	16.80%	12.60%
Weighted average cost of capital			14.00%

To conclude, computing a firm's weighted average cost of capital can involve a wide variety of techniques, some simple and some very complex. We would even have difficulty on a conceptual basis in defending the idea of a single cost of capital for a firm as a whole rather than a cost of capital for each and every investment. What we have presented here is one of the simpler approaches to calculating a firm's cost of capital. Even so, it is the approach taken by most firms (see an example in appendix 4B).

The Value Drivers: Going Deeper

The foregoing discussion demonstrates the process of estimating a firm's value based on the amount and timing of its free cash flows. The approach, while not without its limitations, provides an excellent way for management to think about managing for shareholder value.

If we believe that the capital markets assign a value to a firm based on the free cash flows generated—and there is good reason for such a belief—then the free cash flow valuation method helps us understand what drives firm value. Equally important, we can determine which of the value drivers have the greatest effect on firm value. For instance, when we tested the sensitivity of the Ashley Corporation's value to the sales growth rates, value actually decreased as sales increased. Based on the assumed sales growth rates (see table 4.2), the present value of the firm's free cash flows was $82.6 million. On the other hand, if sales did not increase at all (zero growth across all years) the present value of the free cash flows would be $87.6 million. In other words, increased sales would lower the potential value by $5 million. Stated in another way, the present value of the growth opportunities is negative $5 million.

How could this be? Simply, the company was not earning its cost of capital. As sales increased, profits increased, but not enough to cover the cost of capital on the additional asset investments. Thus, given management's projections, for every one-dollar increase in sales, firm value would be lowered—not what management should be doing. Only if the profit margins were increased to 7.2 percent would the firm value remain unchanged as sales increase. We can think of the 7.2 percent as the *threshold profit margin*—the operating profit margin where value neither increases nor decreases as sales change. If the firm earned an operating profit margin above 7.2 percent, then as sales increased, firm value would increase. Otherwise, despite intentions to the contrary, management is destroying value by growing the company.

What we have just observed provides a different way of looking at the problem. Instead of thinking of value as being equal to the present value of all future cash flows, we can solve for firm value by computing two distinct components of the cash flow stream:

$$\text{Firm value} = \begin{matrix} \text{Present value of} \\ \text{free cash flows} \\ \text{from existing assets} \end{matrix} + \begin{matrix} \text{Present value of} \\ \text{free cash flows} \\ \text{from growth opportunities} \end{matrix}$$

For new high-potential firms, much of the firm value can lie in the second component of this equation. In contrast, more mature companies derive most of their value from the first component—the present value of the free cash flows from existing assets. We should note that the only way for the second part of the valuation equation to be positive is for the firm to earn a return on the incremental invested capital that exceeds the firm's cost of capital. The Ashley Corporation is a great case in point. We estimated that in the three years prior to the valuation, firm value had been reduced $30 million in spite of the company's being profitable. This same story has been played out in numerous companies in the 1970s and 1980s.

We also found that Ashley Corporation's value was highly sensitive to changes in the firm's operating profit margins, as would be expected from what has been said. The shareholders' equity values relative to different operating profit margins were as follows (thousands of dollars):

	Operating Profit Margins	Equity Value	Change in Base Case Equity Value
	6.00%	$27,369	−$20,715
	6.50	37,731	−10,353
Base case	7.00	48,084	0
	7.50	58,436	10,352
	8.00	68,789	20,705
	8.50	79,141	31,057
	9.00	89,494	41,410

We see that a half percentage point change in the operating profit margin can raise or lower value by about $10 million, or about 20 percent of the equity value given the current strategic plans.

Finally, firm value for the Ashley Corporation was sensitive to investments in fixed assets; the firm was fixed-assets intensive. For example, a 10 percent decrease in incremental fixed assets (e.g., a reduction from 40 percent of sales to 36 percent of sales) resulted in a $5 million increase in firm value. Thus, not only should management manage its income statement better, but it could also benefit the firm's shareholders by better managing the firm's fixed assets.

The sensitivity of the Ashley Corporation's value was examined relative to changes in the other value drivers as well, but we need not continue. The point is clear: Firm value is affected by certain critical factors, called value drivers. Understanding the significance of these value drivers is one of the most important things management can do in its endeavor to maximize shareholder value.

As clearly shown in the Ashley Corporation example, value drivers provide a direct connection between financial decisions and firm value, and as such offer the best focus for managing shareholder value creation. However, while sales growth is a value driver, what we also need to know is, What drives the value driver? In other words, there is a temptation for management to feel good about the exercise of free cash flow analysis, but that doesn't get down to the "shop floor." Thus, management must—if value based management is to make any difference—know what is behind the value drivers.

Figure 4.1 shows the efforts of one company's managers to link different layers of value drivers to business unit value. In this regard, they commented,

Figure 4.1 Value Drivers: The Key to an Economic Road Map

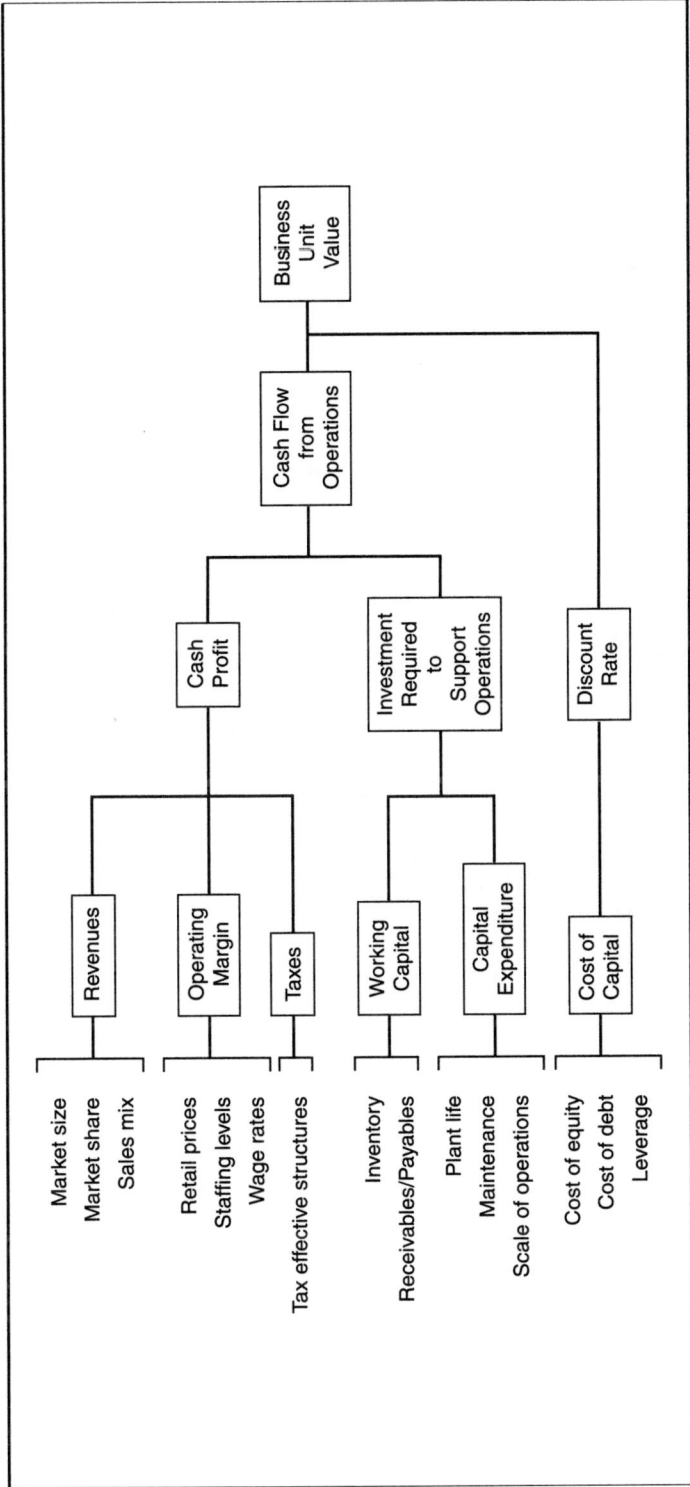

We simulate required performance improvement or degradation to match current market price. We also simulate the impact of changes in performance on value. Each business identifies value drivers that improve cash flow, such as reducing cost, reducing inventories, collection procedures, increasing process yield, and improving cycle time.

It is this type of approach that allows management to manage a firm for value. Only by knowing the important linkages between decisions being made and their effects on the firm's economic value can any difference be made through value based management.

The Shareholder, Free Cash Flows, and Other Things

If the goal is to increase a firm's share price, what should management try to communicate to its investors?[10] If someone asked whether a company's share price was too high, too low, or about right, how would a manager respond? The opinion that "it depends on the circumstances" is most likely wrong. (While we would grant a few exceptions to our blanket statement, we think they are rare indeed.)

Most CEOs believe that one of their primary roles is to be the firm's spokesperson to the public, which includes the firm's investors. However, while most employees are taught that the customer is always right, many CEOs act as if the investors were almost always wrong. Some complain about the market's short-term focus and the pressure they feel to put the firm's short-term interests above the long-term future. Rarely, according to them, have they met an analyst who fully appreciates their firm's potential. However, we believe that many managers underestimate investors and their ability to price a business fairly when they are well informed.

We do not mean to criticize managers for taking seriously their role as the chief advocates of their companies. Prospective shareholders might desire more honesty, but existing shareholders would not appreciate an executive who is continually talking down their shares. After all, a higher share price makes it easier for firms to finance investments.

Besides the usual historical financial measures, investors also want information about the firms' future prospects, and they want more nonfinancial information. As we explained in chapter 2, institutional investors want firms to provide more details about their corporate governance practices, such as boardroom procedures and ethical guidelines. How should managers respond to these varied demands for information by the financial community?

The answer depends largely on what kinds of information we believe the financial markets want and need. In a study by Shelley Taylor & Associates (a consulting firm located in Palo Alto), the biggest institutional investors in the United States and Europe rated one piece of information above all others: free cash flow. Most executives, however, refuse to believe this finding. Instead, they continue to rely on noncash accounting measures to guide decisions while destroying value in the process.

This management perspective has discouraged firms from being forthright with shareholders. Although the disclosure of cash flow itself is easy enough, Shelley Taylor's research suggests that information that would help investors measure future cash flows is guarded closely. Investors want more information about specific business segments and how a firm's results compare with their internal performance measures.

The Shelley Taylor study also explodes a few myths, especially those relating to corporate governance. Of nineteen kinds of corporate governance information considered important, only one—executive pay—ranked among the top twenty issues investors care about. In addition, they are primarily concerned about *how* an executive's compensation relates to performance and only secondarily about the amount paid.

Knowing what investors care about is one thing; knowing how to inform them is another. For a start, managers often face conflicting objectives. Detailed information about strategy and business segments, for example, can help competitors if too much detail is disclosed, hurting shareholders in the process. This has long been cited as an advantage of German- or Japanese-style capitalism, where banks that own lots of shares are the only shareholders that get detailed information.

One way firms are overcoming this problem is to hold private meetings with groups of institutional investors. Provided the information is not abused, regulators allow this kind of exchange. Recent legislation has in fact made it harder to sue a company merely because something unexpected happens. This change should make it less threatening for managers to talk about their plans.

The more significant conflict, however, arises from management's reluctance to share more information with shareholders. Making their goals public exposes them to more scrutiny, and despite all the publicity about shareholder value and accountability, chief executive officers understandably dislike being in a "fish bowl," much like the owners of privately held companies dislike the increased scrutiny when they take a company public. Even so, several large accounting firms have begun a search for other measures to complement the financial measures that are already widely used.

Summary

The concept of free cash flow serves as the foundation—and a good one—for value based management. No matter what we choose to do, free cash flows should be at the heart of any effort to understand how management can contribute to a company's value.

Free cash flow is equal to the cash flow from operations less any incremental investments in working capital and capital expenditures. But what makes free cash flows important is that they represent the amounts distributed to the firm's investors, and as such, represent the core determinant of firm value.

In defining firm value, we frame the analysis as follows:

$$\text{Firm value} = \frac{\text{Present value of}}{\text{free cash flows}} + \frac{\text{Value of}}{\text{nonoperating assets}}$$

and

$$\text{Shareholder value} = \text{Firm value} - \text{Future claims}$$

The determinants of value, or value drivers, include

- Amount of sales
- Sales growth rate
- Operating profit margin
- Asset-to-sales relation
- Cash taxes

We create economic value by earning a rate of return on invested capital that exceeds the firm's weighted cost of capital. Alternatively, we can create value by not enlarging the firm (or even better, downsizing it) when the return on capital is less than the cost of capital. Management should be committed to strategies that create value, that is, to strategies where the present value of the growth opportunities is positive.

From recent studies we know that free cash flow is considered to be an important piece of information for investors, and we believe it will become even more so with time. Thus, management has an obligation to make public the amount of the firm's free cash flows, including a breakdown by major segments of the business. Only then can the firm's owners best know how management is doing at the job of creating economic value for the investors.

Appendix 4A

Johnson & Johnson Financial Statements ($ millions)

Balance Sheets

Assets	Dec. 31, 1998	Dec. 31, 1999
Current assets		
Cash and equivalents	$ 1,994	$ 2,363
Marketable securities	789	1,516
Net accounts receivable	3,752	4,233
Inventories	2,898	3,095
Other current assets	2,053	1,993
Total current assets	$11,486	$13,200
Property, plant, and equipment, net	6,395	6,719
Other investments	437	441
Intangibles	7,364	7,571
Other assets	1,610	1,232
Total Assets	$27,292	$29,163
Liabilities and Shareowners' Equity		
Current liabilities		
Loans and notes payable	$ 2,753	$ 1,806
Accounts payable	1,877	2,003
Accrued liabilities	3,012	2,972
Accrued salaries	445	467
Taxes payable	206	206
Total current liabilities	$ 8,293	$ 7,454
Long-term debt	1,729	2,450
Deferred tax	578	287
Other liabilities	2,615	2,759
Common equity		
Common stock	$ 1,535	$ 1,535
Retained earnings	13,602	15,755
Less: Treasury stock	(1,060)	(1,077)
Common equity	$14,077	$16,213
Total Liabilities and Equity	$27,292	$29,163

Income Statement ($ millions)

	1999
Sales	$27,471
Cost of products sold	8,442
Gross profit	$19,029
Selling, general and administrative expense	12,194
Operating income before depreciation	$ 6,835
Depreciation and amortization	1,444
Operating profits	$ 5,391
Interest expense	197
Nonoperating income	24
Income taxes	1,586
Earnings available for common	$ 3,632

Appendix 4B

Texas Instruments Cost of Capital Computations

In 1996, Texas Instruments' management estimated the firm's weighted average cost of capital to be 11 percent, calculated as follows:

Cost of Debt

$$\frac{\text{After-tax}}{\text{cost of debt}} = \frac{\text{Before-tax}}{\text{cost of debt}} \times (1 - \text{Tax rate}) = 6.5\% \times (1 - 0.35) = 4.23\%$$

Cost of Equity

$$\frac{\text{Cost of}}{\text{equity}} = \frac{\text{Risk-free}}{\text{rate}} + \frac{\text{Company}}{\text{beta}} \times \frac{\text{Market}}{\text{risk premium}}$$

$$= 6\% + (1.2 \times 6.05\%) = 13.25\%$$

Proposed Capital Structure

25 percent debt and 75 percent equity

Weighted Average Cost of Capital

	Percentage of Capital	After-Tax Cost	Weighted Cost
Debt	25%	4.23%	1.06%
Equity	75%	13.25%	9.94%
Weighted average cost of capital			11.00%

References

Boston Consulting Group. *Shareholder Value Management: Improved Measurement Drives Improved Value Creation.* Book 2. Boston: BCG, 1994.

Davies, Erin. "What's Right About Corporate Cash Flow; Afloat in a Sea of Green." *Fortune* (March 31, 1997): 28.

Ehrhardt, Michael C. *The Search for Value: Measuring the Company's Cost of Capital.* Boston: Harvard Business School Press, 1995.

Ibbotson, Roger G., and Rex A. Singuefield. *Stocks, Bonds, Bills, and Inflation: Historical Returns.* Chicago: Ibbotson Associates, 1999.

"Of Pigs and Pokes." *The Economist* (March 14, 1998): 69.

Rappaport, Alfred. *Creating Shareholder Value.* 2d ed. New York: Free Press, 1998.

Stewart, G. Bennett, III. *The Quest for Value.* New York: HarperBusiness, 1991.

Chapter 5

Pick a Name, Any Name: Economic Profit, Residual Income, or Economic Value Added

> EVA is based on something we have known for a long time: what we call profits, the money left to service equity, is not profit at all. Until a business returns a profit that is greater than its cost of capital, it operates at a loss. Never mind that it pays taxes as if it had a genuine profit. The enterprise still returns less to the economy than it devours in resources. . . . Until then it does not create wealth; it destroys it.
>
> **—Peter Drucker,** *The Information Executives Truly Need* **(1995)**

*O*ur objective in this chapter is to give the reader a good grasp of the concept of economic value added (EVA) and the calculations associated with it. Of the different methods for measuring shareholder value creation, it can safely be said that none has received more attention than EVA.[1]

While EVA can be used for several purposes, its main use is as a period-by-period performance measurement. But, as we will see later, Stern Stewart & Co. believes the use of EVA should be more than merely a financial exercise conducted within the inner chambers of a firm's financial suite.

The specific goals for this chapter are to

- Understand the fundamental concept on which EVA is built, that is, residual income or economic profits, two terms that are used interchangeably

- Establish the relation between residual income (economic profits) and free cash flows

- Explain the logic and rationale for EVA, along with the procedures for computing EVA

- Define market value added and demonstrate its importance for management

The Fundamental Concept: Residual Income or Economic Profits

In chapter 3, we briefly introduced a concept called *residual income,* which we suggested as an alternative performance measurement to the traditional return on net assets (RONA). We now return to this notion; however, we will now use two terms interchangeably, these being *residual income* and *economic profits.* These are terms that have been created by economists and managerial accountants. The *financial* accountant, in contrast, speaks only of *accounting profits.* Thus, there is a real difference in perception as to just what is meant by *profits.* For the financial accountant, profits are measured as revenues less operating expenses less the cost of debt financing in the form of interest expense, where interest expense (and preferred stock dividends if incurred) is the only financing cost to be recognized. There is no cost, as such, for equity capital; after all, the shareholders are the owners to whom the profits flow. For economists, however, there are no profits until the required rates of return of *all* investors have been met, including the equity owners—true profits come only after subtracting all financing costs, both for debt capital *and* equity capital, where cost is defined as the opportunity cost of the funds if they were to be invested in another firm of similar risk. In other words, those who speak of residual income maintain that a business activity must not only break even but also earn enough to justify the cost of all the capital used in pursuing the activity. Only then has the firm broken even. Thus,

$$\text{Accounting profits} = \text{Sales} - \text{Cost of goods sold} - \text{Operating expenses} - \text{Interest expenses} - \text{Taxes}$$

but

$$\underset{\text{profits}}{\text{Economic}} = \text{Sales} - \underset{\text{goods sold}}{\text{Cost of}} - \underset{\text{expenses}}{\text{Operating}} - \text{Taxes} - \underset{\text{capital used}}{\text{Charge for all}}$$

or

$$\underset{\text{profits}}{\text{Economic}} = \underset{\text{profits after taxes}}{\text{Net operating}} - \underset{\text{capital used}}{\text{Charge for all}}$$

where the charge for all capital used is the after-tax interest cost on the firm's debt and a cost for its equity capital as well.

To summarize, the economic profits metric is intended to measure how well the firm has performed in terms of generating profits in a particular period, given the amount of total capital that was used to generate those profits. Otherwise, the firm's providers of capital could have liquidated their investment in the firm and put the liberated capital to some other use. Only if there are profits that exceed these opportunity costs would economists, and most managerial accountants, say that the firm "made money," or in other words, earned residual income or economic profits. To put it simply, for the economist, the traditional accounting profits metric does not completely measure a firm's profits.

Residual Income and Free Cash Flows

When it comes to shareholder value, many of us were raised on the notion that a stock's value is equal to the present value of the future dividends (discounted dividends model). In appendix 5A, we show that given certain assumptions the present value of residual income and the present value of future dividends are one and the same.

We have also been taught that the value of an investment is equal to the present value of its cash flows (the net present value rule). Of even more relevance to our study, in chapter 4 we defined a firm's value as the present value of the expected free cash flows. The idea that value is equal to present value of cash flows is without a doubt one of the cornerstones of finance. Thus, it is important to know how residual income relates to discounted free cash flows in determining firm value. Only by reconciling these two approaches (sounds like a good accountant) can we know that value is independent of the perspective taken and that the two methods are essentially tied to the same financial theory. In fact, they are conceptually equivalent. We can show that

$$\underset{\text{value}}{\text{Firm}} = \underset{\text{future free cash flows}}{\text{Present value of}} = \underset{\text{capital}}{\text{Invested}} + \underset{\text{future residual income}}{\text{Present value of}}$$

Thus, firm value can be viewed in either of two ways: (1) value is equal to the present value of all future expected cash flows; or (2) value is equal to the capital that has been invested in a company plus the present value of all future residual income. In the latter case, residual income is the value being created by management beyond the total capital invested in the company by its investors. For instance, for a firm with a market value of $50 million, compared to $40 million of capital invested in the company, the $10 million difference represents the market's expected future residual income stated on a present value basis. That is, the incremental $10 million in value is the result of the investors anticipating that the firm will earn returns above the cost of capital.

An Illustration of Valuation

To compare valuing a company in terms of free cash flows and in terms of residual income, consider the hypothetical Griggs Corporation. The company anticipates that sales in the forthcoming year (2001) will be $20 million on total beginning capital (debt and equity) of $10 million. Management expects an after-tax operating profit margin (operating profits after taxes ÷ sales) of 6.25 percent, which suggests that the after-tax operating profits would be $1.25 million on the $20 million in sales ($20 million × 0.0625) in the year 2001. Given the $10 million in beginning invested capital, the firm's return on beginning-of-year capital is 12.5 percent ($1.5 million in operating profits ÷ $10 million of invested capital).

Further assume that management is planning to reinvest 60 percent of its income to grow the company. Given its return on capital of 12.5 percent, the firm will be growing at 7.5 percent (60 percent of the 12.5 percent return on capital). Also, for each dollar of sales growth, fifty cents of additional investment will be required in working capital and fixed investments each year. We assume that the 7.5 percent growth rate will continue for five years, the time over which management believes the firm can maintain its current competitive advantage, also the time it can continue to earn a rate of return above its cost of capital of 10 percent. Then, after five years under the current corporate strategy, no value will be created by continued growth, Hence, there is no reason to grow the firm after the fifth year—at least not in terms of creating shareholder value.

Based on the foregoing information, we can estimate the Griggs Corporation's value either by finding the present value of the firm's free cash flows or by computing the present value of its future residual income added to the invested capital. These calculations are shown in table 5.1. In the left-hand portion of the table, we see the free cash flows (operating profits after taxes less additional investments in working capital and fixed assets) for the five-year planning period 2001–2005 as well as their present values. In 2006 the firm's net operating profit after taxes is forecasted to be $1,795,000. Since there are no plans to grow the firm in year 2006 and beyond, no additional investments are required.[2] As a result, free cash flow is equal to operating profit of $1,795,000, which is expected to continue in perpetuity. The value of a $1,795,000 annual perpetual cash flow stream at the end of year 2005 is $17.95 million, determined as follows:

$$\text{Present value}_{2005} = \frac{\text{Free cash flow in year 2006}}{\text{Cost of capital}} = \frac{\$1,795,000}{10\%} = \$17,950,000$$

We can then discount the 2005 year-end value to today's present value (beginning of year 2001):

$$\text{Present value}_{2001} = \frac{\text{Year 2005 value}}{(1 + \text{cost of capital})^5} = \frac{\$17.95 \text{ million}}{(1 + 0.10)^5} = \$11.142 \text{ million}$$

As shown in table 5.1, the present value of all the free cash flows—and the firm's value—is $13.314 million.

A similar process is shown in the right-hand part of table 5.1, where we find firm value for Griggs by taking the present value of the annual residual incomes and add them to the beginning capital as of today. Residual income in each year is equal to net operating profits after taxes less a charge for the beginning capital. The charge is equal to the cost of capital times the amount of beginning capital. For year 2001 residual income is $250,000, that is, $1.25 million operating profit less a 10 percent charge (cost of capital) on the $10 million beginning capital ($1.25 million – (0.10 × $10 million) = $250,000). The method of finding the present values of the residual incomes is identical to that used for free cash flows, which results in a present value of $3.314 million for all the future expected residual income. We then add today's invested capital of $10 million to the present value of the residual income, for a total

Table 5.1 Griggs Corporation Valuation ($ thousands)

Free Cash Flow Valuation

Year	Sales	Operating Profits After Taxes	Investments	Free Cash Flows	Present Value of Free Cash Flows
2001	$20,000	$1,250	$750	$500	$ 455
2002	21,500	1,344	806	538	444
2003	23,113	1,445	867	578	434
2004	24,846	1,553	932	621	424
2005	26,709	1,669	1,002	668	415
		Present value of free cash flows (2001–2005)			$ 2,172
2006	28,713	1,795	0	1,795	$11,142
				Free cash flow value	$13,314

Residual Income Valuation

Year	Beginning Capital	Residual Income	Present Value of Residual Income	Return on Beginning Capital (%)
2001	$10,000	$250	$227	12.5
2002	10,750	269	222	12.5
2003	11,556	289	217	12.5
2004	12,423	311	212	12.5
2005	13,355	334	207	12.5
2006	14,356	359	2,229	
Total present value of residual income			$ 3,314	
Original invested capital			10,000	
Residual income value			$13,314	

firm value of $13.314 million—the exact outcome found with the free cash flow method.

We have also shown the rate of return on invested capital (net operating profits after taxes ÷ beginning capital) in the last column of table 5.1, which confirms that the firm is earning 12.5 percent on its capital, compared to a 10 percent cost of capital. Thus, the $3.314 million created in value comes from earning a return that exceeds the investors' 10 percent cost of capital and from the increasing amounts of capital used each year to grow the company. If, on the other hand, we had projected earning only a 10 percent rate of return on the capital, the value of the firm would be $10 million, which means that the present value of the residual incomes would be zero. The value of the firm would be equal to the invested capital, no more or no less.

In summary, the present value of a firm's free cash flows is the same as the present value of its residual income plus the capital invested in the business by its investors. In theory, there is no difference between the two approaches, at least not when it comes to measuring firm value. But if there is no difference between a free cash flow valuation and value based on residual income, then why bother? What does residual income give us that free cash flows do not?

The weakness of free cash flow analysis is that it does not provide a readily apparent measure of *annual* operating performance. Free cash flow can be negative for one of two reasons: (1) investment is high in a profitable business, or (2) operating profitability is low in an unprofitable business. In 1992, when Wal-Mart was one of the leading value-creating firms, the firm had a free cash flow of –13 percent of capital while earning a rate of return of 8 percent above its cost of capital. At the same time, Kmart had a free cash flow equal to 7 percent of capital but earned a return on capital of 3 percent *below* the firm's cost of capital. Thus, free cash flows can be uninformative or even misleading on the surface. The saying that "happiness is a positive cash flow" may not be as true as we have been led to believe. Consequently, residual income is intended to provide a better measure of period performance while maintaining consistency with free cash flow valuation. But, as we will see later, even that hope may not be realized.

EVA: Fine-Tuning Residual Income

The acronym EVA was first used for economic value added in 1989 (Finegan 1989), but it was not until four years later that it began receiving major attention, largely as a result of a feature article in *Fortune* magazine (Tully 1993). The *Fortune* article provided a basic presentation of the EVA concept and its computation; interviewed Joel Stern and Bennett Stewart of Stern Stewart & Co., the leading proponents of EVA use; and offered examples of major U.S. corporations that were successfully using EVA as a measure of corporate performance. From that auspicious beginning, EVA has captured the interest of many in the business community, including such firms as Coca-Cola Co., Eli Lilly, Bausch & Lomb, Sony, Matsushita, Briggs & Stratton, and Herman Miller. Even the Chinese—specifically, China Eagle Securities Research Institute—are trying to adapt EVA to use in evaluating security investments (ChinaOnline 2000). The noted economist Michael Jensen, at Harvard Business School, has commented, "The *Fortune* story really put EVA on the map as the leading management tool." Since that time, the financial press has regularly discussed the EVA concept, usually telling of a recent experience of some adopter. Based on a Lexis Nexis search for articles on EVA, the number has consistently grown, from 152 in 1994 to 672 in the twelve months ending June 1999.[3] Many of these references have appeared in such widely read magazines and newspapers as *Fortune,* the *Wall Street Journal,* and the *London Times,* and in a large number of special-interest magazines. *Fortune* has called EVA "today's hottest financial idea." Peter Drucker has stated that EVA is a measure of "total factor productivity" whose growing popularity reflects the new demands of the information age. In the words of Robert Boldt, the investment officer at CalPERS, a $135 billion pension fund, "Accounting benchmarks just don't do the job. Only EVA gives a real picture of value creation." As a result, CalPERS determines its focus list of underperforming companies based on a firm's long-term stock performance, its corporate governance practices, *and* on an economic value-added calculation.

Even the public accounting profession is beginning to take note of EVA, which we find a little surprising given that EVA calls into question the value of earnings as a measure of corporate performance—the very measure that most traditional accountants consider to be the "final answer." We remember an incident in 1993 when we spoke to a group of partners of a major accounting firm regarding value-based management. In the presentation we suggested that earnings was not the best measure of a firm's performance, that they should begin thinking about some form of economic profits that incorporated an opportunity cost of funds for the equity investors' capital. We presented the rationale and provided an illustration of EVA. Before the presentation was complete, it was apparent to us that these listeners, who had spent their careers in auditing and tax work, were not particularly receptive to anything that departed from their traditional reliance on earnings as a performance measure. But then, a mere three years later, an American Institute of Certified Public Accountants workshop on the future of financial management actually predicted that EVA would replace earnings per share in the regular stock and earnings reports in the *Wall Street Journal*.[4] While we should not assign too much significance to these happenings, we believe they do reflect real overall changes in viewpoint.

What Is EVA?

To understand the economic value added measure, one can best begin by placing it within the context of the earlier discussion of residual income or economic profits. EVA is simply a modified, or according to many EVA users, a new and improved measure of economic profits. Figure 5.1 shows the relations between various financial measures.

As reflected in the "earnings" line of the figure, financial accountants developed the income statement based on an accrual system for matching revenues with the relevant costs and expenses. In the next line, we add back after-tax interest expenses to get the firm's operating profits—the earnings available to all the firm's investors. Next, the financial economist or managerial accountant subtracts a charge for the use of the *total* capital invested, not just for debt as the financial accountant would do. Finally, EVA proponents make additional adjustments to the financial statements in an effort to better reflect the economic sense of the data. Generally accepted accounting principles (GAAP) do not matter to an EVA proponent if they are not considered to matter to investors in the capital markets.

Figure 5.1 Relations Between Financial Measures

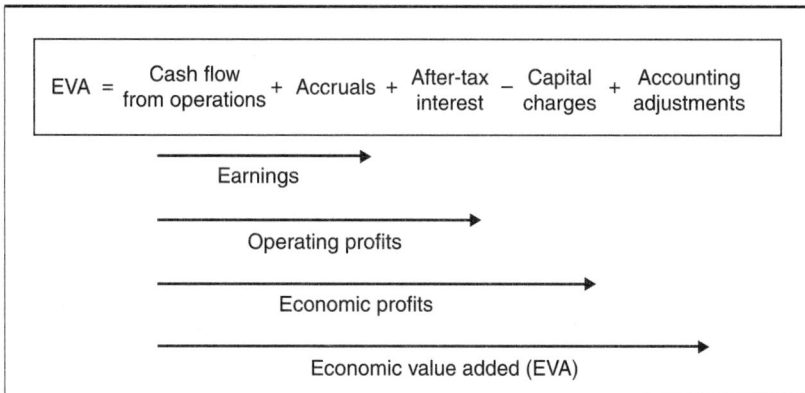

$$\text{EVA} = \frac{\text{Cash flow}}{\text{from operations}} + \text{Accruals} + \frac{\text{After-tax}}{\text{interest}} - \frac{\text{Capital}}{\text{charges}} + \frac{\text{Accounting}}{\text{adjustments}}$$

Earnings

Operating profits

Economic profits

Economic value added (EVA)

While Joel Stern and Bennett Stewart view the residual income metric as a definite improvement over conventional accounting profit measures, they would contend that something is still missing. They argue strongly—probably too strongly, in some accountants' view—that many traditional accounting activities are not relevant when it comes to explaining value creation. Accountants, according to Stern and Stewart, serve some important functions, but providing the framework needed to know if a firm is creating or destroying value is not one of them. Since investors are interested in cash flows, not profits per se, all the measures of accruals and reserves created by accountants are of questionable value. In fact, Stern and Stewart would view them as a deterrent to understanding how the firm is doing from an economic viewpoint. Thus, they believe all this "noise" or "distortion" needs to be removed when computing a company's economic profits and in estimating the amount of capital invested by the firm's investors. Stated plainly, they would encourage analysts not to accept the traditional accounting measures of operating profits and asset book values at face value.

Measuring a Firm's EVA

On the surface, EVA looks much like the economic profits measure. Specifically, EVA is computed as follows:

$$EVA = NOPAT - (k \times CAPITAL)$$

where

$$
\begin{aligned}
NOPAT &= \text{Firm operating profits after taxes but before} \\
&\quad \text{financing costs and noncash bookkeeping entries} \\
&\quad \text{except depreciation[5]} \\
k &= \text{Firm's weighted average cost of capital} \\
CAPITAL &= \text{Total cash invested in the firm over its life,} \\
&\quad \text{net of depreciation}
\end{aligned}
$$

Alternatively, EVA is frequently expressed as

$$EVA = (r - k) \times CAPITAL$$

where r is the firm's return on capital, computed as follows:

$$\text{Return on capital} = \frac{NOPAT}{CAPITAL}$$

Or, if we want more information about a firm's return on invested capital, we can measure the return on capital as follows:

$$\frac{\text{Return on}}{\text{invested capital}} = \frac{\text{NOPBT}}{\text{Sales}} \times \frac{\text{Sales}}{\text{CAPITAL}} \times \left(1 - \frac{\text{Cash taxes}}{\text{NOPBT}}\right)$$

where NOPBT is the firm's net operating profits before taxes.

This latter format is similar to the old DuPont method mentioned in chapter 3 for assessing a firm's accounting return on net assets (RONA). Here we see that the return on invested capital is a function of (1) the firm's before-tax operating profit margin (NOPBT ÷ Sales), (2) the capital turnover rate (Sales ÷ CAPITAL), and (3) the cash tax rate (Cash taxes ÷ NOPBT). Thus, the return on invested capital is determined by how the firm manages its income statement, its balance sheet, and its taxes.

Based upon the foregoing measurements, we can observe if a firm is creating or destroying value (if EVA is positive or negative). Specifically, we know that management can increase firm value in one of the following ways:

- Increase the rate of return earned on the existing base of capital; that is, generate more operating profits without tying up any more capital in the business.

- Invest additional capital in projects that return more than the cost of obtaining the new capital.

- Liquidate capital from, or at least curtail further investment in, operations where inadequate returns are being earned.

Some companies produce significantly positive EVAs by investing in a large number of projects with returns only modestly above the cost of capital. Other firms achieve excellent results by investing in a limited number of high-return projects. Also, much of the restructuring of the late 1980s and 1990s was about improving returns—evidently with success. According to Goldman Sachs U.S. Research Group, the spread between the return on invested capital and the cost of capital for the S&P Industrials has increased from zero in 1986 to over 4 percent in 1997 (Goldman Sachs 1998).

Calculating NOPAT and CAPITAL

Although computing EVA is not fundamentally different from calculating economic profits, it is the adjustments going into a computation of EVA that make it unique. These adjustments, or what Stern

---

Briggs & Stratton and EVA

Each year in its annual report, Briggs & Stratton includes a section they call "Performance Measurement," which shows the firm's EVA computation for the three prior years. The 1999 computations and explanations are presented below.

Performance Measurement

Management subscribes to the premise that the value of the company is enhanced if the capital invested in the company's operations yields a cash return that is greater than that expected by the providers of capital.

Conventional financial statements and measurements, such as earnings per share and return on shareholders' investment, are of less interest to the providers of capital than indicators of cash flow generation and effective capital management. Consequently, we adhere to a measurement of performance that guides divisional and corporate management in evaluating current decisions and long-term planning strategies toward the goal of maximizing cash operating returns in excess of the cost of capital. The following table summarizes the results for the three most recent fiscal years (in thousands):

Stewart & Co. calls *equity equivalents,* are made for the express purpose of converting both NOPAT and CAPITAL from an accounting book value to economic book value. While Stern Stewart speaks of some 160 or so possible equity equivalents for a particular firm, 10 to 15 adjustments are more typical. In any case, there are only three reasons for making adjustments:

- To convert from accrual to cash accounting (eliminating many of the reserves that traditional accountants have created in the financial statements, for example, reserves for bad debt or LIFO reserves)

- To capitalize market-building expenditures that have been expensed in the past (converting from a liquidating perspective to a going-concern perspective, e.g., capitalizing expensed R&D)

	1999	1998	1997
Return on Operations			
Income from operations	**$180,136**	$124,688	$103,719
Adjust for:			
Cost of providing early retirement window	–	–	37,101
Other income except interest income	**4,666**	5,089	1,485
Increase (decrease) in:			
Bad debt reserves	**(21)**	15	(22)
LIFO reserves	**(4,200)**	(794)	769
Warranty accrual	**7,413**	2,548	760
Adjusted operating profit	**$187,994**	$131,546	$143,812
Cash taxes[a]	**65,255**	41,102	56,146
Net adjusted cash operating profit after taxes	**$122,739**	$ 90,444	$ 87,666
Weighted Average Capital Employed[b]	**$697,887**	$716,112	$748,005
Economic Return on Capital	**17.6%**	12.6%	11.7%
Cost of Capital[c]	**10.3%**	10.0%	10.9%
Economic Value Added	**$ 50,857**	$ 18,833	$ 6,133

a. The reported current tax provision is adjusted for the statutory tax impact of interest income and expense.
b. Total assets less non-interest-bearing current liabilities plus the bad debt, LIFO and warranty reserves, minus future tax benefits.
c. Management's estimate of the weighted average of the minimum equity and debt returns required by the providers of capital.

- To remove cumulative unusual losses or gains after taxes (converting from successful-efforts accounting to full-cost accounting)

But even these three purposes cannot tell us whether an adjustment *should* be made in practice. Deciding when an adjustment should be made requires some common sense. Specifically, Stern Stewart & Co. recommends adjustments only when:

1. The adjustment is material.
2. The data is available at a reasonable cost.
3. The adjustment is understandable by the employees using EVA.
4. The adjustment can be effectively communicated to the marketplace.
5. The adjustment is replicable by another party.

Table 5.2 Measuring a Firm's NOPAT and CAPITAL

Computing NOPAT	
Financing Perspective	Operating Perspective
Income available for common stockholders	Net operating profits before taxes (NOPBT), excluding unusual losses or gains
+ Interest expense after taxes	
+ Implied interest expense on non-capitalized leases after taxes	+ Implied interest on noncapitalized leases

− Interest and other passive investment income after taxes	− Cash taxes
	  Provision for income taxes
	  − Increase in deferred tax reserve

+ Preferred dividend	+ Marginal taxes saved (paid) on unusual losses (gains)
+ Minority interest provision	+ Marginal taxes saved on interest expense on debt and implied interest on noncapitalized leases − Marginal taxes paid on interest and other passive investment income

+ Changes in equity equivalents
  Increase in deferred tax reserve
  Increase in LIFO reserve
  Goodwill amortization
  Increase in bad debt reserve
  Increase in (net) cumulative expensed intangibles, e.g., R&D and product development
  Unusual loss (gain) after taxes
  Increase in other reserves, such as for inventory obsolescence, warranties, deferred income
	+ Changes in equity equivalents
	  Increase in LIFO reserve
	  Increase in bad debt reserve
	  Goodwill amortization
	  Increase in (net) cumulative expensed intangibles, e.g., R&D and product development
	  Increase in other reserves, such as for inventory obsolescence, warranties, deferred income

= NOPAT	= NOPAT

There are two equivalent approaches—from a financing perspective and from an operating perspective—for calculating NOPAT and CAPITAL. Table 5.2 provides a framework for computing NOPAT and CAPITAL. Both perspectives yield the same answers. While we cannot include all the possible adjustments (equity equivalents) to be made, those shown represent important ones in most cases.

EVA Computed: An Illustration

To illustrate the process, we calculate the EVA for the hypothetical Hobbs-Meyer Corporation for the year 2001. The firm's financial statements are shown in table 5.3. Equally important is the information taken from the footnotes to the financials. (Most of the equity equivalents are

Table 5.2 (continued)

Computing CAPITAL	
Financing Perspective	Operating Perspective
Common equity	Total assets
+ Interest-bearing debt	− Marketable securities and construction in progress
+ Present value of noncapitalized leases	− Non-interest-bearing current liabilities
+ Capitalized leases	+ Present value of noncapitalized leases
− Marketable securities and construction in progress	+ Equity equivalents LIFO reserve
+ Preferred stock	Bad debt reserve
+ Minority interest	Cumulative goodwill amortization Unrecorded goodwill

+ Equity equivalents
  Deferred tax reserve
  LIFO reserve
  Bad debt reserve
  Cumulative goodwill amortization
  Unrecorded goodwill
  (Net) cumulative expensed
    intangibles, e.g., R&D and
    product development
  Cumulative unusual loss (gain)
    after taxes
  Other reserves, such as for
    inventory obsolescence,
    warranties, deferred income
	(Net) cumulative expensed
	  intangibles, e.g., R&D and product
	  development
	Cumulative unusual loss (gain) after
	  taxes
	Other asset-contra reserves, such as
	  for inventory obsolescence,
	  warranties

= CAPITAL	= CAPITAL

found in the footnotes to the financials, not in the statements themselves.) For example, from the footnotes we learn the following:

- The firm uses LIFO (last in/first out) for reporting its inventories and cost of goods sold and the reserves are $175,000 and $200,000 for 2000 and 2001, respectively.

- The company has commitments in the form of noncapitalized leases. The present values of these leases are $200,000 and $225,000 in each of the two years. The implied or imputed interest on these leases in the year 2001 is estimated at $21,000.

- The firm acquired another business, using a pooling of interest, which resulted in unrecorded goodwill of $40,000. However, in other acquisitions, goodwill was recorded and is being amortized as an expense. Goodwill for 2001 was $7,000, but the cumulative goodwill the firm has expensed is $73,000 through year-end 2000 and $80,000 by the end of 2001.

Table 5.3 Hobbs-Meyer Corporation, Balance Sheets and Income Statement, 2000 and 2001 ($ thousands)

	Dec. 31, 2000	Dec. 31, 2001
Cash	$ 16	$ 20
Marketable securities	4	5
Accounts receivables	300	350
Bad debt reserve	(20)	(25)
Net receivables	$ 280	$ 325
Inventory	2,650	3,350
Total current assets	$2,950	$ 3,700
Land	210	263
Plant and equipment	2,475	3,114
Gross fixed assets	$2,685	$ 3,377
Accumulated depreciation	(500)	(690)
Net fixed assets	$2,185	$ 2,687
Goodwill	50	43
Total assets	$5,185	$ 6,430
Accounts payables	$1,040	$ 1,350
Accruals	406	530
Income taxes payable	120	125
Short term debt	110	25
Current portion long-term debt	25	27
Total current debt	$1,701	$ 2,057
Senior long-term debt	210	190
Capitalized leases	880	1,010
Total debt	$2,791	$ 3,257
Deferred income taxes	78	94
Deferred income	15	20
Preferred stock	20	25
Minority interest	25	25
Common stock	$ 56	$ 57
Paid in capital	170	175
Retained earnings	2,030	2,777
Common equity	$2,256	$ 3,009
Total debt and equity	$5,185	$ 6,430

Table 5.3 (continued)

	Dec. 31, 2001
Sales	$20,650
Cost of goods sold	15,900
Depreciation expense	210
Gross profit	$ 4,540
Selling and administrative	$ 3,400
Goodwill amortization	7
Operating profit	$ 1,133
Interest expense	135
Interest income	5
Extraordinary gains	40
Preferred dividends	3
Provision for minority interests	5
Income before taxes	$ 1,035
Income tax provision	488
Income available for common stockholders	$ 547

The firm's cost of capital is 10 percent and its marginal tax rate is 34 percent.

Given the financial information we have about Hobbs-Meyer, we can calculate the firm's EVA for the year ending 2001. These computations, first for NOPAT and then for CAPITAL, are shown in table 5.4. Both the financing and the operating perspectives are presented so that we can compare the two approaches. The following explanations are offered.

NOPAT: Financing Perspective. We begin with the income available to common stockholders and add back all the financing-related expenses and interest income, e.g., interest expenses and preferred stock dividends. As part of the financing expenses, we include an imputed interest cost associated with the noncapitalized leases. These adjustments are all restated on an after-tax basis. We then add all the *increases* in equity equivalents (1) to convert from an accrual to a cash basis, those being increases in reserves, deferred income, and goodwill amortization, and (2) to remove the effects of unusual gains. The resulting NOPAT is $686,000.

Table 5.4 Hobbs-Meyer Corporation NOPAT and CAPITAL Computations ($ thousands)

NOPAT: Financing Perspective	
	2001
Income available for common	$547
Plus:	
Interest expense after taxes	89
Implied interest on noncapitalized leases after taxes	14
Preferred dividend	3
Minority interest provision	5
Less: Investment income after taxes	(3)
Plus: Changes in equity equivalents	
Increase in deferred tax reserves	16
Increase in LIFO reserve	25
Increase in bad debt reserve	5
Increase in deferred income	5
Goodwill amortization	7
Unusual losses (gains) after taxes	(26)
NOPAT	$686

NOPAT: Operating Perspective		
Operating profits		$1,133
Implied interest on noncapitalized leases		21
Net operating profits before taxes (NOPBT)		$1,154
Less: Cash taxes		
Provision for income taxes	488	
− Increase in deferred tax reserve	16	
− Marginal taxes on unusual gains	14	
+ Marginal taxes on interest expense	46	
+ Marginal taxes on implied interest	7	
− Marginal tax paid on investment income	2	
Cash taxes		$ 510
Plus: Changes in equity equivalents		
Increase in LIFO reserve		25
Increase in bad debt reserve		5
Goodwill amortization		7
Increase in deferred income		5
NOPAT		$ 686

NOPAT: Operating Perspective. With this approach, we begin with the before-tax operating profits and add the before-tax implied interest on noncapitalized leases. We then convert the provision for taxes in the income statement, reported on an accrual basis, to a cash basis. We also recognize any tax effects of financing costs and unusual

Table 5.4 (continued)

CAPITAL: Financing Perspective		
	2000	2001
Common equity	$2,256	$3,009
Plus:		
Interest-bearing debt	345	242
Capitalized leases	880	1,010
Present value of noncapitalized leases	200	225
Preferred stock	20	25
Minority interest	25	25
Less: Marketable securities	(4)	(5)
Plus: Equity equivalents		
Deferred tax reserve	78	94
LIFO reserve	175	200
Bad debt reserve	20	25
Cumulative goodwill amortization	73	80
Unrecorded goodwill	40	40
Cumulative unusual gains after taxes	(139)	(165)
Deferred income reserve	15	20
	$ 262	$ 294
CAPITAL	$3,984	$4,825
CAPITAL: Operating Perspective		
Total assets	$5,185	$6,430
Less:		
Marketable securities	(4)	(5)
Non-interest-bearing current liabilities	(1,566)	(2,005)
Plus: Present value of noncapitalized leases	200	225
Plus: Equity equivalents		
LIFO reserve	175	200
Bad debt reserve	20	25
Cumulative goodwill amortization	73	80
Unrecorded goodwill	40	40
Cumulative unusual losses (gains) after taxes	(139)	(165)
	$ 169	$ 180
CAPITAL	$3,984	$4,825

gains. Finally, we add the *increases* in equity equivalents to convert from an accrual to a cash basis. Again, we find NOPAT to be $686,000.

CAPITAL: Financing Perspective. To compute CAPITAL according to the financing perspective, we take the common equity investment and add all sources of debt, except for non-interest-bearing current liabilities (e.g., accounts payable and accrued operating expenses), preferred stock, and minority interests. We subtract out any nonoperating assets, in this case, marketable securities. Finally, we add the equity equivalents—not merely the increases, as we did with NOPAT, but the total amounts. We find CAPITAL to be $3,984,000 and $4,825,000 at year-ends 2000 and 2001, respectively.

CAPITAL: Operating Perspective. This time we begin with the firm's total assets as reported on the balance sheet and subtract the marketable securities and the non-interest-bearing debt; add the present value of the noncapitalized leases; and finally add the equity equivalents related to the firm's asset accounts, such as goodwill amortization and cumulative unusual gains. It should be no surprise that the firm's CAPITAL accounts again equal $3,984,000 and $4,825,000, as we found with the financing perspective.

Now that we know NOPAT and CAPITAL for the Hobbs-Meyer Corporation, we can easily compute its EVA for the year 2001:

$$\text{EVA} = \text{NOPAT} - \text{Cost of capital} \times \text{Beginning CAPITAL}$$
$$= \$686,000 - (10\% \times \$3,984,000) = \$288,000$$

Alternatively, we can compute EVA as

$$\text{EVA} = \left(\begin{matrix} \text{Return on} \\ \text{capital} \end{matrix} - \begin{matrix} \text{Cost of} \\ \text{capital} \end{matrix} \right) \times \text{Beginning CAPITAL}$$

where

$$\text{Return on capital} = \frac{\text{NOPAT}}{\text{CAPITAL}} = \frac{\$686,000}{\$3,984,000} = 17.22\%[5]$$

Thus,

$$\text{EVA} = (17.22\% - 10\%) \times \$3,984,000 = \$288,000$$

So we can conclude that Hobbs-Meyer created $288,000 in value for its shareholders by earning a 17.22 percent return on $3,984,000 beginning invested capital, compared to a weighted average cost of capital of 10 percent.

From EVA to MVA

Management's ultimate goal is not to increase the return on invested capital; nor is it to increase a single EVA. An individual EVA does not capture the investors' perception about management's ability to generate positive EVAs in future years. After all, it is the present value of the future EVAs that determine a firm's market value. For this reason, we need an additional measure for learning how the markets are assessing a company's outlook at generating future EVAs. That measure is market value added (MVA).

Herman Miller, Inc., and EVA

Herman Miller, Inc., is a multinational provider of office, health-care, and residential furniture, and furniture management services. The firm has been one of the strongest proponents of EVA. For the past three years, management has reported the firm's EVAs in the annual reports. Shown below is their EVA calculations and the accompanying comments.

Calculation of Economic Value Added

($ Thousands)	1999	1998	1997
Operating income	$224,313	$208,295	$130,683
Divestiture	–	–	14,500
Interest expense on noncapitalized leases[a]	4,071	4,166	4,509
Goodwill amortization	3,001	6,161	4,725
Other	4,621	13,765	5,093
Increase (decrease) in reserves	(4,293)	1,290	18,649
Capitalized design and research	3,657	2,101	2,819
Adjusted operating profit	$235,370	$235,778	$180,978
Cash taxes[b]	(83,607)	(90,703)	(72,091)
Net operating profit after taxes (NOPAT)	$151,763	$145,075	$108,887
Weighted-average capital employed[c]	$551,600	$606,018	$617,727
Weighted-average cost of capital[d]	11%	11%	11%
Cost of capital[e]	60,676	66,662	67,950
Economic Value Added	$91,087	$78,413	$40,937

a. Imputed interest as if the total noncancelable lease payments were capitalized.
b. The reported current tax provision is adjusted for the statutory tax impact of interest expense.
c. Total assets less non-interest-bearing liabilities plus the LIFO, doubtful accounts and notes receivable reserves, warranty reserve, amortized goodwill, loss on sale of the German manufacturing operation, deferred taxes, restructuring costs, and capitalized design and research expense. Design and research expense is capitalized and amortized over five years.
d. Management's estimate of the weighted average of the minimum equity and debt returns required by the providers of capital.
e. Cost of capital is the firm's dollar cost of capital and equals the weighted average capital employed times the weighted average cost of capital.

MVA is the difference between a company's market value and the invested capital. In other words, MVA is the premium the market awards a company over and above the money investors have put into it, based on the market's expectations of future EVAs. Earlier, we indicated that the difference between a firm's market value and the capital is equal to the present value of all future residual income. Since EVA is a modified form of residual income, we can conclude that MVA is equal to the present value of all future EVAs.

There are two possible scenarios that can occur. Either the market value of the capital is greater than the capital invested, which means that MVA is positive, or the market value is less than the capital invested. In the first scenario, investors believe that management will more than earn the firm's cost of capital. As a result, they assign a value greater than the invested capital. But in the second scenario, investors are signaling that they do not believe the firm will satisfy their required rate of return. What we are observing is exactly similar to a net present value (NPV) analysis for an individual project. A project's NPV is positive if the expected internal rate of return is greater than the cost of capital, and negative otherwise. What managers should aim for is maximizing MVA, just as they work to maximize NPV on projects.

The market recognizes and impounds value creation by granting a multiple of invested capital in excess of 1.0. Some call this the *one-dollar test*. Warren Buffett described the use of the one-dollar test in a Berkshire Hathaway letter to shareholders. He wrote, "It is our job to select businesses with economic characteristics allowing each dollar of retained earnings to be translated eventually into at least a dollar of market value."

Marakon Associates, a consulting firm that concentrates on value based performance measuring and planning, states that in its experience 100 percent of the value created for most companies is concentrated in less than 50 percent of the capital employed. If this is true, there remains substantial opportunity for the management of a lot of companies to unlock value (Mauboussin 1995).

In chapter 1, we showed the top and bottom five wealth creators on Stern Stewart & Co.'s annual list of companies ranked by MVA. In table 5.5, we have expanded the list to the "best" 25 wealth-creating companies in 1999 (based on 1998 data). In the table, we present not only the MVA, but also the EVAs are shown. Clearly, there is no perfect link between a firm's MVA and its reported EVA. As we have already suggested, MVA represents the market's assessment of the firm's future EVAs, as opposed to a single historical EVA, as reported here. It

Table 5.5 The 1999 Stern Stewart Performance 1000 Top 25 MVA Companies

MVA Rank	Company Name	MVA	EVA	Capital	Return on Capital (%)	Cost of Capital (%)
1	Microsoft	$328,257	$3,776	$10,954	56.2	12.6
2	General Electric	285,320	4,370	65,298	19.3	11.9
3	Intel	166,902	4,280	23,626	35.4	12.9
4	Wal-Mart Stores	159,444	1,159	36,188	13.2	9.8
5	Coca-Cola	157,536	2,194	13,311	31.2	11.2
6	Merck	153,170	4,175	29,550	30.0	11.9
7	Pfizer	148,245	1,052	14,631	18.3	11.4
8	Cisco Systems	135,650	1,849	6,509	38.2	13.1
9	Lucent Technologies	127,265	1,514	31,448	17.5	11.6
10	Bristol-Myers Squibb	119,350	2,273	15,883	26.8	11.3
11	IBM	116,572	(1,058)	73,891	10.1	11.7
12	Exxon	114,774	(2,262)	84,599	6.2	8.8
13	Procter & Gamble	102,379	1,661	27,997	17.6	10.8

Table 5.5 (continued)

MVA Rank	Company Name	MVA	EVA	Capital	Return on Capital (%)	Cost of Capital (%)
14	Philip Morris	98,657	5,180	47,121	21.2	9.1
15	Johnson & Johnson	92,568	1,712	24,395	19.5	10.9
16	Dell Computer	90,302	1,447	1,004	200.7	14.0
17	Eli Lilly	87,890	1,548	12,276	23.0	10.2
18	Home Depot	81,285	813	11,452	18.3	9.8
19	SBC Communications	79,956	2,219	53,120	13.9	8.5
20	WorldCom	77,032	(3,585)	86,364	6.0	12.6
21	Schering-Plough	75,620	1,298	6,158	38.1	12.0
22	BellSouth	74,322	1,122	38,297	11.3	8.2
23	America Online	70,861	38	2,334	18.9	16.7
24	AT&T	66,667	(1,314)	68,916	7.9	9.8
25	Abbott Laboratories	65,924	1,347	12,001	22.5	9.9

Source: www.sternstewart.com.

is also interesting to notice the diversity of firms making the list, from high-tech to discount stores to home products. However, the high-techs and communication companies certainly are more than well represented on the list.

More Than a Financial Exercise

As you read about and visit with executives who have integrated EVA into their firm's management system, you cannot help but notice the enthusiasm—even excitement—about what the use of EVA has done for the company's culture and processes. Frequently, it is more an ideology and value system than it is a quantitative analysis. For many, it becomes the paradigm through which they see the business. At a seminar hosted by Stern Stewart & Co., Bennett Stewart spoke of the "underpinnings of EVA," or what we think of as the core values that Stern Stewart believes must accompany the effective use of EVA within a firm. Some of these ideas, subject to our paraphrasing, included:

- Corporate governance should include everyone, and everyone should feel part of the creation of shareholder wealth.

- EVA is a company's profit less a required profit; it is as if we own nothing and rent everything, but it is more than a measure of economic profit—it is also a measure of value added by management, as if the company has gone through an LBO.

- EVA is to provide a shared vision; it is *the* financial management system. To get the benefit of EVA, we must use it for *everything;* otherwise it is not effective; it becomes too complex if only used in certain areas.

- Managers should think and be paid like owners, both viscerally and economically. When management creates value, they should share in the value created. EVA says, "Let's share the increase in value," which is different than a bonus. Sharing value, as opposed to receiving a bonus, is what drives behavior.

So to think that EVA is simply about calculating a number—as informative as that might be—misses the point that Stern Stewart & Co. wants us to understand about EVA. In their seminars and in what they write, you hear more about how to think about financial issues than you do on how to compute EVA. As Joel Stern is quick to say, "Anyone can compute a firm's EVA, but it's how EVA is used that makes the difference." Ehrbar (1998), a senior vice president at Stern Stewart & Co., would tell us that simply using EVA as a benchmark of perform-ance probably isn't worth the bother. He, along with Stewart (1991), argues long and hard that if EVA is to matter, it must become *the* finan-cial management system within the organization, including being tied to incentive compensation from the president down to the shop floor. If it is, they suggest, then four benefits will follow:[6]

- EVA relies on a new and improved measurement of return on invested capital that removes all the accountant's journal entries that can distort the economic information about the firm and mis-lead management and investors about how the firm is performing financially.

- EVA provides a new and improved criterion for evaluating a firm's operating and strategic decisions, including strategic planning, allocating capital, pricing acquisitions or divestitures, and setting goals.

- EVA, combined with the right bonus plan, can instill a sense of urgency along with an owner's perspective; managers will think and act like owners because they are paid like owners.

- An EVA system can change a corporate culture by facilitating com-munications and cooperation among divisions and departments. As such, it can be a key element of a firm's internal corporate gov-ernance.

Thus, if applied as Stern Stewart & Co. would advocate, EVA is intended to provide the right management incentives to change behav-ior, including how capital is utilized, rather than just serving as a tool of financial analysis. That is the primary message that Stern Stewart & Co. would want us to hear.

Summary

EVA is based on the concept of residual income. For the financial accountant, there is no cost for equity capital. But for the financial econ-omist and the managerial accountant, there is a cost associated with the use of equity capital—the opportunity cost of these funds. After con-sidering this cost, we obtain residual income. But EVA is more than residual income; it is also intended to eliminate the "distortions" created by traditional accounting, which make no economic sense.

Mathematically, EVA is computed as follows:

$$
\begin{aligned}
\text{EVA} = &\ \text{Net operating profits after taxes} \\
&- (\text{Cost of capital} \times \text{Beginning CAPITAL})
\end{aligned}
$$

where net operating profits after taxes (NOPAT) and CAPITAL have been restated on a cash basis, or as close to it as we can reasonably get.

Firm value can be expressed in terms of EVA, which will yield the same firm value as the present value of free cash flows. That is,

$$
\frac{\text{Firm}}{\text{value}} = \frac{\text{Present value of}}{\text{future free cash flows}} = \frac{\text{Invested}}{\text{capital}} + \frac{\text{Present value of}}{\text{future EVAs}}
$$

EVA causes us to focus on three ways of increasing value:

- Increase the rate of return earned on the existing base of capital; that is, generate more operating profits without tying up any more capital in the business.
- Invest additional capital in projects that return more than the cost of obtaining the new capital.
- Liquidate capital from, or at least curtail further investment in, operations where inadequate returns are being earned.

Some companies produce significantly positive EVAs by investing in a large number of projects with returns only modestly above the cost of capital. Other firms achieve excellent results by investing in a limited number of high-return projects.

Management's ultimate goal is not to increase the return on invested capital; nor is it to increase a single EVA. An individual EVA does not capture the investors' perception about management's ability to generate positive EVAs in future years. After all, it is the present value of the future EVAs that determine a firm's market value. For this reason, we need an additional measure for learning how the markets are assessing a company's outlook at generating future EVAs. That measure is market value added (MVA). MVA is the difference between a company's market value and the invested capital. In other words, MVA is the premium the market awards a company over and above the money investors have put into it, based on the market's expectations of future EVAs.

The primary purpose of EVA is to provide an answer to the question, Is management creating value for its shareholders? However, to think that EVA is simply about calculating a number—as informative as that might be—would miss the point that Stern Stewart & Co. wants everyone to understand about EVA. If EVA is used purely as a financial measure, few of the real benefits are realized from its use. In fact, Stern Stewart contends that EVA offers four advantages if used properly. In short, the intent is to use EVA as a *behavioral* tool to alter capital utilization and other incentives rather than just a tool of financial analysis.

Appendix 5A

Residual Income and Discounted Dividends

To compare residual income and the present value of dividends, we rely on the concept of clean surplus accounting, which means that all gains and losses affecting a firm's book value are also included in its profits.[7] That is, the change in book value from period to period $(BV_t - BV_{t-1})$ is equal to profits (P_t) less the payment of any dividends (D_t) and therefore

$$P_t = D_t + (BV_t - BV_{t-1}) \qquad (A.1)$$

Solving for dividends in year t, we get

$$D_t = P_t - (BV_t - BV_{t-1}) \qquad (A.2)$$

Residual income in period t (RI_t) stated in terms of equity (not firm) value for period t can be expressed as follows:

$$RI_t = P_t - k\, BV_{t-1} \qquad (A.3)$$

where k is the required return on equity, which we assume to be the same for all periods.

The discounted dividend value of a firm's equity at date 0 (E_0) can be written as follows:

$$E_0 = \sum_{t=1}^{\infty} \frac{D_t}{(1+k)^t} \qquad (A.4)$$

If we solve eq. (A.2) for P_t and substitute into eq. (A.3), the results are

$$D_t = RI_t + (1+k)BV_{t-1} - BV_t \qquad (A.5)$$

Now substituting eq. (A.5) for D_t in eq. (A.3), we get the following result:

$$E_0 = \frac{RI_1 + (1+k)BV_0 - BV_1}{(1+k)^1} + \frac{RI_2 + (1+k)BV_1 - BV_2}{(1+k)^2}$$

$$+ \frac{RI_3 + (1+k)BV_2 - BV_3}{(1+k)^3} + \dots \qquad (A.6)$$

By combining the terms in eq. (A.6), we get

$$E_0 = BV_0 + \left(\frac{RI_1}{(1+k)^1} - \frac{BV_1}{(1+k)^1}\right) + \left(\frac{RI_2}{(1+k)^2} - \frac{BV_2}{(1+k)^2} + \frac{BV_1}{(1+k)^1}\right)$$

$$+ \left(\frac{RI_3}{(1+k)^3} - \frac{BV_3}{(1+k)^3} + \frac{BV_2}{(1+k)^2}\right) + \dots \qquad (A.7)$$

Simplifying the equation gives

$$E_0 = BV_0 + \left(\frac{RI_1}{(1+k)^1}\right) + \left(\frac{RI_2}{(1+k)^2}\right) + \left(\frac{RI_3}{(1+k)^3} - \frac{BV_3}{(1+k)^3}\right) + \dots \qquad (A.8)$$

and if we extend the expression out to $t = \infty$ and assume that $\dfrac{BV_\infty}{(1+k)^\infty} \to 0$, then

$$E_0 = BV_0 + \sum_{t=1}^{\infty} \frac{RI_t}{(1+k)^t} \qquad (A.9)$$

Thus, the dividend discount model can be restated in terms of book value and residual income (or economic profits), which is not true for traditional GAAP-based accounting profit. This restatement is possible because residual income incorporates a charge for all capital, both debt and equity, as is done in determining economic profits, P_t.

References

"China to Appraise Companies Using Economic Value Added Method." ChinaOnline LLC, May 12, 2000.

Drucker, Peter. "The Information Executives Truly Need." *Harvard Business Review* (January–February 1995), 73.

Einhorn, Steve. "EVA® and Return on Capital: Roads to Shareholder Wealth." Goldman Sachs & Co. U.S. Research Group, Selected Transcripts, June 9, 1997.

Ehrbar, Al. *EVA: The Real Key to Creating Wealth.* New York: John Wiley & Sons, 1999.

Finegan, P. T. "Financial Incentives Resolve the Shareholder-Value Puzzle." *Corporate Cashflow* (October 1989): 27–32.

Mauboussin, Michael J. "Wealth Maximization Should Be Management's Prime Goal." C. S. First Boston, Equity Research-Americas, December 13, 1995.

O'Byrne, Stephen F. "Does Value Based Management Discourage Investment in Intangibles?" Working Paper, March 1, 1999.

Selection of articles on EVA appearing in the *Journal of Applied Corporate Finance.* Vol. 12, No. 2 (Summer 1999).

Stewart, G. Bennett, III. *The Quest for Value.* New York: HarperBusiness, 1991.

Tully, Shawn. "The Real Key to Creating Wealth." *Fortune* (September 20, 1993): 38–50.

Chapter **6**

Performance Evaluation Using Rates of Return

> The proper choice of criteria [for choosing an investment] depends on the nature of the investor. . . . Two objectives, however, are common to all investors: 1. They want "return" to be high. The appropriate definition of "return" may vary from investor to investor. But, in whatever sense is appropriate they prefer more of it to less of it. 2. They want the return to be dependable, stable, not subject to uncertainty.
>
> —**Harry M. Markowitz,** *Portfolio Selection* **(1959)**

*J*ust as economic value added and market value added are associated with Stern Stewart & Co., cash flow return on investment and cash value added (CVA) are associated with the Boston Consulting Group (BCG) and HOLT Value Associates. BCG works mostly with strategic planners of large publicly held firms, and HOLT Value Associates has devoted itself to advising professional money managers.[1] In both instances, the tools used—cash flow return on investment and cash value added—are the same.

Chapters 4 and 5 focused on cash flows and value added measures of financial performance. The theoretical link between value and value added is illustrated in figure 6.1, which shows that the present value of all future EVAs plus the firm's invested capital is equal to the present value of free cash flows. The key point is that value creation is expressed in dollar terms. Every student of elementary finance knows that there is a rate of return analogue to these dollar-value performance

111

Figure 6.1 Free Cash Flows and EVAs Provide Same Firm Value

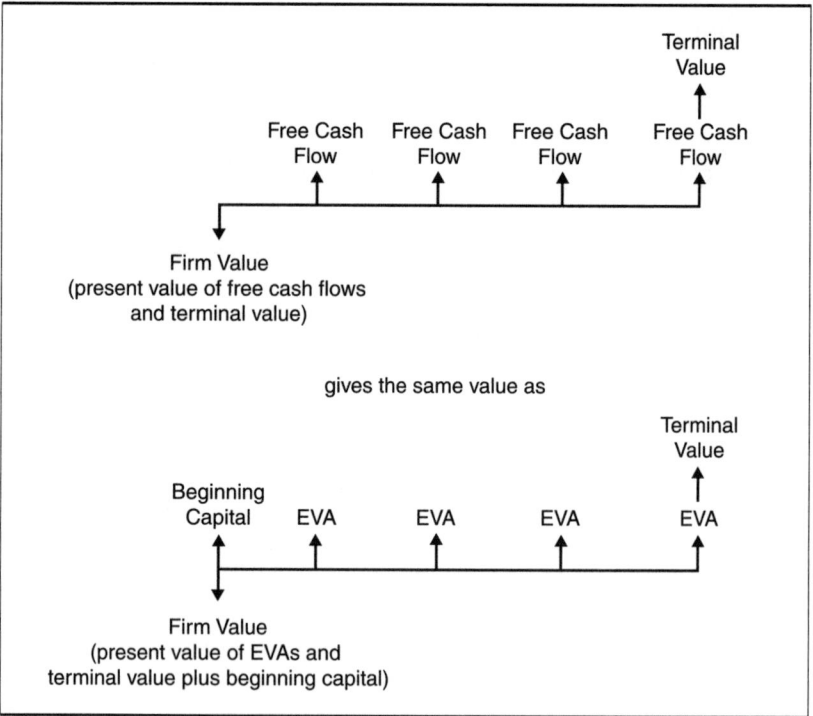

metrics that is generally called internal rate of return. In promoting the use of a rate of return metric, BCG contends that using percentage rates of return facilitates comparison of returns to costs of capital and empirical testing of cash flow models employing those rates of return as primary drivers. It also eliminates the size bias inherent in the use of performance metrics based on dollar values or dollar value added when making comparisons across projects, divisions, or companies.

Although the procedure for estimating a firm's rate of return may become a bit tedious at times, the concept is quite simple. Much like the interest rate earned on a savings account, we want to know the cash-on-cash return being earned. Investors make cash investments and expect to receive cash flows in return. Whether they are satisfied with the investment depends on the rate of return earned on the investment compared to some minimum acceptable return.

Two concepts form the foundation for the models presented in this chapter: total shareholder return (TSR) and total business return (TBR). The operational manifestations of these concepts when applied to value based management are two performance metrics: cash flow return on investment (CFROI), and cash value added (CVA).[2] After carefully defining and developing these metrics we illustrate their use with an example for the Motorola Corporation. Finally, in the chapter appendix, we explain the rationale for some of the more common adjustments made by BCG and HOLT to generally accepted accounting principles (GAAP) financial statements when computing CFROI and CVA.

Taking a Rate of Return Perspective— TSR and TBR

We encounter rate of return performance measures almost daily. For example, the evening news tells us that the Dow Jones average was up (or down) by some percentage. This percent increase (decrease) in the Dow Jones average reflects what financial economists refer to as price appreciation (depreciation), which when combined with dividend yield measures the *rate* of return investors earn from owning a company's stock over a period of time. BCG calls this return measure *total shareholder return* (TSR).

If total shareholder return is to be used as the basis for a system of value based management, then an *internal* counterpart is needed that can be "managed" in an effort to improve a firm's TSR. For BCG, *total business return* (TBR) fills this need. The use of TBR is much like other methods of value based management (free cash flow valuation and economic value added): we can connect a firm's TBR to its value drivers. This connection between TSR and TBR and the related value drivers is shown in figure 6.2, where the basic value drivers are shown to be profitability, as measured by the return on invested capital; growth in new investments; and free cash flows being generated. BCG and HOLT suggest that CFROI is a useful measure of the return a firm earns on its invested capital.

We can think of TBR as a single holding-period return, computed as follows:

$$\text{TBR} = \left(\frac{\text{Free cash flow}}{\text{Beginning value}}\right) + \left(\frac{\text{Ending value} - \text{Beginning value}}{\text{Beginning value}}\right) \quad (6.1)$$

where beginning and ending values are estimates of market values of the firm or business unit at the beginning and end of the period.

Figure 6.2 Total Business Return and the Value Drivers

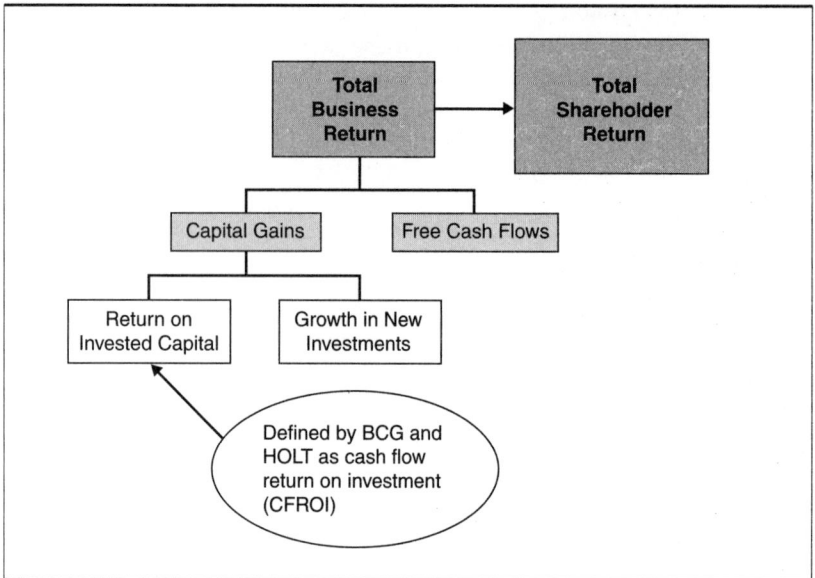

Alternatively, we could use the conventional internal rate of return (IRR) computation to measure the TBR over multiple periods:[3]

$$\begin{array}{c}\text{Beginning} \\ \text{market value}\end{array} = \frac{\begin{array}{c}\text{Year 1} \\ \text{free cash flow}\end{array}}{(1 + \text{TBR})^1} + \frac{\begin{array}{c}\text{Year 2} \\ \text{free cash flow}\end{array}}{(1 + \text{TBR})^2} + \cdots$$

$$+ \frac{\begin{array}{c}\text{Year } N \\ \text{free cash flow}\end{array}}{(1 + \text{TBR})^N} + \frac{\begin{array}{c}\text{Ending value} \\ \text{in Year } N\end{array}}{(1 + \text{TBR})^N}$$

(6.2)

BCG calculates TBR using a unique approach called *total capital time fade model,* or *spot valuation model.*[4] BCG contends that greater accuracy is obtained in valuation estimates by recognizing that a firm's return on investment and its growth rates will fade over time toward a national average. This reflects the belief that investors will not pay for sustained above-average returns. Bartley Madden (1999, pp. 18, 19, 21) of HOLT Value Associates explains,

> When businesses succeed in achieving above-average returns, competitors are attracted by above-average returns and try to serve the customer even more effectively. The competitive process tends to force high-CFROI firms down toward the average. Businesses earning CFROIs below the cost of capital are eventually compelled to

TSR and Procter & Gamble

Procter & Gamble is a strong advocate for using the TSR metric and provides each employee with a booklet entitled *An Employee's Guide to Total Shareholder Return*. The booklet explains the importance of creating shareholder value as measured by TSR. The metric is used both at the company level and within each business unit. P & G employees are encouraged to think about how they can contribute to improving the rate of return for the company's shareholders. The firm's value drivers are as follows:

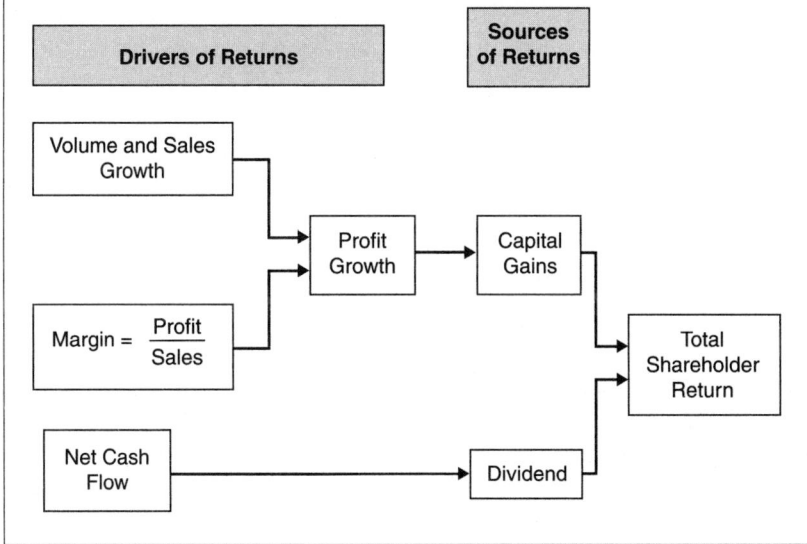

restructure and/or downsize in order to earn at least the cost of capital, or eventually they cease operations. . . . All else equal, more wealth is created when CFROIs above the cost of capital are coupled with larger asset bases. But as a tendency, a higher rate of asset growth drives down CFROIs. So, the complete display of a firm's life cycle includes both CFROIs and real asset growth rates.

For instance, to compute a firm's value, BCG would begin with current CFROI and growth rate as the starting points and then "fade" these numbers to national averages over forty years.[5] BCG prefers to use a firm's current CFROI and growth rate in the analysis rather than the estimate of analysts or planners.

BCG uses the TBR metric in two ways: as the framework for a valuation model, and for performance evaluation. To apply TBR in firm valuations, BCG projects the cash flows both for the firm's assets in place and from any new investments coming from planned growth. TBR is also used purely as a tool for evaluating management performance relative to the market, peers, or the cost of capital. For instance, Proctor & Gamble's management compares its returns against a peer group within the industry, aspiring to be in the top third of the group.

In conclusion, TBR incorporates the returns (CFROIs) both for the assets in place and the growth assets in an effort to capture the link between a firm's performance and shareholder returns. Thus, CFROI is an important determinant of a company's TBR. Also, many firms rely solely on the CFROI of the firm or business unit's assets in place, ignoring growth assets, as their measurement of management performance. They simply want to know how effective management has been in using existing assets, without regard to any value attributable to future plans.

Cash Flow Return on Investment (CFROI)

CFROI represents an economic measure of the company's performance and as such attempts to capture the average underlying rates of return on the firm's investment projects. BCG defines CFROI as "the sustainable cash flow a business generates in a given year as a percentage of the cash invested in the firm's assets." When inflation is a significant factor, both cash flow and cash invested are expressed in deflated or current dollars. BCG cites three primary advantages of CFROI. Specifically, CFROI (1) converts accounting profits into cash flows (i.e., cash generated before capital expenditures); (2) deals with total cash (in current dollars) invested in a business to produce those cash flows rather than with depreciated book values; and (3) recognizes the life over which the assets will produce the cash flows. We explore each of these advantages later in the chapter.

The novice reader of BCG's published materials could be confused by the fact that CFROI can either be calculated (1) as a multi-period rate of return (IRR) over the normal economic life of the assets, or (2) as a single-period rate of return. However, as we will illustrate, there is a relationship between the two calculations (in some cases).

The calculation of CFROI involves five steps:

1. Estimate the average economic life of the firm's assets.
2. Compute the annual inflation-adjusted gross cash flows expected to be received over the life of the firm's assets.

3. Calculate the firm's total inflation-adjusted gross investment, and for the multi-period approach divide the gross investment between depreciating and nondepreciating assets.

4. Project the company's inflation-adjusted terminal value, equal to the nondepreciating asset release of land and working capital.

5. Determine CFROI, either by the multi-period (IRR) method or by using a single-period calculation.

We then compare the CFROI against the firm's real, as opposed to nominal, cost of capital, or against the rates of return for an industry or a peer group. In determining this hurdle rate, BCG chooses not to use the familiar Capital Asset Pricing Model. Instead it derives a market rate that is calculated based on the CFROI, the sustainable asset growth rates, and the current market prices of approximately 300 companies from Standard & Poor's 400 Index companies.[6] BCG notes that the average CFROI for the Standard & Poor's 400 Index firms has consistently been about 6 percent, and the average asset growth rate for these firms approximated 2–3 percent over time. However, since 1990, the range of average returns have risen to 10–11 percent.

Measuring CFROI: Multi-Period (IRR) Approach

CFROI for a firm can be thought of as the internal rate of return (IRR) of all a firm's projects. Figure 6.3 depicts this concept graphically: CFROI is the rate of return that makes the present value of a firm's future cash flows, including a "terminal value" from the release of non-depreciating assets, equal to the company's gross cash investment. Note that CFROI is analogous to project IRR when applied to an entire company. For a firm with assets having an average life of N years, CFROI would be defined as follows:

$$
\begin{aligned}
\text{Firm's gross cash investment} &= \frac{\text{Year 1 cash flow}}{(1 + \text{CFROI})^1} + \frac{\text{Year 2 cash flow}}{(1 + \text{CFROI})^2} + \cdots \\
&+ \frac{\text{Year } N \text{ cash flow}}{(1 + \text{CFROI})^N} + \frac{\text{Terminal value}}{(1 + \text{CFROI})^N}
\end{aligned}
\tag{6.3}
$$

In computing CFROI, BCG assumes that the firm's assets will continue to generate the same current real dollar cash flows over the average life of the assets. Since BCG tries to calculate a measure of

Figure 6.3 CFROI: Multi-Period (IRR) Analysis

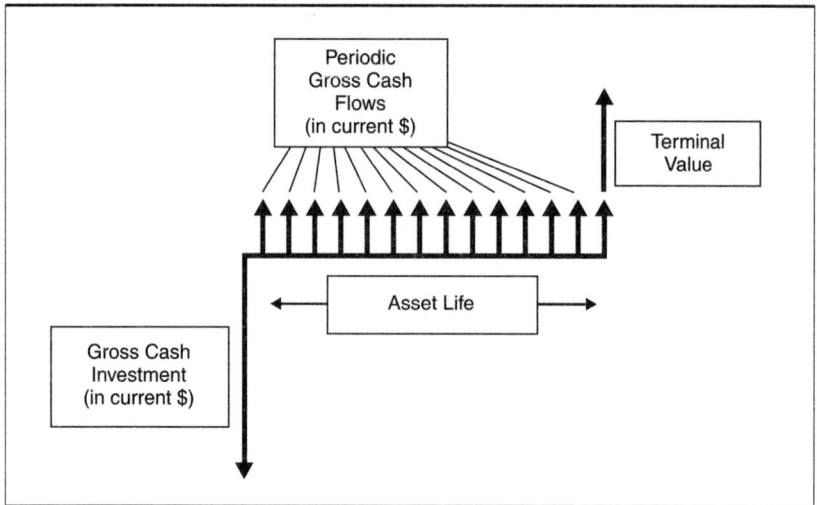

current performance, it assumes that the firm's real cash flows do not rise or fall in future periods.[7] CFROI therefore represents the average return on (performance of) all the business's existing projects at a point in time.

To illustrate, think of a firm that routinely invests $10 million each year in new projects, consisting of $6 million in depreciable assets and $4 million in working capital. The working capital is to be recovered by the end of the project's life in four years. The cash flows from this sequence of investments are shown in figure 6.4, with the total invested capital accumulating to $40 million, annual cash flows equal to $8 million, and the annual recovery of working capital over the four-year life cycle totaling $16 million. Using an IRR calculation, we determine the firm's CFROI on its assets to be 6.36 percent, computed as follows:[8]

$$\$40 \text{ million} = \frac{\$8 \text{ million}}{(1 + \text{CFROI})^1} + \frac{\$8 \text{ million}}{(1 + \text{CFROI})^2}$$

$$+ \frac{\$8 \text{ million}}{(1 + \text{CFROI})^3} + \frac{\$24 \text{ million}}{(1 + \text{CFROI})^4}$$

Measuring CFROI: Single-Period Approach

While computing CFROI on an IRR basis is a valuable measure for business analysis, it does have its shortcomings. BCG suggests that some may view this approach as overly complex. In the foregoing

Figure 6.4 CFROI: Return on All Existing Projects

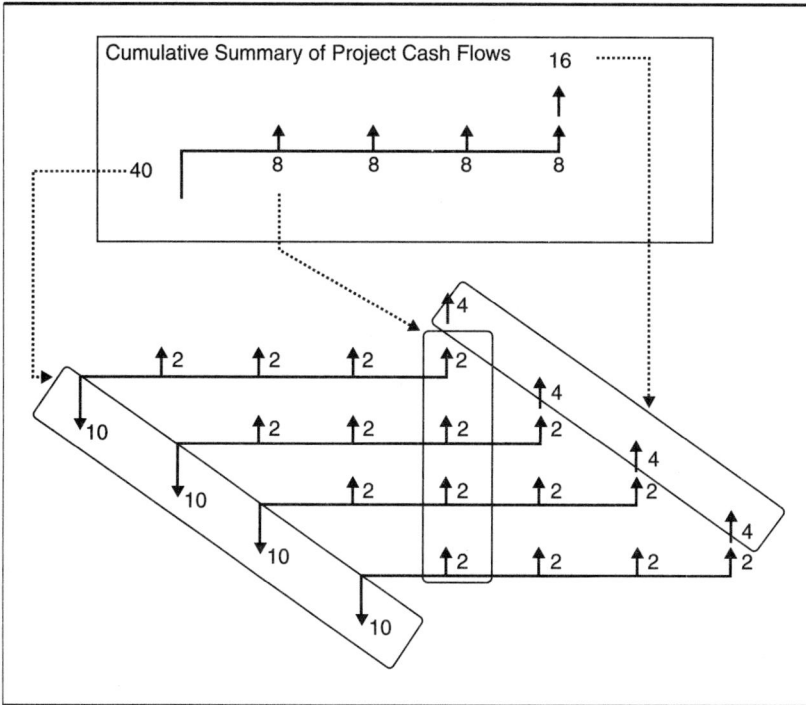

example, the IRR approach was simple enough; however, when we are dealing with live companies, the level of sophistication becomes substantial. Also, with an IRR methodology, a problem can arise if the firm expects to experience negative cash flows (e.g., the business is headed toward bankruptcy).[9] In order to overcome these shortcomings, CFROI can be converted to a simpler single-period ratio. With this approach, we calculate CFROI as follows:

$$\text{CFROI} = \frac{\text{Sustainable cash flows}}{\text{Current dollar gross investment}} \qquad (6.4)$$

where *sustainable cash flow* is the firm's operating gross cash flows (as measured earlier) less sinking fund depreciation. Figure 6.5 depicts these computations graphically and is similar to figure 6.3, which represents the multi-period (IRR) CFROI analysis. However, there are two differences: first, the nondepreciating assets are no longer part of the calculation, and second, the replacement investment is subtracted from

Figure 6.5 CFROI: Single-Period Analysis

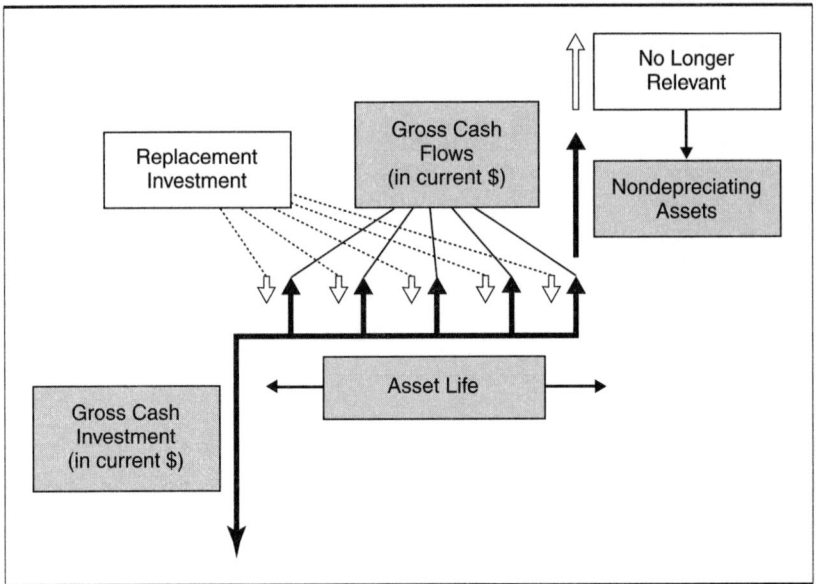

gross cash flows in the form of an annual sinking fund depreciation. However, sinking fund depreciation is not like what a traditional accountant would compute. Sinking fund depreciation is the annual investment that must be made, given the firm's opportunity cost of funds, in order to accumulate a sum equal to the original cost of the depreciable assets at the end of the asset's life. For instance, assuming an asset life of N years, sinking fund depreciation is computed as follows:

$$\begin{array}{l}\text{Current \$ cost of} \\ \text{depreciating assets}\end{array} = \begin{array}{l}\text{Sinking fund} \\ \text{depreciation}\end{array} \sum_{t=0}^{N-1}(1 + \text{Reinvestment rate})^t \quad (6.5a)$$

Alternatively,

$$\begin{array}{l}\text{Sinking fund} \\ \text{depreciation}\end{array} = \begin{array}{l}\text{Current \$ cost of} \\ \text{depreciating assets}\end{array} \times \frac{\text{Reinvestment rate}}{(1 + \text{Reinvestment rate})^N - 1}$$

$$(6.5b)$$

where the reinvestment rate is equal to the five-year past median of the economy CFROI.[10]

Returning to our previous example, where the gross investment was \$40 million, the depreciable assets were \$24 million—the remaining \$16 million was working capital—and the average asset life was four years. Given the firm's opportunity cost of funds of 6.36 percent, the sinking fund depreciation would be $5.457 million per year:

$$\$24 \text{ million} = \frac{\text{Sinking fund}}{\text{depreciation}} \sum_{t=0}^{3} (1 + 0.0636)^t$$

That is, if we invest $5.457 million each year to earn a rate of return of 6.36 percent, we will accumulate the $24 million needed to replace the asset in four years.

Thus, for our example, CFROI is calculated as follows ($ thousands):

Operating gross cash flow	$ 8,000
Less: Sinking fund depreciation	5,457
Sustainable cash flows	$ 2,543
Current dollar gross investment	$40,000

$$\text{CFROI} = \frac{\text{Sustainable cash flows}}{\text{Current dollar gross investment}} = \frac{\$2,543}{\$40,000} = 6.36\%$$

We see that the single-period calculation produces the same CFROI estimate (6.36%) as did the multi-period (IRR) approach. However, this happens *only* when the reinvestment rate is equal to the asset's internal rate of return—that is, where the project's net present value (NPV) is equal to zero.[11]

Developing the Numbers

To this point, we have been given the information needed to compute CFROI, consisting of four pieces of data:

1. The gross investment made by all lenders and investors, measured on a current dollar basis
2. The annual gross cash flows generated by the firm, also converted to current dollars
3. The amount of the firm's nondepreciating assets
4. The anticipated life of the asset

To compute these items, BCG makes a number of adjustments to the firm's accounting statements. The types of adjustments are shown in figure 6.6 (the numbers shown in the figure relate to the example used earlier in the chapter). Let's consider each of the pieces of data in turn.

Figure 6.6 Computing CFROI: An Overview

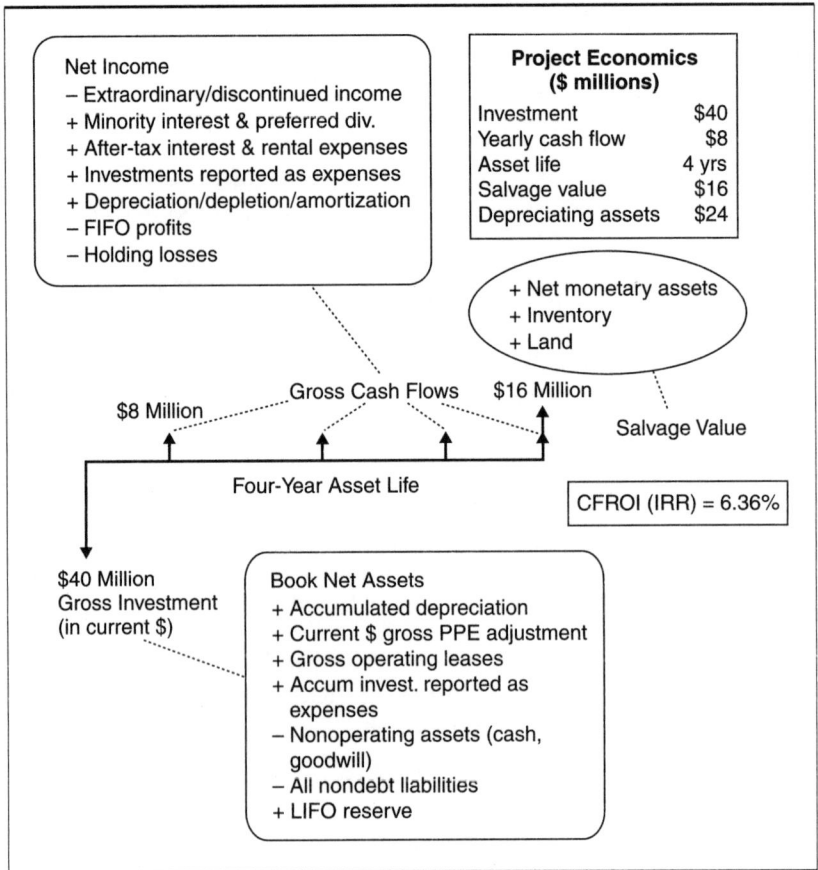

Net Income
  − Extraordinary/discontinued income
  + Minority interest & preferred div.
  + After-tax interest & rental expenses
  + Investments reported as expenses
  + Depreciation/depletion/amortization
  − FIFO profits
  − Holding losses

Project Economics ($ millions)

Investment	$40
Yearly cash flow	$8
Asset life	4 yrs
Salvage value	$16
Depreciating assets	$24

  + Net monetary assets
  + Inventory
  + Land

Gross Cash Flows $16 Million

$8 Million

Salvage Value

Four-Year Asset Life

CFROI (IRR) = 6.36%

$40 Million
Gross Investment
(in current $)

Book Net Assets
  + Accumulated depreciation
  + Current $ gross PPE adjustment
  + Gross operating leases
  + Accum invest. reported as
    expenses
  − Nonoperating assets (cash,
    goodwill)
  − All nondebt liabilities
  + LIFO reserve

Current Dollar Gross Investment

Current dollar gross investment is equal to the cash invested in a business over its life, but restated in current dollars. The calculation of a firm's gross investment (adjusted for inflation) and the reasons for the adjustments are as follows:

Calculations	Reason for Adjustment
Net working capital (current assets less non-interest-bearing current liabilities)	
+ Net fixed assets	
+ Accumulated depreciation, depletion, and amortization	Convert to a cash basis
+ Gross plant current dollar adjustment	Restate ("inflate") historical investments to today's dollars

+ Capitalized value of lease payments	Neutralize the effects of rent/buy decisions
− Other nondebt, noncurrent liabilities (e.g., deferred taxes)	
− Other nondebt, noncurrent dollar adjustments	Restate ("inflate") historical deferred taxes to today's dollars
+ LIFO inventory reserve	Reverse LIFO inventory effect

Thus, we measure the gross investment as the firm's net working capital—net of non-interest-bearing current liabilities, such as accounts payable—plus gross fixed assets, adjusted to current dollars. We capitalize operating leases and then subtract other non-interest-bearing liabilities, such as deferred taxes, which are adjusted for inflation. Finally, we remove LIFO inventory effects, if any. The resulting number is an estimate of the amount of capital invested in the firm over its life.

Current Dollar Gross Cash Flow

Once we know the amount of capital that return-seeking investors have invested in the firm, including interest-bearing lenders, we next determine the annual cash flows that are generated by the firm's current gross investment. BCG defines this number as the current dollar gross cash flow, which represents the total cash provided by the business before reinvestment. The calculations and explanations are as follows:

Calculations	Reason for Adjustment
After-tax net income before minority interest, extraordinary items, and discontinued operations (NOPAT)	
+ Depreciation (and other noncash charges)	Convert to cash basis
+ After-corporate-tax interest expense (including interest on leases)	Neutralize financing decisions
+ Monetary holding gain or loss	Inflation charge on net monetary assets
+ FIFO profit	Inflation charge for using FIFO accounting

Thus, when computing gross investment and gross cash flows, BCG makes a number of adjustments to the data in an effort to capture the economic essence of the firm's performance. The rationale for these adjustments is only briefly noted here but is explored more fully in appendix 6A.

Nondepreciating Assets

We next consider how much of the firm's capital will be released at the end of the assets' lives. In the balance sheet these assets generally include the nondepreciating assets. In effect, they represent the company's salvage value. We would typically compute these assets as follows:

$$\begin{aligned} \text{Nondepreciating} &= \text{Net monetary} + \text{Inventories} \\ \text{assets} & \quad \text{assets} \end{aligned}$$

$$+ \text{LIFO inventory} + \text{Land and} + \text{Land current} \\ \text{reserve} \quad \text{improvements} \quad \text{dollar adjustment}$$

where the net monetary assets are equal to the sum of operating cash, accounts receivables, and other current assets (excluding inventory) less non-interest-bearing current liabilities.

Asset Life

The fourth and final piece of information needed to compute CFROI is the average life of the firm's depreciating assets. The life of a firm's assets is used to determine the time horizon for computing CFROI, much as we did in our earlier hypothetical example, where we knew that all the assets had a four-year life. However, in practice—particularly when we are relying on public information—we cannot *know* the lives of the firm's depreciating assets and must make an estimate.

If we assume that accounting depreciation allocates the cost of a firm's tangible fixed assets over their service life, then we can estimate asset life by dividing depreciable gross plant and equipment by the associated annual depreciation expense:

$$\text{Asset life in years} = \frac{\text{Depreciating gross plant and equipment}}{\text{Annual depreciation expense}} \quad (6.6)$$

By incorporating asset life into the CFROI calculations, we recognize that businesses have different life cycle durations (i.e., high versus low obsolescence factors). This estimate, however, may require some common sense to know that reasonable results are occurring. For example, distortions can arise if the firm uses a method of depreciating its assets other than straight-line, or if a substantial portion of the fixed assets are fully depreciated but not retired. Thus, it may be wise to compare results with industry peers.

Real-World Example: Motorola, 1995–1998

We now demonstrate how CFROI is computed for an actual firm, using Motorola as an illustration. Taking the firm's financial data for years 1995–1998, we compute the firm's CFROI for each year (see table 6.1).

Table 6.1 is an adaptation of a template used by BCG for computing CFROI. In the table, we see how Motorola's current dollar gross cash investment and current dollar gross cash flows are computed. Then CFROI is calculated for each year, first using the single-period method and then the multiple-period (IRR) method. Some brief explanations are in order regarding these calculations:

To determine the average project life, the amount of the company's adjusted gross plant is divided by the annual depreciation. For instance, in 1998 the average project life is estimated to be ten years:

$$\frac{\text{Adjusted gross plant}}{\substack{\text{Depreciation and} \\ \text{amortization}}} = \frac{\$22,888 \text{ million}}{\$2,197 \text{ million}} = \frac{10.4 \text{ years,}}{\text{rounded to 10 years}}$$

Sinking fund depreciation is equal to an annuity that would result in the accumulation of the capital invested in these assets at the end of their life. For example, in 1998 the depreciating assets are worth $26,080 million. Given an average project life of ten years and a company reinvestment rate or cost of capital of 10.86 percent,[12] the sinking fund depreciation is $1,570 million, calculated as follows ($ millions):

$$\substack{\text{Depreciating} \\ \text{assets}} = \substack{\text{Sinking fund} \\ \text{depreciation}} \sum_{t=0}^{N-1} (1 + \text{discount rate})^t$$

$$\$26,080 = \substack{\text{Sinking fund} \\ \text{depreciation}} \sum_{t=0}^{9} (1 + 0.1086)^t$$

$$\$26,080 = \$1,570 \sum_{t=0}^{9} (1 + 0.1086)^t$$

We can now compute Motorola's CFROI, first as a single-period measure and then on a multi-period basis. Again using the 1998 figures for illustrative purposes, Motorola's single-period CFROI is computed as follows ($ millions):

Table 6.1 Motorola CFROI Computations ($ millions)

	1995	1996	1997	1998
Cash	$ 725	$ 1,513	$ 1,445	$ 1,453
Short-term investments	350	298	335	171
Receivables	4,081	4,035	4,847	5,057
Current assets (other)	1,826	2,253	2,513	3,105
Investment & advances (equity)	0	928	848	931
Investment & advances (other)	2,271	1,379	2,442	3,280
Other assets	617	617	803	933
Monetary assets	$ 9,870	$11,023	$13,233	$14,930
Accounts payable	$ 2,018	$ 2,050	$ 2,297	$ 2,305
Income taxes payable	125	246	175	84
Accrued expenses	3,350	3,643	3,838	4,635
Other current liabilities	695	674	1,463	1,507
Liabilities (other)	1,043	1,247	1,285	1,245
Non-interest-bearing current liabilities	$ 7,231	$ 7,860	$ 9,058	$ 9,776
Net monetary assets	$ 2,639	$ 3,163	$ 4,175	$ 5,154
Inventories	$ 3,528	$ 3,220	$ 4,096	$ 3,745
LIFO inventory reserve	0	0	0	0
Nondepreciating assets	$ 6,167	$ 6,383	$ 8,271	$ 8,899
Adjusted gross plant	$17,466	$19,598	$21,380	$22,888
Gross plant current $ adjustment	1,688	1,523	2,047	2,362
Less: Deferred taxes and investment tax credit	968	1,108	1,522	1,188
Less: Deferred taxes current $ adjustment	83	72	118	97
Gross leased property	1,427	1,817	2,067	2,115
Depreciating assets	$19,530	$21,758	$23,854	$26,080
Current dollar gross investment	$25,697	$28,141	$32,125	$34,979

Operating gross cash flow	$ 2,946
Less: Sinking fund depreciation	1,570
Sustainable cash flows	$1,376
Current dollar gross investment	$34,979

$$\text{CFROI} = \frac{\text{Sustainable cash flows}}{\text{Current dollar gross investment}} = \frac{\$1,376}{\$34,979} = 3.93\%$$

Table 6.1 (continued)

	1995	1996	1997	1998
Income before extraordinary items	$ 1,781	$ 1,154	$ 1,180	$ (962)
Depreciation and amortization	1,919	2,308	2,329	2,197
Interest expense (gross)	213	249	216	301
Depreciation in leases	178	227	258	264
Total interest implied in leases	44	52	50	56
Less: Tax benefit of interest	95	111	98	132
Monetary holding gain (loss)	(61)	(60)	(77)	(53)
LIFO charge to FIFO inventories	(63)	(38)	1	28
Special items	0	150	327	1,980
Less: Tax on special items	0	56	121	733
Current dollar gross cash flows	$ 3,916	$ 3,875	$ 4,065	$ 2,946
Asset project life (integer)	9	8	9	10
Reinvestment rate (discount rate)	8.65%	9.37%	10.82%	10.86%
Depreciating assets	$19,530	$21,758	$23,854	$26,080
Sinking-fund depreciation	$ 1,522	$ 1,947	$ 1,697	$ 1,570
Sustainable gross cash flows (gross cash flow – sinking fund depreciation)	$ 2,394	$ 1,928	$ 2,368	$ 1,376
CFROI—single-period method	9.32%	6.85%	7.37%	3.93%
CFROI—IRR method	9.53%	5.94%	6.26%	1.44%
Cost of capital	6.36%	6.50%	6.28%	6.02%

Source: Adapted from Boston Consulting Group.

Next, Motorola's 1998 multi-period (IRR) CFROI can be calculated as follows:

$$\text{Firm's gross cash investment in 1998} = \frac{\text{Year 1 cash flow}}{(1 + \text{CFROI})^1} + \frac{\text{Year 2 cash flow}}{(1 + \text{CFROI})^2} + \dots$$

$$+ \frac{\text{Year } N \text{ cash flow}}{(1 + \text{CFROI})^N} + \frac{\text{Terminal value}}{(1 + \text{CFROI})^N}$$

$$\$34,979 = \frac{\$2,946}{(1 + \text{CFROI})^1} + \frac{\$2,946}{(1 + \text{CFROI})^2} + \dots$$

$$+ \frac{\$2,946}{(1 + \text{CFROI})^{10}} + \frac{\$8,899}{(1 + \text{CFROI})^{10}}$$

Solving for CFROI, we get a meager 1.44 percent with the IRR method, compared to 3.93 percent with the single-period method. Why the difference in results? Recall that the two methods will produce the same answer *only* when the multi-period CFROI is equal to the reinvestment rate used for sinking fund depreciation. When the reinvestment rate is lower than the CFROI, the IRR method will result in a higher CFROI than will the single-period method (see 1995 in table 6.1). When the reinvestment rate is higher than the CFROI, the IRR method will give a lower CFROI than will the single-period method (see 1996–1998 in table 6.1). In any case, we should note the declining CFROIs over time, regardless of the method of computation used.

Motorola's CFROIs are next compared to the company's annual costs of capital (the investment hurdle rate), which are shown on the bottom row of table 6.1. These costs of capital are BCG's market-derived rates for the economy as a whole, adjusted for the individual firm's leverage.

We have now completed our discussion of CFROI. As we indicated from the outset, CFROI is an important piece of information, both as a stand-alone computation and for computing the TBR for a company or division. In the latter case, the current-year CFROI is the departure point for estimating a firm's future free cash flows, where the CFROI is faded over time toward a national average. Thus, the TBR measurement can be no better than its foundation, the CFROI.

CVA: The BCG Alternative to EVA

The CFROI is clearly the major metric used by BCG when measuring firm performance and valuing a company. However, BCG has also developed a measure of economic profit called *cash value added* (CVA), which BCG contends is an improvement over economic value added (EVA) because CVA is based on cash flows, not earnings.

CVA is measured as operating cash flows less sinking fund depreciation (earlier called sustainable cash flows) less a capital charge on the *total* amount of cash invested in the business. The capital charge assigns a cost for the use of all capital the firm is using, which is equal to the firm's cost of capital times the amount of gross capital employed. Thus,

$$\text{CVA} = \frac{\text{Operating}}{\text{cash flows}} - \frac{\text{Sinking fund}}{\text{depreciation}} - \frac{\text{Capital charge on}}{\text{gross investment}} \qquad (6.7)$$

In the Motorola example the CVAs for 1995–1998 are computed as follows ($ millions):

	1995	1996	1997	1998
Current dollar gross cash flows	$ 3,916	$ 3,875	$ 4,065	$ 2,946
Sinking fund depreciation	$ 1,522	$ 1,947	$ 1,697	$ 1,570
Gross investment	$25,697	$28,141	$32,125	$34,979
Cost of capital	6.36%	6.50%	6.28%	6.02%
Capital charge (investment × cost of capital)	$ 1,634	$ 1,829	$ 2,017	$ 2,106
CVA	$ 759	$ 98	$ 351	$ (730)

As expected given the significant reductions in Motorola's CFROI, Motorola's ability to create value has decreased, culminating in a negative $730 million CVA in 1998.

Summary

In this chapter, we have shown the basic approach for measuring a company's performance using rates of return. Specifically, we translated total shareholder return (TSR) into total business return (TBR) and then into cash flow return on investment (CFROI), a major component of TBR and an important performance measure by itself.

We have particularly been interested in the rate of return, CFROI, as developed by Boston Consulting Group and HOLT Value Associates. CFROI is the sustainable cash flow a business generates in a given year as a percentage of the cash invested in the firm's assets. When inflation is a significant factor, both cash flow and cash invested are expressed in deflated or current dollars. Thus, CFROI is an economic measure of the company's performance that reflects the average underlying rates of return on all existing investment projects.

CFROI for a firm can be thought of as a weighted average internal rate of return (IRR) of all the projects making up the business as a whole:

$$\frac{\text{Firm's gross cash investment}}{\text{}} = \frac{\text{Year 1 cash flow}}{(1 + \text{CFROI})^1} + \frac{\text{Year 2 cash flow}}{(1 + \text{CFROI})^2} + \cdots$$

$$+ \frac{\text{Year } N \text{ cash flow}}{(1 + \text{CFROI})^N} + \frac{\text{Terminal value}}{(1 + \text{CFROI})^N}$$

Alternatively, it can be computed as a single-period rate of return as follows:

$$\text{CFROI} = \frac{\text{Sustainable cash flows}}{\text{Current dollar gross investment}}$$

where sustainable cash flows are the firm's operating gross cash flows less sinking fund depreciation.

BCG believes that measuring value creation in terms of rates of return is much better than measuring it with any form of economic profit, such as economic value added (EVA). In fact, BCG argues that since CFROI is a cash-based measure, it correlates well with price/book multiples, more so than non-cash-based measures such as return on net assets (RONA), return on equity (ROE), and economic value added (EVA). BCG also contends that the other methods inherently discourage growth because they are *net*-asset-based and are stated in book/historic value. BCG attributes CFROI's success—apart from the conversion of accounting data into cash-based measures—to its reflecting the economic reality that firms have differing asset lives and asset mixes (depreciating and nondepreciating assets).

BCG has committed extensive resources to verifying empirically the robustness of its models, particularly testing the correlation of the model results with total shareholder returns. Based on this work, BCG claims that the CFROI and its model TBRs,[13] which rely heavily on a BCG time fade valuation model, possess twice the empirical accuracy of competing approaches, including EVA. BCG also claims that its framework is more robust in that the derivation involves data from many more companies than any other approach. However, independent third parties have not replicated these claims of empirical accuracy. Until that substantiation is completed, we are reluctant to join a debate on the numerous statistical and empirical issues involved. However, in chapter 9, we provide what empirical evidence is available relating to the various VBM methodologies.

Appendix 6A
Adjusting the Data

*I*n computing a firm's current dollar gross investment and its current dollar cash flows, a number of adjustments are made to adapt the data from GAAP accounting to have a more economic flavor. Some of the more frequently made adjustments were noted previously. However, the rationale for these adjustments was only given in passing. Here we offer BCG's explanation as to why these adjustments are made.

Removing the Age Bias
One of the more significant characteristics of the CFROI metric is the use of gross, rather than net, investments when estimating the amount of capital provided by investors. To measure the capital employed by the firm, BCG adds back accumulated depreciation in order to "gross-up" net fixed assets and thereby remove any possible age bias, or what BCG calls the *old plant/new plant trap*. For consistency, it also "grosses-up" the annual cash flows by any depreciation, amortization, and depletion expense to convert from an accrual system to a cash basis.

BCG maintains that using net assets can give mixed signals to management. As we explained in chapter 3, annual book depreciation causes the net asset base to shrink, which can artificially increase an accounting-based measure of returns on net assets (RONA) over time as book depreciation accumulates. In turn, asset growth may be discouraged, as it will decrease an accounting measurement of return. A company may have a high RONA with a deteriorated or obsolete asset base to run future business. The opposite is true in the short term when new assets are purchased. This problem can be exaggerated where accelerated depreciation methods are employed. Thus, BCG recommends adding back depreciation to avoid this potential source of bias.

Figure 6A.1 offers a visual comparison of how returns on capital based on net assets (e.g., RONA) might compare to returns based on gross investments (e.g., CFROI). While the example is hypothetical, it is representative of what we could expect as a firm replaces old assets with newer ones.

Figure 6A.1 Old Plant/New Plant Trap

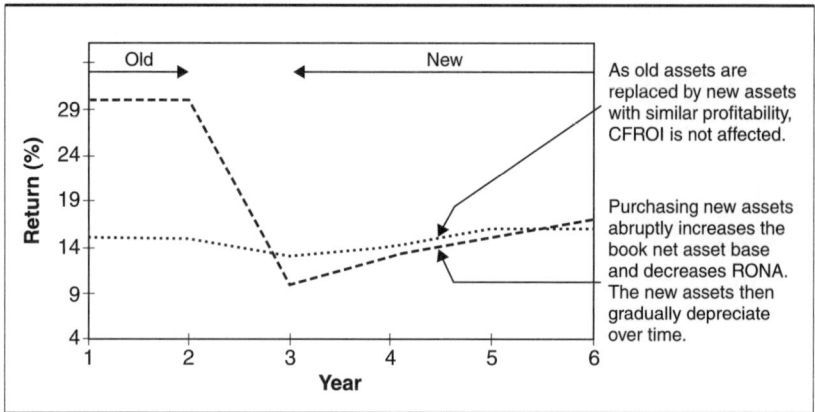

Inflation Adjustments

Inflation adjustments to gross assets are made for two reasons. First, since income statements are presented in today's dollars, the firm's invested capital or assets should also reflect equivalent purchasing power units.[14] Second, assets are replaced in today's dollars, so estimating replacement capital expenditures over the investment cycle requires inflation adjusting. In addition to the assets' being inflation-adjusted, long-term, non-interest-bearing liabilities, such as deferred taxes, are inflation-adjusted as well and then subtracted from the firm's gross investment.

Cash flows are also adjusted for any monetary holding gains or losses to reflect the gains or losses of purchasing power to investors from companies that hold monetary assets. Since monetary assets/liabilities are short-term in nature, the adjustment is based on the annual gross domestic product (GDP) deflator change multiplied by the net monetary assets.

Operating Leases

Operating leases are essentially an alternative form of capital investment. Equipment acquired using finance leases or purchased through some combination of debt and equity appears on asset side of the balance sheet. Assuming assets leased on an operating basis are required to run the business, they too should be capitalized and included in the asset base to calculate CFROI. For example, a retail store that is leased would typically show a high return on assets (and

CFROI) if the property lease were not capitalized. Clearly, the real estate is needed to sell the wares and as such is part of a shareholder risk/return assessment; it therefore should be included as an operating asset. To adjust cash flows for the effect of capitalized operating leases, the related depreciation and interest (net of tax) associated with these capitalized leases are added back to gross cash flow.

LIFO Reserve and FIFO Inventories

To reflect the actual cash investment in inventories, BCG adds back the last in/first out (LIFO) reserve in determining the gross cash investment.

Since the first in/first out (FIFO) method values inventory assuming the first inventories are sold first, it has a tendency to lower the cost of goods sold if the cost of making the product increases over time (because of inflation). To account for this effect on the income statement, BCG adjusts the cash flows accordingly. Inventories reported on a FIFO basis are multiplied by the change in the producer price index (PPI) and subtracted from the cash flows to reflect more accurately the cash cost of goods sold.

Goodwill

BCG believes that goodwill should *not* be viewed as part of a firm's operating capital because including goodwill in the asset base causes CFROI and RONA to follow a pattern similar to the one in figure 6A.1. BCG suggests that by excluding goodwill, CFROI will be more consistent through time. Otherwise, the return will decrease dramatically at first and increase yearly as the goodwill is amortized and the assets age. Consequently, a high-performing RONA company may become an under-performing RONA company as a result of an acquisition. After all, BCG suggests, the operating performance of a company does not suffer because it has made an acquisition. However, BCG *does* recommend that intangibles be included in the TBR calculation as a cash flow, where they clearly affect valuation and shareholder performance over time.

References

Boston Consulting Group. *Shareholder Value Metrics*. Booklet 2. 1996.

Ijiri, Yuji. "Recovery Rate and Cash Flow Accounting." *Financial Executive* (March 1980): 54–60.

Madden, Bartley J. *CFROI Valuation: A Total System Approach to Valuing the Firm*. Oxford: Butterworth-Heinemann, 1999.

Markowitz, Harry M. *Portfolio Selection*. New Haven: Yale University Press, 1959.

Ross, Stephen A., Randolph W. Westerfield, and Jeffrey Jaffe. *Corporate Finance*. 5th ed. New York: Irwin McGraw-Hill, 1999.

Chapter **7**

Project Evaluation Using the New Metrics

> A business proposal—such as a new investment, the acquisition of another company, or a restructuring plan—will raise the firm's value only if the present value of the future stream of net cash benefits the proposal is expected to generate exceeds the initial cash outlay required to carry out the proposal.
>
> **—Gabriel Hawawini and Claude Viallet,**
> *Finance for Executives* **(1999)**

For many companies the new value based management (VBM) metrics have successfully replaced the standard accounting-based tools (earnings per share, return on investment, and earnings growth) to measure the performance of the ongoing operations of the business enterprise as a whole. In an effort to maintain consistency with the tools used to measure anticipated performance of new projects it is tempting to try and use the new metrics as a replacement for the standard discounted cash flow tools of project evaluation (net present value and internal rate of return). Furthermore, we noted in chapters 5 and 6 that the VBM metrics are straightforward adaptations of traditional discounted cash flow (DCF) tools. As such they should yield the same predictions regarding project value (if properly used) as traditional discounted cash flow tools of analysis. The caveat "if properly used" is an important one, as we discuss at some length.

In this chapter we examine the period-by-period performance of new capital investment projects using economic value added (EVA), cash value added (CVA), and cash flow return on investment (CFROI).

135

We demonstrate how GAAP depreciation can distort these performance measures. Switching to present value depreciation (defined later) eliminates the source of the performance distortion, but may give rise to a conflict of interest problem. Specifically, estimating present value depreciation generally requires the involvement of the firm's management to provide estimates of future cash flows, but these same employees are the ones whose performance is being evaluated. We close the chapter by looking at how EVA has been adapted to fit the oil and gas industry.

Example Capital Investment Project

To illustrate the relationship between traditional measures of project value such as accounting return on net assets (RONA), net present value (NPV), and internal rate of return (IRR) and the VBM tools we consider the investment opportunity in table 7.1. The investment involves spending a total of $16,000 for plant and equipment plus an additional $2,000 for working capital. The plant and equipment are depreciated on a straight-line basis over seven years toward a zero salvage value. The $2,000 invested in working capital will be returned at the end of the project's seven-year life. The investment is expected to produce net operating profits after taxes (NOPAT) of $1,200.78 per year. Adding GAAP straight-line depreciation to NOPAT provides an estimate of the project's free cash flows of $3,486.49 per year. Finally, the opportunity cost of capital for the investment is 10 percent.

Traditional Measures of Project Value

Table 7.1 indicates that the project is a break-even proposition with a zero NPV and an IRR equal to the opportunity cost of capital. Note, however, that the accounting return on net assets (RONA or, in the vernacular of VBM, the return on invested capital—ROIC) varies from 6.67 percent for year one to 28.02 percent for year seven. The increasing rates of return over time evidenced in ROIC reflect the fact that project income remains constant while the depreciated book value used to measure invested capital is declining. Does the fact that ROIC is below the 10 percent opportunity cost of capital during the first three years of the project mean that the project is destroying value in these years? Not necessarily. As we learned in chapter 3, ROIC calculated using GAAP accounting income and asset book values based on GAAP depreciation is an unreliable indicator of value creation since it fails to consider cash

Table 7.1 Traditional Measures of Project Value—IRR, NPV, and ROIC

	0	1	2	3	4	5	6	7
Net operating profits after tax (NOPAT)		$1,200.78	$1,200.78	$1,200.78	$1,200.78	$1,200.78	$1,200.78	$1,200.78
Depreciation expense (straight-line)		2,285.71	2,285.71	2,285.71	2,285.71	2,285.71	2,285.71	2,285.71
Cash flow from operations		$3,486.49	$3,486.49	$3,486.49	$3,486.49	$3,486.49	$3,486.49	$3,486.49
Plant and equipment	($16,000.00)							0.00
Working capital	(2,000.00)							2,000.00
Invested capital	($18,000.00)							
Free cash flows	($18,000.00)	$3,486.49	$3,486.49	$3,486.49	$3,486.49	$3,486.49	$3,486.49	$5,486.49
Book value of capital	18,000.00	15,714.29	13,428.57	11,142.86	8,857.14	6,571.43	4,285.71	2,000.00
Return on invested capital (ROIC) NOPAT$_t$ ÷ Book value of capital$_{t-1}$		6.67%	7.64%	8.94%	10.78%	13.56%	18.27%	28.02%
IRR	10.00%							
NPV	($0.00)							

flows or the time value of money. Perhaps the new tools of VBM do a better job of measuring period-by-period value creation. Let's see.

Using EVA to Evaluate Project Value Creation

Table 7.2 contains estimates of the annual EVAs for the example project introduced in table 7.1. How are we to use EVA to evaluate whether the project is a worthwhile investment? Is value being created in each period of the project's life? The answer to the first question is straightforward. A project's NPV of free cash flows will always equal the present value of its EVAs. Since our example project's NPV based on free cash flows—and the present value of EVAs—are both equal to zero, the project neither creates nor destroys shareholder value. However, the answer to the second question related to the analysis of period-to-period performance is problematic. This point is obvious when we look at our example project's EVAs across time. For instance, in year 1, EVA begins at –$599.23 and then increases each year until in year 7 it reaches $772.20. Thus, the annual EVAs send mixed signals. In years 1–3 we would conclude that the project destroys value, but in years 4–7 we conclude that it contributes positively to firm value. Only by considering all the EVAs across the life of the project can we know if it is worthwhile. The problem we are encountering in interpreting the year-to-year EVAs is directly related to the changing return on invested capital (ROIC) that we noted earlier in table 7.1. Recall that the returns increase over time as a direct result of depreciating invested capital. The link between ROIC and EVA is transparent in the following formulation of EVA (introduced in chapter 5), i.e.,

$$EVA_t = (ROIC_t - k_{wacc}) \times \text{Invested capital}_{t-1} \qquad (7.1)$$

Recall that invested capital is equal to the depreciated book value of the investment based on GAAP accounting depreciation. In our example $ROIC_t$ (and correspondingly EVA) increases over time due to the decreasing book value of the investment. Consequently, even though the EVAs taken together provide an appropriate basis for evaluating the project's NPV, the period-by-period measures are distorted by the use of GAAP accounting depreciation.

Fixing the Problem

Ehrbar (1998) appropriately traces the root of the problem with the use of an annual EVA to evaluate period-by-period performance of

Table 7.2 Analyzing Period-by-Period Performance Using EVA

	0	1	2	3	4	5	6	7
NOPAT		$1,200.78	$1,200.78	$1,200.78	$1,200.78	$1,200.78	$1,200.78	$1,200.78
Depreciation		2,285.71	2,285.71	2,285.71	2,285.71	2,285.71	2,285.71	2,285.71
Plant and equipment	($16,000.00)							(0.00)
Working capital	(2,000.00)							2,000.00
Invested capital	($18,000.00)							
Firm free cash flow	($18,000.00)	$ 3,486.49	$ 3,486.49	$ 3,486.49	$3,486.49	$3,486.49	$3,486.49	$5,486.49
Book value of capital	$18,000.00	$15,714.29	$13,428.57	$11,142.86	$8,857.14	$6,571.43	$4,285.71	$2,000.00
Capital cost		1,800.00	1,571.43	1,342.86	1,114.29	885.71	657.14	428.57
EVA (NOPAT – Capital cost)		($599.22)	($370.65)	($142.08)	$86.49	$315.07	$543.64	$772.21
MVA = PV(EVAs)	($0.00)							
IRR	10.00%							
NPV	($0.00)							

new investments to the GAAP depreciation calculation. He describes the problem as follows:

> For most companies, the straight-line depreciation of plant and equipment used in GAAP accounting works acceptably well. While straight-line depreciation doesn't attempt to match the actual economic depreciation of physical assets, the deviations from reality ordinarily are so inconsequential that they do not distort decisions. That's not true, however, for companies with significant amounts of long-lived equipment. In those cases, using straight-line depreciation in calculating EVA can create a powerful bias against investments in new equipment. That's because the EVA capital charge declines in step with the depreciated carrying value of the asset, so that old assets look much cheaper than new ones. This can make managers reluctant to replace "cheap" old equipment with "expensive" new gear.

The Boston Consulting Group (BCG) refers to this tendency to avoid investing in new equipment and hold onto old equipment as the "old plant–new plant trap."

Stern Stewart recommends a heuristic approach to resolving the problem described in the above quote. Specifically, Ehrbar described the procedure to us in a telephone interview as follows:

> If an investment's cash flows are slow at coming on line, Stern Stewart uses *suspension accounting treatment* or *strategic treatment*. The approach is similar to the concept of construction in progress used in the utilities industry. For instance, if we make an investment that will not come on line for three years, we would hold the capital investment in a suspense account for that time. However, we would accrue interest on the capital at the rate of the firm's weighted cost of capital while it is held in suspension, so that the capital is not free to management. Then the higher capital would be used in the EVA computations in later years when the cash flows are being realized. (Based on a telephone conversation on June 15, 2000)

Bierman (1988) and later O'Byrne (2000) propose an analytical solution to the problem of measuring period-by-period performance using EVA. They suggest the substitution of present value depreciation for traditional GAAP depreciation. Specifically, present value depreciation for the year is defined as the change in the present value of the project's future cash flows, where project cash flows are discounted using the internal rate of return (IRR), i.e., for year t we estimate

$$\text{Present value depreciation}_t = \sum_{T=t+2}^{7} \frac{\text{FCF}_T}{(1+\text{IRR})^{T-1}} - \sum_{T=t+1}^{7} \frac{\text{FCF}_T}{(1+\text{IRR})^{T}} \quad (7.2)$$

We illustrate this procedure in table 7.3 for our example project. In year 0 the present value of project free cash flows is $18,000 and it declines to $16,314 by the end of year 1. Thus, present value depreciation for year 1 is the difference in these two present values or –$1,686. We apply Bierman's concept of present value depreciation to our example problem and report the results in table 7.4. Here we find that the reconstituted EVAs are all equal to zero, which is consistent with the fact that the project yields a zero NPV. Furthermore, the present value of the revised EVA estimates is still equal to the project's NPV of zero.

Using CVA and CFROI to Evaluate Project Value Creation

The Boston Consulting Group (BCG) offers the cash value added (CVA) metric as a replacement for EVA along with the claim that CVA "removes the accounting distortions inherent in EVA."[1] Recall from chapter 6 that we calculate CVA for period t as operating cash flow less sinking fund depreciation[2] less a capital charge on the gross cash invested in the business, i.e.,

$$\text{CVA}_t = \text{NOPAT}_t + \begin{matrix}\text{Accounting}\\\text{depreciation}_t\end{matrix} - \begin{matrix}\text{Sinking fund}\\\text{depreciation}_t\end{matrix} - \begin{matrix}\text{Capital charge on}\\\text{the gross (initial)}\\\text{capital invested in}\\\text{the business}\end{matrix} \quad (7.3)$$

Using the example found in table 7.1, we see that NOPAT is equal to $1,200.78 for years 1–7. Next we calculate sinking fund depreciation, which is equal to the annual investment that must be made in order to accumulate a balance of $16,000 by the end of year 7. The rationale underlying this calculation is that annual depreciation will grow in value over the life of the investment to equal the original investment and can be used to replace the worn-out plant and equipment. Note that this calculation incorporates consideration for the firm's 10 percent opportunity cost of funds in calculating the periodic investments, i.e.,

$$\$16,000 = \begin{matrix}\text{Sinking fund}\\\text{depreciation}\end{matrix} \sum_{t=0}^{6} (1+.10)^t \quad (7.4)$$

Table 7.3 Estimation of Present Value Depreciation

Present Value Depreciation	Year	Present Value Remaining Cash Flows	Free Cash Flows in Year						
			1	2	3	4	5	6	7
	0	$18,000	$3,486.49	$3,486.49	$3,486.49	$3,486.49	$3,486.49	$3,486.49	$5,486.49
$ 1,686.49	1	$16,314		3,486.49	3,486.49	3,486.49	3,486.49	3,486.49	5,486.49
1,855.14	2	$14,458			3,486.49	3,486.49	3,486.49	3,486.49	5,486.49
2,040.65	3	$12,418				3,486.49	3,486.49	3,486.49	5,486.49
2,244.72	4	$10,173					3,486.49	3,486.49	5,486.49
2,469.19	5	$ 7,704						3,486.49	5,486.49
2,716.11	6	-$ 4,988							5,486.49
2,987.72	7	$ 2,000 ◀—— Value of working capital							
$16,000.00 ◀—— Total depreciation									

Table 7.4 Revised Calculation of EVA Using Present Value Depreciation

	0	1	2	3	4	5	6	7
Book value of invested capital	$18,000.00	$16,313.51	$14,458.38	$12,417.72	$10,173.01	$7,703.82	$4,987.72	$2,000.00
Cash flow from operations		$ 3,486.49	$ 3,486.49	$ 3,486.49	$ 3,486.49	$3,486.49	$3,486.49	$3,486.49
Present value depreciation		1,686.49	1,855.14	2,040.65	2,244.72	2,469.19	2,716.11	2,987.72
NOPAT (revised)		$ 1,800.00	$ 1,631.35	$ 1,445.84	$ 1,241.77	$1,017.30	$ 770.38	$ 498.77
Capital cost (revised)		(1,800.00)	(1,631.35)	(1,445.84)	(1,241.77)	(1,017.30)	(770.38)	(498.77)
Return on invested capital (revised)		10.0%	10.0%	10.0%	10.0%	10.0%	10.0%	10.0%
EVA (revised using present value depreciation)		$ 0.00	$ 0.00	$ 0.00	$ 0.00	$ 0.00	$ 0.00	$ 0.00
IRR	10.00%							
MVA = PV(Revised EVAs)	$0.00							
NPV	$0.00							

The resulting sinking fund depreciation is $1,686.49. The final element of the CVA calculation is the charge for the use of invested capital. This calculation differs from EVA in that for CVA we base the capital cost on the full or gross investment in the project ($18,000) for every year.

In table 7.5 we see that for our example CVA is zero for all seven years. Since CVA_t is equal to NPV for every year of the project's life, it does (for this example) provide sufficient information to evaluate the project's contribution to shareholder value. BCG compares CVA and EVA for an example very similar to the one used here (i.e., one with level cash flows and zero NPV) and makes the following observation:

> The CVA calculation shows a value equal to zero each year, which accurately reflects the underlying reality that the plant is consistently generating a cost of capital return. The adjustments incorporated in CVA avoid the behavioral biases inherent in the EVA calculation in both early and later years and provide the right signals to operating management. (BCG 1994, p. 16)

However, their comparison is between CVA and EVA computed using GAAP straight-line depreciation. As we have already observed, the problem with EVA can be resolved where we use Bierman's (1988) notion of present value as opposed to GAAP depreciation. However, for our example investment problem and the one used by BCG, CVA using sinking fund depreciation produces the same results as EVA based on present value depreciation.

Before leaving our discussion of CVA we devise and compute a multi-period counterpart that we call MCVA. Just as market value added (MVA) is the present value of all future EVAs, we define MCVA as the present value of all future CVAs, i.e.[3]

$$\text{MCVA} = \sum_{t=1}^{7} \frac{CVA_t}{(1 + k_{\text{wacc}})^t} = \text{NPV} \qquad (7.5)$$

The equivalence of MCVA and NPV is illustrated in the example calculations found in table 7.5, where both are found to be $0.00.

BCG also advocates the use of a rate of return metric that they call the cash flow return on investment, or CFROI. They define CFROI as "the sustainable cash flow a firm generates in a given year as a percent of the cash invested to fund assets used in the business." (BCG 1994, p. 33). For year t we can calculate $CFROI_t$ as follows:

Table 7.5 Calculation of CVA, CFROI, and MCVA

	1	2	3	4	5	6	7
Free cash flow = NOPAT + Accounting depreciation	$3,486.49	$3,486.49	$3,486.49	$3,486.49	$3,486.49	$3,486.49	$5,486.49
Sinking fund depreciation	(1,686.49)	(1,686.49)	(1,686.49)	(1,686.49)	(1,686.49)	(1,686.49)	(1,686.49)
Gross invested capital	18,000.00	18,000.00	18,000.00	18,000.00	18,000.00	18,000.00	18,000.00
Estimated capital cost	(1,800.00)	(1,800.00)	(1,800.00)	(1,800.00)	(1,800.00)	(1,800.00)	(1,800.00)
Cash value added (CVA)	$ 0.00	$ 0.00	$ 0.00	$ 0.00	$ 0.00	$ 0.00	$ 0.00
Cash flow return on investment (CFROI)	10%	10%	10%	10%	10%	10%	10%
Present value of CVAs (MCVA)	$0.00						

$$\text{CFROI}_t = \frac{\text{Free cash flow}_t - \text{Sinking fund depreciation}}{\text{Gross invested capital}} \qquad (7.6)$$

Table 7.5 contains the CFROIs for our example project. The CFROI$_t$ for each of the project's seven years of life are the same and equal 10 percent, i.e.,

$$\text{CFROI}_t = \frac{\$3,486.49 - \$1,686.49}{\$16,000 + \$2,000} = \frac{\$1,800}{\$18,000} = 10\%$$

CFROI$_t$ is the same for all years and is equal to the cost of capital. Thus, for this particular example CFROI$_t$ provides a correct signal of the value created by the project over its useful life. Is this always the case?

Unequal Cash Flows and Positive NPV

Let's now consider an investment project that is similar to our earlier one, except that cash flows are no longer the same from year to year and the NPV is positive. We have the same investment outlay of $18,000, where $16,000 is for plant and equipment and $2,000 is for working capital that will be recouped at the end of the project life in seven years. However, the project's free cash flows are now $3,365.71 for the first three years, increasing to $4,168.51 for the remaining four years. The cost of capital remains at 10 percent. The present value analysis for this project is shown in panel A of table 7.6, where we see the project has an IRR of 12 percent and a positive NPV of $1,324.

In panel B of table 7.6 we calculate the project's EVAs for each year using present value depreciation as proposed by Bierman (1988) and demonstrated earlier in table 7.3. These EVAs are all positive, which is consistent with the fact that the project has a positive NPV. Also, the project's MVA equals the project's NPV and all seven ROIC$_t$ estimates are equal to the project's 12 percent IRR.[4]

We next compute the CVAs for the project (panel C of table 7.6). The calculation of CVA is identical to what was done with our earlier project that had a zero NPV and equal cash flows. We even use the same discount rate, the firm's cost of capital. Furthermore, in panel C we see that the present value of the CVAs, i.e., MCVA, is again equal to the project's NPV. However, the individual CVA$_t$ no longer provide a consistent indication of the value of the project. While the project has a positive NPV and should be accepted, the CVAs are negative for the first two years, turning positive in year 3. A manager whose incen-

Table 7.6 Example with Unequal Cash Flows

					Years			
	0	1	2	3	4	5	6	7
Panel A. Project NPV and IRR								
Free cash flows	$(18,000.00)	$ 3,365.71	$ 3,365.71	$ 3,365.71	$ 4,168.51	$ 4,168.51	$ 4,168.51	$ 6,168.51
Cost of capital	10%							
NPV	$1,323.94							
IRR	12%							
Panel B. Revised EVA Using Present Value Depreciation								
Present value of invested capital	$ 18,000.00	$16,794.46	$15,444.24	$13,931.98	$11,435.43	$ 8,639.28	$ 5,507.56	$ 2,000.00
Free cash flow		$ 3,365.71	$ 3,365.71	$ 3,365.71	$ 4,168.51	$ 4,168.51	$ 4,168.51	$ 4,168.51
Present value depreciation		(1,205.54)	(1,350.22)	(1,512.26)	(2,496.55)	(2,796.15)	(3,131.72)	(3,507.56)
NOPAT		$ 2,160.17	$ 2,015.49	$ 1,853.45	$ 1,671.97	$ 1,372.36	$ 1,036.79	$ 660.96
Capital costs		(1,800.00)	(1,679.45)	(1,544.42)	(1,393.20)	(1,143.54)	(863.93)	(550.76)
EVA		$ 360.17	$ 336.05	$ 309.03	$ 278.77	$ 228.82	$ 172.87	$ 110.20
Return on invested capital (NOPAT/Beginning capital)		12%	12%	12%	12%	12%	12%	12%
MVA = PV(Revised EVAs)	$ 1,323.94							

continued

Table 7.6 (continued)

		Years						
	0	1	2	3	4	5	6	7
Panel C. CVA								
Gross invested capital		$18,000.00	$18,000.00	$18,000.00	$18,000.00	$18,000.00	$18,000.00	$18,000.00
Free cash flow		$ 3,365.71	$ 3,365.71	$ 3,365.71	$ 4,168.51	$ 4,168.51	$ 4,168.51	$ 4,168.51
Sinking fund depreciation		(1,686.49)	(1,686.49)	(1,686.49)	(1,686.49)	(1,686.49)	(1,686.49)	(1,686.49)
Capital cost		(1,800.00)	(1,800.00)	(1,800.00)	(1,800.00)	(1,800.00)	(1,800.00)	(1,800.00)
CVA		$ (120.77)	$ (120.77)	$ (120.77)	$ 682.03	$ 682.03	$ 682.03	$ 682.03
CFROI		9.33%	9.33%	9.33%	13.79%	13.79%	13.79%	13.79%
MCVA = PV(CVA)	$1,323.94							

tive compensation is based on CVA might be inclined to reject the project, particularly if he expects to leave the firm in the next two years. In short, the use of sinking fund depreciation, which works for a project with equal annual cash flows, does not always work for investments with unequal cash flows. The problem with sinking fund depreciation is that it is a constant (see eq. 7.2) and when project cash flows vary from year to year, the resulting CVA_t can provide misleading signals regarding the period-by-period value creation potential of the project. Note also (as in table 7.2) that EVA calculated using GAAP depreciation has the same problem.

Finally, in panel C of table 7.6, we compute the project's cash flow return on investment (CFROI) for each year of the project's life. The CFROI for years 1–3 is 9.33 percent, and 13.79 percent for years 4–7. During the first three years the CFROI indicates that the project fails to earn the cost of capital of 10 percent while it earns more than the cost of capital during years 4–7. Thus, just like CVA, uneven project cash flows can lead to problems for the CFROI metric.[5]

A Multiple-Period EVA for the Oil and Gas Industry

The issues that give rise to problems for all traditionally defined VBM metrics (uneven cash flows and nonzero NPVs) are particularly acute for mining and energy exploration and production (E&P) companies. In these industries it often takes many years of investment outflows before projects begin to return cash to the company. This situation creates negative EVAs for the early (development) years of the project followed by positive EVAs as the fruits of the investment are harvested.

Recent attempts to resolve the problem posed by lumpy project cash flows and the use of annual EVAs to evaluate period-by-period performance have involved converting the traditional EVA calculation from a single- to a multiple-period performance measure. For example, Elliott (1997) describes adjustments to EVA along these lines, and McCormack and Vytheeswaran (1998, p. 117) describe the rationale underlying the multi-period EVA as follows:

> Since management needs an internal performance measure that is a contemporaneous indicator of the wealth created, the remedy seems straightforward. The increase in the NPV of the company's reserves should be added both to its NOPAT and to its capital, in effect mark-

ing the reserves to market value.

McCormack and Vytheeswaran (1998) develop a revised version of EVA that captures the full valuation consequences of oil and gas discoveries in the period in which those discoveries are made. To see how their model works, consider an E&P development project that is expected to produce 1,000 barrels of oil over a five-year period, entails an investment of $10,000, and provides a project NPV of $522.43. Further details are as follows:

Cost of capital	10%
Total reserves	1,000 barrels
Production volume (year 1)	300 barrels
Decline in production	5% per year
Price/barrel	$20.00
Initial investment	$10,000.00
Depletion rate/barrel	$10.00
Operating cost/barrel	$5.00
Tax rate	35%

Table 7.7 shows estimated revenues, operating costs, cash flows, and annual EVAs for the traditional EVA calculation and the McCormack and Vytheeswaran adjusted EVA.

$$\text{Adjusted EVA}_t = \text{NOPAT}_t + (\text{PV}_t - \text{PV}_{t-1}) - (\text{BV}_t - \text{BV}_{t-1}) - k_{\text{wacc}}\text{PV}_{t-1} \quad (7.7)$$

where PV_t is the present value of future cash flows from operations as of period t, BV_t is the book value (historical cost) of the firm's invested capital as of period t, and k_{wacc} is the firm's cost of capital. Note that the cost of invested capital is based on the estimated market value, PV_{t-1}, and the incremental value created each period is the change in the net present value of additional reserves discovered in the period.

Panel B of table 7.7 shows that for the traditional way of calculating EVA, a negative EVA in the first year of the project's operation was followed by positive EVAs for years 2–7. The present value of all the EVAs is, of course, the net present value of the project, or $522.43.

Is the annual EVA calculated in the traditional way an accurate reflection of the wealth created for the shareholders year by year? McCormack and Vytheeswaran argue that these EVAs are actually *lagging* indicators of wealth creation, as the net present value of the project will be reflected in the stock price as soon as the 1,000-barrel discovery

Table 7.7 McCormack and Vytheeswaran's Adjusted EVA for Oil and Gas Firms

	0	1	2	3	4	5
Panel A. Calculation of Free Cash Flow						
Net volumes (barrels)		$ 300	$ 250	$ 200	$ 150	$ 100
Price/barrel		20	20	20	20	20
Gross revenues		$6,000	$ 5,000	$4,000	$3,000	$2,000
Less: Depletion cost		(3,000)	(2,500)	(2,000)	(1,500)	(1,000)
Less: Cash operating costs		(1,500)	(1,250)	(1,000)	(750)	(500)
Net Operating Income		$1,500	$1,250	$1,000	$ 750	$ 500
Less: Taxes		(525)	(438)	(350)	(263)	(175)
Net operating profit after taxes (NOPAT)		$ 975	$ 813	$ 650	$ 488	$ 325
Free cash flow = NOPAT + Depletion cost	$(10,000)	$3,975	$3,313	$2,650	$1,988	$1,325
Panel B. Calculation of Traditional EVA and Adjusted EVA						
NOPAT	—	$ 975	$ 813	$ 650	$ 488	$ 325
Invested capital (at cost or book value)	10,000	7,000	4,500	2,500	1,000	—
Capital charge (Invested capital × Cost of capital)		(1,000)	(700)	(450)	(250)	(100)
EVA = NOPAT − Capital charge	—	$ (25)	$ 113	$ 200	$ 238	$ 225
MVA = PV(future EVAs)	$522.43					
$PV(t)$ = Estimated market value of reserves	10,522	7,600	5,047	2,902	1,205	—
$\Delta PV(t) = PV(t) - PV(t-1)$ = ΔMarket value of reserves		(2,923)	(2,553)	(2,145)	(1,697)	(1,205)
Capital cost CCPV ($k_{waac} \times PV(t-1)$)		(1,052)	(760)	(505)	(290)	(120)
$\Delta BV(t) = BV(t) - BV(t-1)$ = ΔBook value of reserves		(3,000)	(2,500)	(2,000)	(1,500)	(1,000)
Adjusted EVA = NOPAT(t) + $\Delta PV(t)$ − $\Delta BV(t)$ − CCPV$(t-1)$	$522.43	—	—	—	—	—

is announced. Looking at the adjusted EVA in panel B of table 7.7 we see that the entire valuation consequence of the project is reflected in the announcement year (year 0) and the subsequent values are zero. This pattern of adjusted EVAs is entirely consistent with changes in the firm's equity value corresponding to the discovery and subsequent announcement of the new reserves.

What makes this type of adjustment difficult is the estimation of the change in value of the firm's reserves (i.e., the present value of the firm's future cash flows from operations). However, for E&P companies the problem is made easier by virtue of the SEC requirement that E&P companies file an estimate of this quantity annually in the SEC-10 report.[6] The fact that the estimate is made by independent engineers is also important, for it separates this important component of the firm performance metric from the firm's management whose efforts are being evaluated.

McCormack and Vytheeswaran agree that the addition of the estimated change in value of reserves less exploration costs is needed. However, they argue that the SEC-10 estimate of the value of reserves is too rough and can be improved upon in important ways. First, the same discount rate (10 percent) is used for every company regardless of the operating risks associated with the properties or the financial risks faced by the firm that owns the reserves. Second, the discounted cash flow valuation of the reserves fails to recognize managerial flexibility in producing and selling those reserves. This flexibility creates real options that make the reserves more valuable than the discounted expected value of future production.[7]

Summary

What we've learned about the use of VBM tools for new project analysis is that single-period performance measures made popular by VBM vendors for the evaluation of the performance of ongoing firm operations can easily be misinterpreted and misused when used to evaluate the period-by-period performance of new investment opportunities. Nothing is wrong with single-period measures of performance (such as EVA, CVA, and CFROI), per se; the problem lies in the use of single-period measures as indicators of value creation potential for long-lived projects. The simple answer is to use project NPV. NPV is completely consistent with EVA and CVA when we consider the present value of all future project EVAs and CVAs.

Two modifications of EVA (by McCormack/Vytheeswaran and by Bierman and O'Byrne) correct for the problems that arise in the use of traditionally defined EVA in project analysis. However, the "fix" comes at a high cost in terms of the required information. The difficulty with the McCormack/Vytheeswaran model is that it relies on the availability of verifiable data on the present value of the firm's assets that is generally not available (with the possible exception of the oil and gas industry, where SEC filings serve as a useful proxy). This is especially true at the divisional level, where the greatest effect from implementing an EVA incentive system would arguably occur. The problem with using economic depreciation, as recommended by Bierman and O'Byrne, is that the estimates required in implementing the system come from the firm's management. Since managerial compensation depends upon these estimates, managers would have an economic incentive to manipulate their estimates opportunistically. We return to a discussion of this problem in chapter 8, where we review compensation issues in the context of VBM.

Appendix 7A

The Equivalence of MVA and NPV

Market value added (MVA) is the term used by Stern Stewart & Co. to measure the incremental value that a firm's management has added to the capital that has been invested in a firm. Stern Stewart annually calculates MVA for the 1,000 largest firms and uses it to identify the top wealth creators. The calculation involves first computing the market value of a firm's equity and adding to this sum the value of its liabilities. From this sum is subtracted an estimate of the total invested capital (book value of the firm's assets adjusted for a number of accounting practices that tend to make this book value an underestimate of invested capital, e.g., the expensing of R&D expense). However, MVA has another interpretation where we assume that the market value of the firm is equal to the discounted present value of the firm's future cash flows. We demonstrate that MVA is analogous to the net present value (NPV) of the firm as a whole.

To illustrate the relationship between MVA and NPV consider a single-period investment project in which a firm invests I_0 dollars in return for operating income at the end of the period equal to NOI_1. The firm pays tax at a rate T, the asset is fully depreciated in one period leaving no residual or salvage value (i.e., depreciation expense for the period equals I_0), and the firm faces an opportunity cost of capital of k_{waac}. In this simple setting, the year one EVA_1 can be defined as follows:

$$EVA_1 = NOI_1(1 - T) - k_{waac}I_0 \qquad (A.1)$$

MVA then equals

$$MVA = \frac{NOI_1(1 - T) - k_{wacc}I_0}{(1 + k_{wacc})^1}$$

To see the equivalence of MVA and NPV, note that the project's free cash flow (FCF) is defined as follows:

$$FCF_1 = NOI_1(1 - T) + I_0 \qquad (A.3)$$

where depreciation expense equals I_0. Solving (A.3) for $\text{NOI}_1(1 - T)$ and substituting the result into (A.2)

$$\text{MVA} = \frac{\text{FCF}_1 - I_0 - k_{\text{wacc}}I_0}{(1 + k_{\text{wacc}})^1} = \frac{\text{FCF}_1 - I_0(1 + k_{\text{wacc}})}{(1 + k_{\text{wacc}})^1} = \text{FCF}_1 - I_0 = \text{NPV}$$

The equivalence of MVA and NPV can easily be extended to multiple future periods.

References

BCG (Boston Consulting Group). *Shareholder Value Management: Improved Measurement Drives Improved Value Creation.* Book 2. July 29, 1994.

Bierman, Harold. "Beyond Cash Flow ROI." *Midland Corporate Finance Journal.* 5, 4 (1988): 36–39.

Dixit, Avinash K., and Robert S. Pyndick. *Investment Under Uncertainty.* Princeton, N.J.: Princeton University Press, 1994.

Ehrbar, Al. *Stern Stewart's EVA: The Real Key to Creating Wealth.* New York: Wiley, 1998.

Elliott, Lisa. "Is EVA for Everyone?" *Oil & Gas Investor* 17, 2 (1997): 46–51.

Jensen, Michael, and William Meckling. "Divisional Performance Measurement." Chap. 12 in *Foundations of Organizational Strategy.* Cambridge, Mass.: Harvard University Press, 1998.

McCormack, John, and Jawanth Vytheeswaran. "How to Use EVA in the Oil and Gas Industry." *Journal of Applied Corporate Finance* 11 (1998): 109–131.

Hawawini, Gabriel, and Claude Viallet. *Finance for Executives: Managing for Value Creation.* Cincinnati: South-Western College Publishing, 1999.

O'Byrne, Stephen. "Does Value Based Management Discourage Investment in Intangibles?" In *Value-Based Metrics: Foundations and Practice,* ed. James L. Grant and Frank J. Fabozzi. Frank J. Fabozzi & Associates (2000).

Trigeorgis, Lenos. *Real Options: Managerial Flexibility and Strategy in Resource Allocation.* Cambridge, Mass.: MIT Press, 1996.

Chapter **8**

Incentive Compensation: What You Measure and Reward Gets Done

Academics and practitioners from a wide range of backgrounds agree that bringing about sustainable, productive changes in organizations is difficult. They disagree, however, on why this is the case. Consequently, they disagree on the most effective approaches to analyzing and solving organizational problems, and on the most effective approaches to implementing solutions. At the heart of the disagreement are differences over the factors that motivate individuals to change their behavior. Behavioral changes on the part of individuals are required for organizational change, and compensation systems affect behavior. Thus, it is critical to consider the role that compensation systems play in the process of organizational change.

> **—Karen Hopper Wruck, "Compensation, Incentives,**
> **and Organizational Change" (2000)**

When managers become owners, they begin to think a lot harder about taking money out of mature businesses and investing in growth areas. And I think that happens as a fairly natural consequence of greater ownership. It's certainly not happening because all of a sudden we put in new controls at headquarters. In fact, today we have fewer controls than we had as part of Kraft. What's different is that the proposals for change are coming from the bottom up rather than from the top down.

> **—Robert Kidder, CEO of Duracell (1998)[1]**

> We had a cross-functional team, which for some time had been examining what we saw as a shortcoming of our incentive system—that executive pay was linked to sales and net income. There just wasn't a very good correlation at all with shareholder value.
>
> **—Randall Tobias, CEO of Eli Lilly (1996)[2]**

*E*very business faces the problem of motivating its employees to create value for the firm's owner(s). The problem is particularly acute for the non-owner-managed corporation because the owners (i.e., the stockholders) do not exercise direct control over the firm's operations. Two fundamental approaches can be taken. The first involves careful monitoring or oversight of employee behavior. Although this approach can be effective, it becomes very cumbersome and consequently very expensive to implement in large organizations where decentralized decision making is required to make timely choices in the face of competition. Thus, the effectiveness of "watching over the employee's shoulder" is limited. The second approach involves developing a compensation policy that attracts, retains, and motivates high-performing personnel. This approach forms the basis for value based management systems and is the subject of this chapter.

Before we proceed we should point out that a compensation system is not limited to monetary payments. Wruck (2000) notes what human beings value or dislike more than monetary compensation within a business organization and that monetary considerations cannot capture all that affects their motivation and incentives. However, for managers considering the redesign of their firm's compensation system, monetary rewards are particularly important and provide a productive place to start. The importance of money is not that it is valued more highly than other types of rewards, but that money is fungible, that is, it can be converted into whatever it is that the employee values most highly. Thus, with the important caveat that compensation systems must deal with more than the allocation of monetary rewards,[3] we focus our discussion on the monetary component of a firm's compensation system.

O'Byrne (1997) identifies four basic objectives for a firm's compensation policy:

- *Alignment:* to give managers an incentive to choose strategies and investments that maximize shareholder value

- *Leverage:* to give managers sufficient incentive compensation to motivate them to work long hours, take risks, and make unpleasant decisions, such as closing a plant or laying off staff, to maximize shareholder value

- *Retention:* to give managers sufficient total compensation to retain them, particularly during periods of poor performance due to market and industry factors

- *Shareholder cost:* to limit the cost of management compensation to levels that will maximize the wealth of current stockholders

While each firm may describe its compensation policy objectives in a slightly different manner, these four objectives are universal.[4] All four of these objectives are important to the design of an effective compensation policy; however, value based management systems have generally focused on the alignment and leverage objectives. Consequently, these objectives form the basis for our discussion.[5]

Compensation plans vary in their complexity across firms, industries, and levels of employees in the firm's hierarchy. Consider the typical CEO's compensation package, which Murphy (1999) describes as base salary, an annual bonus tied to accounting performance, stock options, and long-term incentive plans (including restricted stock plans and multi-year accounting performance plans). In very broad terms we can think of the base salary as fixed compensation in that it does not vary with firm performance. The remaining components of the CEO's compensation package are variable or at risk because they depend on some measure of firm performance. Value based management systems are concerned with the design of measurement and pay-for-performance systems that determine the variable components.

Most of this chapter is devoted to the use of the annual performance measures of value based management to determine the annual bonus component of managerial compensation. This focus is directly related to the emphasis placed on this component in the value based management literature. One of the principal points we make is that annual pay-for-performance bonuses based on the tools of value based management can fail to provide a long-term value perspective. In fact, we demonstrate that these systems can lead to myopic investment decisions if other forms of long-term measurement and reward such as stock options and grants do not accompany them.

We first discuss the three fundamental issues that every compensation program must address. Next, we examine actual executive compensation practices using the work of Murphy (1999). We discover that pay-for-performance compensation programs are far less prevalent than we might have thought. Finally, we discuss some possible explanations for the reluctance of many firms to use pay-for-performance compensation programs.

Determining a Firm's Compensation Policy

A firm's compensation policy must answer three fundamental questions: (1) what level of compensation is to be paid, (2) how the compensation is to be to linked to performance (i.e., the functional form), and (3) how the compensation is to be paid (i.e., its composition), including cash payments versus benefits (insurance, working conditions, leisure time, and so forth) and the use of cash versus equity (stock options and grants) for incentive pay.[6]

What Should Be the Level of Compensation?

A competitive labor market requires, at a minimum, that executives be paid what they might earn in a comparable job working elsewhere. In essence, the level of compensation a firm pays will determine the quality and quantity of workers the firm can attract. Furthermore, market forces that are outside the firm's control largely determine the level of compensation paid. It is standard practice for firms to use compensation survey data as the basis for determining the level of compensation paid to their employees. For example, Dana Corporation's 1999 proxy statement indicates that the firm "compares Dana's compensation practices to those of a group of comparable companies. The comparison group . . . currently consists of 22 companies." (p. 11) According to Murphy (1999) the use of compensation surveys is nearly universal as a means for determining base salaries.

The proponents of value based management argue that paying a competitive level of compensation is not sufficient to ensure the creation of shareholder value. Specifically, they argue, one must link pay to performance. The fundamental premise underlying value based management systems is simple: what a firm measures and rewards gets done. So, if the goal is to create shareholder value, one should select a performance measure that is consistent with that objective and use it to determine compensation.[7] Thus, value based management systems focus on the functional form of compensation.

How Should Pay Be Linked to Performance?

Functional form refers to the relation between pay and performance. The sensitivity of pay to performance depends upon two attributes of the firm's compensation program: (1) the fraction of total compensation that is tied to performance, and (2) the formula used to relate pay to performance. There are no hard-and-fast rules for determining the mix of variable versus fixed compensation. However, in practice we observe that the firm's highest-ranking employees have a larger fraction of their total compensation at risk and dependent on firm performance. For most firms this simply mirrors the responsibilities of the firm's top managers and their ability to control firm performance. Furthermore, because the at-risk or variable component of compensation is the key to determining the sensitivity of compensation to performance, we focus on this factor as it influences incentive compensation.

Formula for Determining Incentive Pay

The procedure used to determine the level of incentive compensation varies little regardless of the particular performance measure that is chosen.[8] Let's begin by looking at an unbounded incentive compensation payout formula:[9]

$$\frac{\text{Incentive}}{\text{pay}} = \frac{\text{Base}}{\text{pay}} \times \frac{\text{Fraction of}}{\text{pay at risk}} \times \frac{\text{Actual performance}}{\text{Target performance}} \quad (8.1)$$

Since no maximum or minimum level of compensation is specified, the incentive pay is unbounded. Also, we see that the incentive compensation in eq. (8.1) is a function of the amount of the employee's compensation that is at risk or subject to firm performance (the product of base pay and the fraction of pay at risk)[10] and the firm's actual performance for the period relative to a target level of performance. In practice, this basic system might be the same for all employees but differ in terms of the level of employee base pay and the percentage of that base pay that is at risk or subject to incentive compensation.

How does the basic model of incentive pay work? Consider the case of an employee whose base pay is $50,000 with an additional 20 percent of this base pay, or $10,000, at risk (i.e., dependent on firm performance). For convenience we have defined base pay as the employee's fixed compensation, or salary that is fixed regardless of the firm's performance.[11] Thus, the employee's total compensation is equal to the base component of $50,000 plus some fraction of the at-risk pay. If we assume that the ratio of actual to target performance is 1.1, then her incentive or at-risk pay for the year is $11,000 and total compensation for the period is equal to $61,000.[12] Alternatively, if the firm's performance is just equal to the target level of performance, then incentive compensation is equal to $10,000 and total compensation is equal to $60,000.

Figure 8.1 illustrates how incentive compensation varies with firm performance. In this example, incentive compensation is unbounded because it varies directly with actual performance relative to target performance with no floor (minimum) or cap (maximum).[13] Such a system provides the firm's employees with an incentive to improve firm performance regardless of the level of firm performance.

Most firms, however, do not use an unbounded incentive pay program. Instead they use a system that provides for a minimum or threshold level of performance (in relation to the target level) before the incentive plan kicks in and a maximum level of performance (again in relation to the target) above which no incentive pay is rewarded. These minimum and maximum performance levels are sometimes referred to as "golfing points" because of the adverse incentives they have on employee work effort.

Figure 8.2 contains an example of an 80/120 plan for which the minimum or threshold level of performance for which incentive compensation is paid is equal to 80 percent of the target level of performance. The maximum performance for which incentive pay is rewarded is 120 percent of the target performance. Consequently, incentive compensation is only paid for performance levels that fall within the 80/120 range. In addition, there is a wide range of firm performance for which no incentive pay is awarded (i.e., performance above 120 percent or below 80 percent of the target level). Thus, this type of program has incentive effects that are limited to the range of performance for which the payout varies with performance.

Figure 8.1 Pure (Unbounded) Incentive Pay-for-Performance System

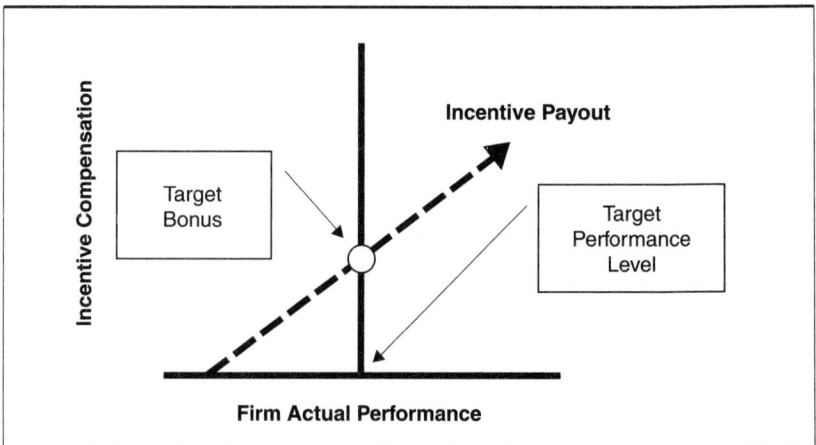

Figure 8.2 An 80/120 (Bounded) Incentive Pay-for-Performance
System

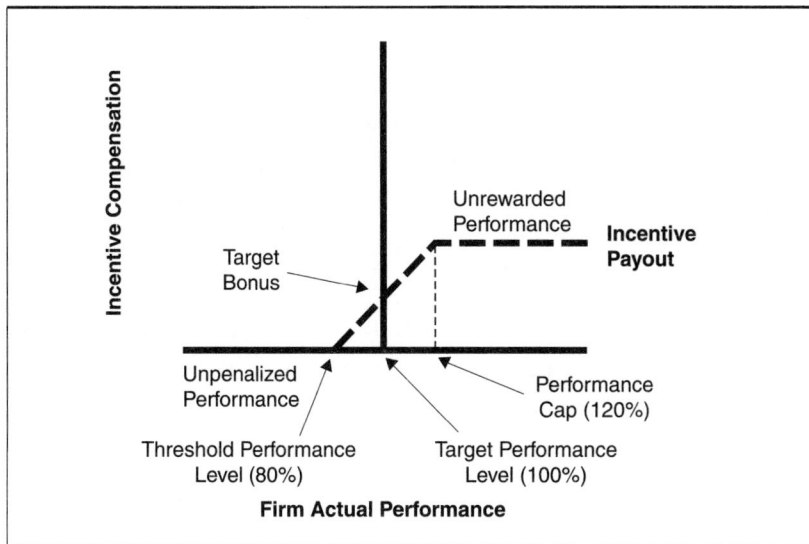

Bounded incentive compensation plans, Watts and Zimmerman (1986) argue, can provide adverse incentives to managers. For example, as it becomes obvious that the firm's performance for the evaluation period (usually one quarter or one year) will fall below the 80 percent threshold, employees have no direct pay-for-performance incentive to work harder in order to raise firm performance during the remainder of the performance evaluation period. In fact, they have an incentive to reduce current-period performance even further in the hopes that it will lower the target level for the coming period. In addition, reducing current-period performance may allow shifting some or all of the lost performance to the following evaluation period, when they hope to be rewarded for it.

A similar problem arises on the upper end of the performance spectrum. For example, if it looks like the firm's performance is going to surpass the maximum payout level then the employees once again lose the incentive to improve performance. First, they are not paid for performance above the maximum, and second, they may be able to postpone business until the coming period, when it can be counted toward incentive pay for that period.[14]

A growing body of evidence suggests that managers do behave opportunistically in reacting to bounded compensation plans. The evidence suggests that managers bank earnings when it appears that they will surpass the performance cap, but there is no evidence that they take an earnings bath when threshold performance is unlikely (Degeorge et al. 1998; Gaver et al. 1995; Healy 1985; Holthausen et al. 1995).[15]

Single-Period Performance Measures and Managerial Incentives

To this point we have referred to firm performance without specifying how it is to be measured. A wide variety of performance metrics might be used, including accounting-based measures such as earnings, earnings growth, and revenue growth, in addition to the value based management system metrics. However, virtually all of these measures are based on the results of a single period's historical performance. This fact raises a very serious problem that Jensen and Meckling (1986, p. 13) summarize in the following way:

> Because EVA is a flow measure, it does not solve the capital value problem. This means that if future annual EVA of a project is sufficiently large, it will pay a company to take a project whose early years' EVA is negative. Market value, the discounted value of net cash flows less the investment required to generate them, is the appropriate value to maximize. Thus, while EVA is the best flow measure of performance currently known, it is not the universal answer to the search for the perfect performance measure.

The problem can create adverse incentives for managers whose decisions are based on personal financial incentives over a decision horizon that is shorter than the life of the projects being considered.

Managerial Decision Horizons and the Use of EVA and CVA. We can illustrate the nature of the "stock versus flow" problem noted in the preceding quotation using the example investment project (similar to those discussed in chapter 7) in table 8.1. We assume an initial investment of $18,000, consisting of plant and equipment of $16,000 to be depreciated on a straight-line basis ($2,285.71 per year) over a seven-year life, and working capital equal to $2,000 to be recouped at the end of the project's life. The project has a 10 percent required rate of return.

We begin our analysis of project cash flow and its value in table 8.1 with the project's expected net operating profits after taxes (NOPAT). Observe that NOPAT is the same throughout the first three years of the project's life, then increases to a higher level for the final four years. We then add back depreciation to compute free cash flow. Note that book

Table 8.1 EVA- and CVA-Based Incentive Compensation for a Positive NPV Project

	0	1	2	3	4	5	6	7
Net operating profit after taxes (NOPAT)		$ 1,140.00	$ 1,140.00	$ 1,140.00	$1,320.00	$1,320.00	$1,320.00	$1,320.00
Depreciation		2,285.71	2,285.71	2,285.71	2,285.71	2,285.71	2,285.71	2,285.71
Plant and equipment	$(16,000.00)							0.00
Working capital	(2,000.00)							2,000.00
Invested capital	$(18,000.00)							
Firm free cash flow	$(18,000.00)	$ 3,425.71	$ 3,425.71	$ 3,425.71	$3,605.71	$3,605.71	$3,605.71	$5,605.71
NPV	$132.81							
Book capital	$ 18,000.00	$15,714.29	$13,428.57	$11,142.86	$8,857.14	$6,571.43	$4,285.71	$2,000.00
Capital cost		1,800.00	1,571.43	1,342.86	1,114.29	885.71	657.14	428.57
Return on invested capital		6.33%	7.25%	8.49%	11.85%	14.90%	20.09%	30.80%
EVA		$ (660.00)	$ (431.43)	$ (202.86)	$ 205.71	$ 434.29	$ 662.86	$ 891.43
EVA-based compensation (1% of EVA)		(6.60)	(4.31)	(2.03)	2.06	4.34	6.63	8.91
Cumulative PV of EVA compensation		$ (6.00)	$ (9.57)	$ (11.09)	$ (9.68)	$ (6.99)	$ (3.25)	$ 1.33
CVA		$ (60.77)	$ (60.77)	$ (60.77)	$ 119.23	$ 119.23	$ 119.23	$ 119.23
CVA-based compensation (1% of CVA)		(0.61)	(0.61)	(0.61)	1.19	1.19	1.19	1.19
Cumulative PV of CVA compensation		$ (0.55)	$ (1.05)	$ (1.51)	$ (0.70)	$ 0.04	$ 0.72	$ 1.33

capital declines over time as the plant and equipment are depreciated, and the capital cost each year is the beginning book capital (ending capital in the prior year) times the cost of capital (10 percent). The results are as follows:

- The project's net present value (NPV) is $132.81.

- Return on invested capital is equal to NOPAT divided by the beginning capital and grows from 6.33 percent to 30.80 percent over the life of the project.

- Economic value added (EVA) is NOPAT less the capital cost. EVA is negative initially but increases over the life of the project from –$660.00 to $891.43.

- EVA-based compensation is assumed to equal 1 percent of EVA for the period.

- Cumulative present value of the compensation is the sum of the present values of the annual EVA compensation for one, two, and so forth, years. If a manager's horizon were four years, then the cumulative present value effect of accepting the project on his bonuses is –$9.68, whereas it rises to $1.33 for a seven-year horizon.

- Cash value added (CVA) is the project's free cash flow less the sinking fund depreciation less the capital charge on the full cost of the project.[16]

- CVA compensation and the cumulative present value of CVA compensation are calculated in the same way as the EVA compensation.

Since the project has a positive net present value of $132.81, it is expected to create shareholder value. Note, however, that the EVAs and CVAs for the project are negative for years 1 through 3. Consequently, regardless of whether incentive compensation is based on EVA or CVA, the project has a negative impact on managerial compensation. This fact is depicted graphically in figure 8.3, where we plot the sum of the present values of the annual bonuses for each year.[17] Note, however, that since the magnitude of the EVAs is so much greater than that of the CVAs, it takes seven years for the cumulative present value of the EVA bonuses to sum to a positive number, whereas it takes only five years for the CVA-based bonuses to produce a positive present value sum.

Consider the financial incentive of a manager who is considering such a project but who does not plan to remain with the firm for more than, say, three or four years.[18] This individual will not want to under-

Figure 8.3 Cumulative Present Value of EVA-Based Compensation for a Positive NPV Project

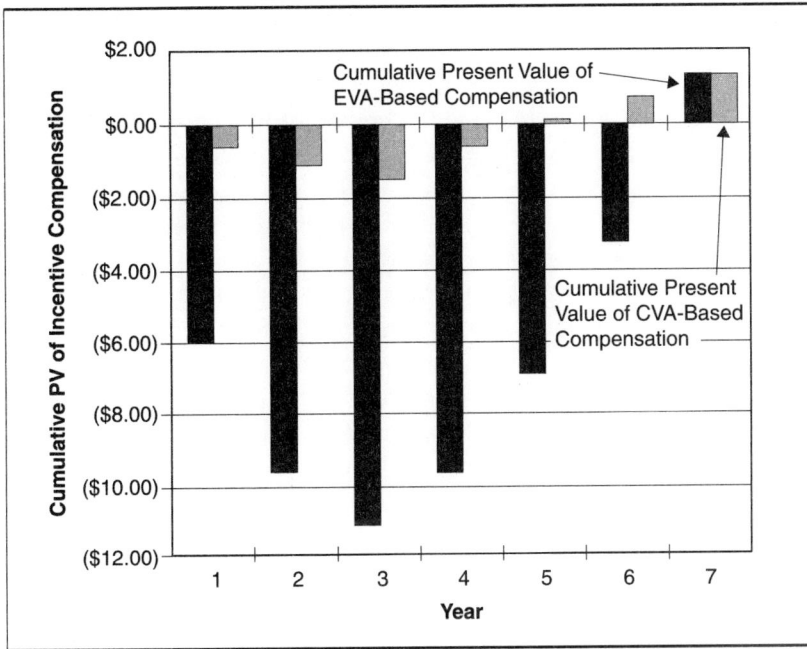

take the project even though it offers a positive net present value regardless of whether EVA or CVA is used to evaluate annual performance. This is because the project's annual performance metrics in any given year do not reflect the value of future performance. As a result, a manager who is compensated based on EVA and with a decision horizon less than six years will reject the project even though it offers a positive NPV.[19] The CVA manager will only accept the project if she has a decision horizon of five or more years.

It is important to note, however, that when the manager's decision horizon is equal to the life of the project under consideration, she will be motivated to make decisions that are consistent with NPV. That is, the cumulative present value of her bonuses based on either EVA or CVA are positive for a manager with a seven-year horizon, indicating that she will want to undertake the positive NPV project. This result is not surprising since, as we stated in chapter 7, the present value of project EVAs or CVAs over the entire life of the project is equal to the project's NPV. Thus, the cumulative present value of future bonuses over the entire life of the project is simply a percentage (1 percent in our example) of NPV. Correspondingly, if NPV is positive (negative) the cumulative present value of the manager's bonuses over the life of the project will also be positive (negative).

Now consider the managerial incentives associated with a negative NPV investment that offers high initial returns followed by poor returns. Table 8.2 shows such an example. The project has a *negative* NPV of –$301.40, but because of the higher returns on invested capital earned in the early years of the project's life it provides positive EVAs and CVAs in these early years. As a result, a manager who is compensated based on EVA and has a decision horizon of three years or less will want to undertake the project even though it has a negative NPV. Similarly, if CVA is used to determine compensation, a manager with a decision horizon as long as six years will find the project attractive. Once again, if the manager's decision horizon is equal to the project's life, he will have an incentive to make choices that are consistent with NPV regardless of whether EVA or CVA is used to measure annual performance. These results are shown graphically in figure 8.4.

To summarize, when either EVA (calculated using GAAP depreciation) or CVA (both single-period performance measures) is used to measure performance, managers with horizons shorter than the life of the project can have a financial incentive to behave counterproductively. Specifically, such a manager will be motivated to accept some projects that have good near-term prospects but have a negative NPV (e.g., the project in table 8.2) and reject positive NPV projects that have good long-term prospects but do not provide much cash in their early years (e.g., the project found in table 8.1). The primary source of the problem, of course, is the length of the manager's decision horizon. Also, the distribution of the cash flows across time can contribute to the problem. Notice that in both tables 8.1 and 8.2 the returns on invested capital are increasing and decreasing over time, respectively. For the positive NPV project in table 8.1, the returns start below the 10 percent cost of capital and gradually climb until they exceed the cost of capital by a wide margin. This relation is reversed in table 8.2 for the negative NPV project. Thus, anytime the return on invested capital varies from year to year and is sometimes above the cost of capital and sometimes below, we have the potential for conflicts between single-period measures (flow measures) and the net present value of the project (a stock measure).

Extending Managerial Horizons Using a Bonus Bank. One method that has been suggested for addressing the problem of managerial decision horizons and the single-period nature of the EVA and

Table 8.2 Example EVA- and CVA-Based Incentive Compensation for a Negative NPV Project

	0	1	2	3	4	5	6	7
Net operating profit after taxes (NOPAT)		$ 1,950.00	$ 1,521.00	$ 1,186.38	$ 925.38	$ 721.79	$ 563.00	$ 439.14
Depreciation		2,285.71	2,285.71	2,285.71	2,285.71	2,285.71	2,285.71	2,285.71
Plant and equipment	$(16,000.00)							0.00
Working capital	(2,000.00)							2,000.00
Invested capital	$(18,000.00)							
Firm free cash flow	$(18,000.00)	$ 4,235.71	$ 3,806.71	$ 3,472.09	$3,211.09	$3,007.51	$2,848.71	$4,724.85
NPV	($301.40)							
Book capital	$ 18,000.00	$15,714.29	$13,428.57	$11,142.86	$8,857.14	$6,571.43	$4,285.71	$2,000.00
Capital cost		1,800.00	1,571.43	1,342.86	1,114.29	885.71	657.14	428.57
Return on invested capital		10.83%	9.68%	8.83%	8.30%	8.15%	8.57%	10.25%
EVA		$ 150.00	$ (50.43)	$ (156.48)	$ (188.91)	$ (163.92)	$ (94.14)	10.57
EVA-based compensation (1% of EVA)		1.50	(0.50)	(1.56)	(1.89)	(1.64)	(0.94)	0.11
Cumulative PV of EVA compensation		$ 1.36	$ 0.95	$ (0.23)	$ (1.52)	$ (2.54)	$ (3.07)	$ (3.01)
CVA		$ 749.23	$ 320.23	$ (14.39)	$ (275.40)	$ (478.98)	$ (637.77)	$ (761.63)
CVA-based compensation (1% of CVA)		7.49	3.20	(0.14)	(2.75)	(4.79)	(6.38)	(7.62)
Cumulative PV of CVA compensation		$ 6.81	$ 9.46	$ 9.35	$ 7.47	$ 4.49	$ 0.89	$ (3.01)

Figure 8.4 Cumulative Present Value of EVA-Based Compensation for a Negative NPV Project

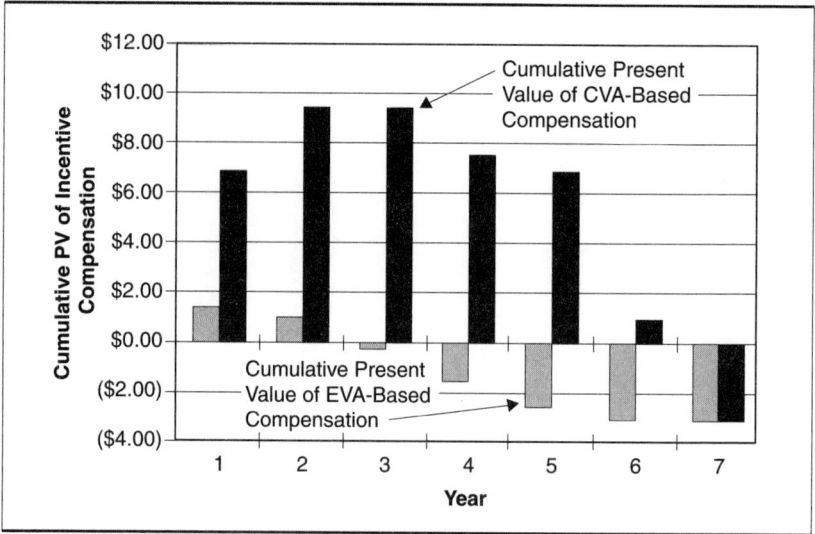

CVA measurements is to use a bonus bank system.[20] A bonus bank entails paying out employee bonuses over an extended period of time. For example, with a three-year bonus bank the bonus earned this year would be paid out one third this year, one third next year, and one third the following year.[21] A bonus bank system pushes the manager's decision horizon out to the length of the bonus bank period because poor performance in the future will reduce the employee's bonus bank balance. However, to be completely effective the bonus bank must extend the manager's decision horizon over the entire life of the projects being analyzed. In practice, bonus banks seldom extend beyond five years.[22]

Setting EVA Targets Based on Year-to-Year Improvements

Bonus plans based on residual income type measures (of which EVA is a special case) have existed for many years. For example, in 1922, General Motors adopted a bonus plan that provided a bonus pool equal to 10 percent of profit in excess of a 7 percent return on capital. This plan survived with little modification for twenty-five years (Sloan 1963). Walt Disney used a similar compensation plan for Michael Eisner beginning in 1983, whereby an annual bonus of 2 percent of net income in excess of a 9 percent return on equity was granted. This plan was used for almost fifteen years with only minor modification. Both these plans provided for a fixed percentage interest in residual income that can be problematic.

Specifically, O'Byrne (2000) notes four reasons why this simple bonus plan based on a fixed percent of firm performance is rarely used today: (1) Paying a percent of the level of residual income does not allow for the payment of bonuses where the firm is suffering negative performance. (2) If no bonus is paid in years with negative performance, managers have an incentive to defer revenues and profits to later periods when a bonus will be earned. This is the gaming problem we alluded to earlier regarding figure 8.2. (3) Giving management a bonus based on the first dollar earned provides an inefficient trade-off between the strength of the incentive to the manager and the cost to the shareholder. For very low levels of the performance metric the bonus is very small and may provide a very limited incentive to management; however, in very successful years the same percentage bonus may lead to payments that shareholders feel are in excess of what is necessary to attract capable managers. This argues for a bonus payout function that provides for a declining bonus percentage as performance increases. For example, the bonus payout might be, say, 5 percent of EVA up to a threshold level of EVA, then 4 percent for a second range of performance, and so forth. (4) Paying bonuses based on the level of the performance measure fails to account for a lack of improvement. This criticism is based on the notion that continuing to earn a positive EVA does not deserve a reward. However, where EVA truly measures excess or economic profit, one might reason that for managers who must operate in contested markets just maintaining the current level of EVA might be a significant accomplishment.

In response to the problems associated with paying a fixed percent of EVA in managerial bonuses Stern Stewart & Co. recommends that bonuses be paid based upon changes in EVA rather than the level of EVA for the period (Stern, Stewart, and Chew 1998). However, this leaves unanswered the question as to what should be the firm's target level of EVA or target change in EVA? Stern Stewart's recommendation that the firm pay for improvements seems reasonable in the absence of any information regarding what is possible or feasible. However, we should recognize that although increasing EVA is generally better than decreasing it, there are circumstances when EVA for a given year is expected to decline (e.g., immediately following a major capital commitment to a project that will not begin producing cash flows for many years). This is the same problem we discussed earlier in chapter 7. That is, single-period historical performance metrics can be insufficient indicators of the creation of value where shareholder value is based on the performance of the firm in all future periods. Thus, we are left with the conclusion that single-period measurements of performance are necessary, but we should not think that they can be applied mechanically without judgment—not even those of more recent acclaim, such as EVA and CVA.

Using Equity to Lengthen Managerial Decision Horizons

If managers believe that stock prices are driven by the present value of future cash flows, then a natural way to lengthen their decision horizons is to pay them with stock or options on shares of stock.[23] This is in fact what many firms are doing in increasing numbers. For example, stock options currently account for more than half of total CEO compensation in the largest U.S. companies and about 30 percent of senior operating managers' pay. Furthermore, options and stock grants now constitute almost half of directors' pay. These facts reflect the notion that equity-based pay can be a natural complement to short-term performance-based bonuses. Viewed in this way equity-based compensation, like value based management, is yet another approach that can be used to try to align shareholder and manager interests.

In principle, stock price seems to be the correct measure if the objective is to link performance to what shareholders care about. However, equity-based compensation does have its limitations. Baker, Jensen, and Murphy (1988) describe the issues arising out of the use of equity compensation in the following way:

> Compensation practitioners argue that fundamental changes in the "corporate culture" occur when employees are made partial owners of the firm. The effects of these plans include "rooting for the home team" and a growing awareness of and interest in the corporate bottom line. We do not understand how these effects translate into increased productivity, nor do we have a well-developed economic theory of the creation and effects of corporate culture.

The practical issue here is what compensation experts refer to as *line of sight,* and the associated theoretical problem is what economists call the *free rider problem.* Line of sight refers to managers' belief that their actions have the power to affect stock price. If a manager cannot see the effect of his actions on the firm's share price, it is questionable whether owning stock will lead to any change in behavior that increases shareholder value. The associated free rider problem arises where employees who own stock or stock options benefit from the actions of others that drive up share price. These employees have a free ride because they did nothing but ride on the coattails of others whose actions drove share price upward.[24]

The issues that Baker, Jensen, and Murphy (1988) raised in the preceding quotation are less important for the firm's top-level managers. For this reason we find the use of stock options and grants is far more prevalent among a firm's top executives and members of its board of directors than among other levels of employees. We conclude that equity-based compensation is not a substitute for bonus plans that reward current period performance but complement them by helping extend the decision horizons of the firm's top managers.

What Should Be the Composition of Employee Compensation?

The amount of incentive pay is determined by firm performance and the particulars of the payout function (e.g., whether it is bounded or not and whether the firm uses a bonus bank).[25] However, the form of the compensation is also an important component of a firm's compensation program. Specifically, the firm can pay in cash, stock/options or some mixture of the two. If the firm chooses stock, the employees are rewarded for current performance and may also receive an additional incentive to improve the firm's long-term performance.

The issues we raised with respect to the use of options or equity-based compensation do not argue against their use as a substitute for cash in an incentive compensation program. That is, $100 in cash is equivalent to $100 worth of stock or in-the-money call options worth $100. The question is whether equity-based compensation offers any *additional* positive incentives to managers beyond the positive effects associated with the incentive compensation that gave rise to the use of the equity-based compensation in the first place.

Equity-based compensation programs are widely supported in industry practice. Furthermore, this form of incentive compensation is particularly effective at the very highest levels of management. For these managers the line of sight from their actions to stock price is visible (even if hazy). Thus, the issues we raised concerning the incentive effects of equity-based compensation relate to its use at the lower organizational levels within the firm, where the line of sight between managerial decisions and stock price can be more easily obscured. For the lower levels of the firm's management some type of incentive pay based on operating performance measures that are under the control of the managers being compensated is more appropriate. Thus, we conclude that the composition of the firm's compensation package will vary across the levels of management, with the higher levels receiving more equity and the lower levels receiving more cash.

How Do Executives Get Paid?

Murphy (1999) documents the heterogeneity of incentive pay plans in use based on the annual incentive plans of 177 large U.S. corporations found in the Towers Perrin Annual Incentive Plan Design Survey for 1997. For example, 68 of the 177 firms surveyed base their performance assessment on a single measure, with earnings constituting the most widely used performance measure. Furthermore, only 6 of the 68 single-measure firms and 4 of the 109 firms that utilize two or more performance measures specifically mentioned EVA.[26] Murphy also summarizes the performance standard (i.e., the basis for target or planned performance) used by the same 177 firms. A striking feature is the widespread use of budgets in setting the threshold for the payment of incentive pay. For example, for firms that use a single criterion for judging performance, over half the industrial firms base their performance standards on budgets while 28 percent and 35 percent of the finance and insurance firms and utilities, respectively, follow this practice. When we look at firms that use multiple criteria for assessing performance, budgets are the most common performance standard used.

The budget-based standard is problematic because it creates a situation in which negotiating skills can affect the level of compensation earned. That is, the budget standard used to compare against realized firm performance when determining the basis for incentive compensation generally results from a negotiation process between the employees whose performance is being reviewed and the manager doing the review. Clearly, there is an incentive for the employee being reviewed to negotiate for a lower threshold level of budgeted performance. Thus, the negotiating skills of the employee enter into the setting of targets or standards used in determining when incentive compensation is paid. One major attraction of value based management systems is their use of an external performance standard such as the cost of capital to set performance expectations. This removes at least one source of internal politics from the compensation program.

Murphy (1999) found that the 80/120 type of bounded incentive plan is the most common plan in use. Furthermore, the most common shape of the payout function in the "incentive zone" (e.g., 80–120 percent of targeted performance) is discretionary, followed in popularity by linear (as in figures 8.1 and 8.2), and convex functions. The bonus is generally paid at some threshold level of performance and is capped above some level.

To conclude, the majority of the 177 firms in the survey do not use value based management systems. Most, in fact, base their compensation on accounting-based performance measures where performance targets are set in the budgeting process. Furthermore, the majority of firms do not pay incentive pay until some minimum threshold level of performance has been achieved and stop paying once a maximum level of performance is achieved.

Why Isn't Pay for Performance the Norm?

We have just observed that value based management systems are not the predominant form of incentive compensation. However, there is more to the story. Baker, Jensen, and Murphy (1988, p. 607) characterize the compensation systems in wide use in corporate America in terms of "the overwhelming use of promotion-based incentive systems, egalitarian pay systems apparently motivated by horizontal equity considerations, the asymmetric effects of rewards and punishments, tenure and up-or-out promotion systems, survey-based and seniority-based pay systems, profit sharing, holiday bonuses . . . and the general reluctance of employers to fire, penalize, or give poor performance evaluations to employees."

There are a number of possible explanations for the use of compensation systems that are not directly linked to individual performance. For example, it would be very easy to point the finger at managers who seek to protect themselves from pressures to perform, and this may be a part of the problem in some cases. However, we would like to highlight a very real problem that can limit the effectiveness of every system of value based management. This problem is related to the accuracy of performance measurement. If we cannot make accurate appraisals of performance contributions of employees or business units, this can lead to frustration on the part of the managers who are engaging in the evaluation process, and can have counterproductive effects on those being evaluated, who may feel that their efforts and those of their fellow employees are not properly rewarded.

Measurement accuracy is also relevant from the perspective of the firm's shareholders. For example, we demonstrated in chapter 7 that a single period's performance can be an insufficient (noisy) indicator of value created during the period. This problem is less severe in some industries than in others. Thus, measurement accuracy or the link between a single period's performance and the creation of shareholder value might explain the preponderance of the use of value based management systems among stationary or slow-growing firms, such as in basic manufacturing, and their absence in high-growth firms that operate in rapidly changing markets.

Summary

A firm's compensation policy is a critical component of its internal control system. That is, where owners (stockholders) do not manage the firms they own, it is essential that the firm have in place an internal control system to monitor employee performance and reward those efforts that increase shareholder wealth. In this chapter, we have discussed a fundamental component of every firm's internal control system, its compensation program. The basic paradigm espoused by the proponents of value based management is that what a firm measures and rewards gets done. Consequently, if the firm is to be run so as to maximize shareholder value, the compensation program must measure employee activities that contribute toward this goal and reward them. The measurement element focuses on the discussion from previous chapters, where we talked about EVA, CVA, CFROI, and the like. The reward component was the focal point of this chapter.

Employee compensation at most firms consists of both a fixed and a variable component. The variable component is generally tied to some measure of firm performance that is connected to the firm's primary goal (maximizing shareholder value, in this instance). Thus, incentive-based compensation, pay-for-performance, or at-risk pay is the compensation component of interest when designing a value based management system.

The level of incentive pay is usually linked to a comparison of actual versus target (planned) performance. However, many firms limit the range of performance over which incentive pay is rewarded. This can have adverse effects on employee motivation as employees respond to the circumstance where actual firm performance comes in below or above the threshold level of performance for which incentive pay will be rewarded. One solution to the adverse effects of floors and caps on incentive compensation is to remove them and create a long-term bonus bank into which employee incentive pay is placed and then paid out over a period of three to five years. The purpose of the bonus bank is to counter the incentive of employees to focus on near-term performance at the expense of longer-term performance.

Once the level of incentive pay has been determined, there is still an issue as to whether it should be paid in cash or equity (shares of stock or options). Paying with equity has the potential for motivating employees to behave like owners because they now share in the benefits of the wealth they help create. Furthermore, where equity values are based on the present value of future cash flows over the indefinite horizon, managers who hold stock have an incentive to optimize long-term performance. However, the downside is that all employees are not capable seeing the impact of their actions on stock prices. In fact, it is only the highest levels of management that can sense that their actions are guiding the success of the firm's shares in the equity market. Thus, one would generally expect stock- or equity-based pay to be most prevalent for the highest levels of management and cash based compensation to be used more often for lower levels of employees. Thus cash and stock are complementary forms of payment rather than substitutes, and most firms will end up using both forms of payment to distribute incentive compensation.

References

Baker, George P., Michael C. Jensen, and Kevin J. Murphy. "Compensation and Incentives: Practice vs. Theory." *Journal of Finance* 43, 3 (1988): 593–616. Reprinted in *Foundations of Organizational Strategy*, ed. Michael C. Jensen. Cambridge, Mass.: Harvard University Press, 1998.

Bruns, William J., and Kenneth A. Merchant. "The Dangerous Morality of Managing Earnings." *Management Accounting* (August, 22–25, 1990).

Deci, Edward. "The Effects of Contingent and Noncontingent Rewards and Controls on Intrinsic Motivation." *Organizational Behavior and Human Performance*, 8 (1992).

Degeorge, Francois, Jayendu Patel, and Richard Zeckhauser. "Earnings Management to Exceed Thresholds." *Journal of Business* 72, 1 (1999): 1–33.

Edwards, Laurie. "You Can't Beat Cash." *Across the Board* 30, 7 (1993): 20–22.

Gaver, Jennifer J., Kenneth M. Gaver, and Jeffrey R. Austin. "Additional Evidence on Bonus Plans and Income Management." *Journal of Accounting and Economics* 19 (1995): 3–28.

Gibbons, Robert, and Kevin J. Murphy. "Does Executive Compensation Affect Investment?" *Continental Bank Journal of Applied Corporate Finance* 5, 2 (1992): 99–109.

Healy, Paul M. "The Effect of Bonus Schemes on Accounting Decisions." *Journal of Accounting and Economics* 7 (1985): 85–107.

Holthausen, Robert W., David F. Larcker, and Richard G. Sloan. "Annual Bonus Schemes and the Manipulation of Earnings." *Journal of Accounting and Economics* 19 (1995): 29–74.

Jensen, Michael C., ed. *Foundations of Organizational Strategy*. Cambridge, Mass.: Harvard University Press, 1998.

Jensen, M. C., and W. Meckling. "Divisional Performance Measurement." Presented at the Harvard Colloquium on Field Studies in Accounting, June 18–20, 1986. Unpublished working paper, University of Rochester, Rochester, N.Y. Reprinted in *Foundations of Organizational Strategy*, ed. M. C. Jensen.

Kohn, Alfie. "Incentives Can Be Bad for Business." *INC* (January 1988), 93–94.

Kole, Stacey R. "The Complexity of Compensation Contracts." *Journal of Financial Economics* 43 (1997): 79–104.

Martin, John, J. William Petty, and Steve Rich. "Managerial Horizons, EVA-Based Compensation, and Shareholder Wealth." Unpublished manuscript, Hankamer School of Business, Baylor University, January 2000.

Martin, Justin. "Eli Lilly Is Making Shareholders Rich. How? By Linking Pay to EVA." *Fortune,* September 9, 1996.

Murphy, Kevin. "Executive Compensation." In *Handbook of Labor Economics,* ed. Orley Ashenfelter and David Card. Vol. 3. New York: North Holland, 1999.

O'Byrne, Stephen F. "Executive Compensation." Chap. E9 in *Handbook of Modern Finance,* ed. Denis Logue. New York: Warren, Gorham & Lamont, 1997.

———. "Does Value Based Management Discourage Investment in Intangibles?" In *Value-based metrics: Foundations and practice,* ed. Frank J. Fabozzi and James L. Grant. Frank J. Fabozzi & Associates (2000).

Rappaport, Alfred. "New Thinking on How to Link Executive Pay with Performance." *Harvard Business Review* (March–April 1999): 91–101.

Rich, Anne J., Carl S. Smith, and Paul Mihalek. "Are Corporate Codes of Conduct Effective?" *Management Accounting* (September 1990): 34–35.

Sloan, Alfred P., Jr. *My Years with General Motors.* New York: Doubleday, 1963.

Stern, Joel, Bennett Stewart, and Donald Chew. "The EVA Financial Management System." In *The Revolution in Corporate Finance,* ed. Joel Stern and Donald Chew, 474–489. 3d ed. Malden, Mass.: Blackwell, 1998.

Watts, Ross L., and Jerold L. Zimmerman. *Positive Accounting Theory.* Englewood Cliffs, N.J.: Prentice Hall, 1986.

Wruck, Karen Hopper. "Compensation, Incentives and Organizational Change: Ideas and Evidence from Theory and Practice." In *Breaking the Code of Change,* ed. Michael Beer and Nitin Nohria. Boston: Harvard Business School Press, 2000.

Zimmerman, J. "EVA and Divisional Performance Measurement: Capturing Synergies and Other Issues." *Bank of America Journal of Applied Corporate Finance* 10, 2 (1997): 98–109.

PART **III**

HOW WELL DOES VALUE BASED MANAGEMENT WORK?

It is now more than ten years that firms have been using value based management systems. Firms have adopted, modified, dropped, and readopted various systems, and the evidence is growing that VBM does indeed lead to the creation of shareholder value. Firms that adopted VBM have cut costs, reduced investment in assets, and increased cash flows. However, the evidence also shows that VBM may not be right for every firm. It appears that VBM works best for firms that need to shed assets rather than for those facing growth opportunities. However, it remains to be seen whether VBM can be more than a tool for motivating managers to focus on underutilized assets. In part III we review the evidence. Much of this research tests the link between one or more VBM metrics and a firm's stock price (returns). This line of research is conceptually flawed and offers only limited information of interest to firms interested in adopting a VBM system. We find studies of the performance of firms that have adopted a VBM system to be very informative. These studies indicate that VBM does indeed lead managers to make significant decisions that affect firm operating performance. Furthermore, we report the lessons learned from a best-practices study of a group of VBM adopters.

Chapter 9

The Empirical Evidence: Does Value Based Management Really Work?

Our belief at Goldman Sachs [is] that an analysis of return on capital and its cost are important ingredients in assessing the investment merit of companies.

—Steve Einhorn, Head of Global Investment Research at Goldman Sachs (1997)

EVA, as a single-period measure, may be one of the better ways of representing what a company achieved in the past but falls short of quantifying what the expectations are for the future.

—Michael J. Mauboussin, CS First Boston (1994)

*T*he financial press is replete with stories extolling the benefits of value based management (VBM) programs. In fact, the publication of this book attests to the level of interest in VBM in the business community. But do the programs really work? Do VBM systems help firms create shareholder value, and do they improve upon traditional methods of performance measurement? Ultimately, these are empirical questions that demand empirical observations and tests. In this chapter, we consider the evidence bearing on these important issues. Specifically we review evidence that addresses the following questions:

- Does the discounted cash flow (DCF) theory of valuation provide reliable estimates of stock prices? Throughout this book we have pointed out that the DCF theory of valuation underpins all the tools of VBM. Thus, it is imperative that the DCF theory be able to provide reasonable guideposts for action if VBM is to be of use in creating shareholder value.

- Do VBM metrics provide reasonable predictions of the market prices of common stock? Here the issue revolves around how closely management's performance tools are linked to stock prices. That is, even if the answer to the first question is affirmative, we still don't know whether our performance measures are sufficiently closely linked to equity prices to make them useful tools for managing for shareholder value.

- Does VBM affect the performance of adopters? Ultimately, we would like to see firms that adopt a VBM system change managerial behavior so as to lead to improvements in operating performance that investors reward in the marketplace.

- Does VBM improve upon traditional accounting measures of performance such as return on assets, earnings, and earnings growth? Although the proponents of VBM spend a great deal of time pointing out the shortcomings of traditional measures of accounting returns, the astute reader has no doubt realized that the tools of VBM are built upon the firm's accounting information system (albeit with sometimes lengthy modifications).

The first of these issues has been addressed by studies that test the predictability of market prices for common stock using the present value of future cash flows. These studies constitute indirect tests of the connection between VBM and stock prices in that they do not directly test the association between a particular VBM metric and stock price. The second question has been addressed by studies that directly test for the association between VBM metrics and stock prices. The third issue revolves around the effects of adopting a VBM system on various measures of firm operating and market-based performance. The final issue is a tougher one to address because it calls for a comparison of the effectiveness of VBM systems with more traditional accounting-based systems. Nonetheless, there is some evidence that has been brought to bear on this last issue from the accounting literature.

This chapter examines studies that tested the usefulness of discounted cash flow models in predicting observed market prices of common stock, studies that tested the predictive power of various VBM metrics to estimate market prices, and studies that tried to document the effects of VBM adoption on firm behavior and performance.

Does Discounted Cash Flow Theory Reliably Predict Stock Prices?

Some financial economists and many investors contend that the stock market is too volatile and erratic to be consistent with the discounted cash flow model of equity valuation.[1] It is often alleged that investors give far too much weight to swings in short-term earnings and that this concern for short-term results spills over into stock market prices, causing excessive price volatility. This concern is not new. In 1936, J. M. Keynes stated, "Day-to-day fluctuations in the profits of existing investments, which are obviously of an ephemeral and nonsignificant character, tend to have an altogether excessive, and even an absurd, influence on the market." And in 1938, John B. Williams noted, "Prices have been based too much on current earning power, too little on long-run dividend paying power."

A different view is taken by many financial economists, who believe that the stock market takes a long-term view of a firm's future cash flow generating potential. They further claim that when investors react to a current earnings announcement they are responding to information about the future that they feel is imbedded in the current earnings report. Ultimately, the answers can only be found in the data. Do discounted cash flow estimates of share values provide reasonable and reliable estimates of observed market prices? By this we mean estimates that are *good enough* so that we might use the determinants of the DCF values (cash flow drivers and discount rates) as the basis for managing the firm for shareholder value.

To address this issue we review two studies that test how well DCF models predict stock prices. Both studies utilize the Kaplan and Ruback (1995) model, which is but one variant of the DCF valuation model. We chose these studies as representative of this body of research because they are recent and carefully done. In addition, we review the findings of a recent study from the accounting literature that tests the residual income valuation model, which can be shown to be consistent with the standard DCF dividend model of equity value. Finally we present some direct evidence bearing on the usefulness of dividend discount models in explaining observed stock prices. The evidence suggests that stock prices at any point in time are indeed reliably related to the present value of expected future cash flows. However, the relation is far from exact. We conclude that the evidence supports the use of VBM methods aimed at improving the determinants of the present value of future cash flows, albeit with caution.

Valuing Firms That Engage in Highly Leveraged Transactions

Kaplan and Ruback (1995) provided a well-known test of the robustness of discounted cash flow predictions of stock market prices by analyzing the market values of highly leveraged transactions (leveraged buyouts and leveraged recapitalizations) to the present value of their corresponding cash flow forecasts. This study serves as a prototype for this type of research and demonstrates the difficulties encountered in trying to test the usefulness of the discounted cash flow model of firm valuation.

The Research Plan

The objective of the Kaplan and Ruback (1995) study was to compare the discounted value of the cash flow forecasts (DCF values) for a set of fifty-one highly levered transactions with their actual transaction values. In the language of the statistician, the dependent variable that we are trying to predict is the "transaction value" (which corresponds roughly to the market value of the firm) and the independent variable that we are using to make the prediction is the DCF value of expected cash flows.[2]

The DCF estimate of the transaction value is computed using what the authors refer to as the Compressed Adjusted Present Value Model (CAPV), which is a simplified version of the Modigliani and Miller (1963) tax-adjusted firm valuation model. Very simply, this valuation model calculates firm value as the value of the firm's cash flows as if it had no financial leverage plus the present value of the interest tax savings resulting from the firm's use of debt financing.[3]

The Data

A sample consisted of fifty-one highly leveraged transactions (large management buyouts and leveraged recapitalizations) that took place between 1983 and 1989. The reason for selecting this group of firms was the availability of sufficient financial information to perform a complete valuation (from SEC filings). This information included at least four years of post-transaction projections of (1) operating income before interest, depreciation, amortization, and taxes; (2) depreciation and amortization; (3) planned capital expenditures; and (4) anticipated changes in net working capital.

The Results

Table 9.1 provides a summary of the study's findings using three forecast accuracy statistics for three different DCF forecasts. The three measures of forecast accuracy are found in the first column. The first row contains the percentage of the forecasts that fell within plus or minus 15 percent of the transaction (market) value. The last two measures of forecast accuracy are the mean square error and mean absolute error.[4] The reason that we don't simply report an average forecast error is that the positive errors would be offset by negative errors, resulting in a downward biased error measure. Consequently, we either average the absolute values of the forecast errors to estimate the mean absolute forecast error or square the forecast errors before averaging to calculate the mean square forecast error. The three DCF forecasts (columns 2–4) differ in terms of how the beta coefficient used in the Capital Asset Pricing Model is determined. The firm beta forecast uses the firm's own beta coefficient; the industry beta forecast uses an industry average beta; and the market beta forecast uses a beta of 1.

The results suggest that the DCF methods do a reasonable job of predicting actual transaction values but with substantial error. For example, approximately 60 percent of the DCF forecasts made using industry or market betas were within ±15 percent of the transaction value. Note, however, that the average absolute prediction error was roughly 20 percent for each of the DCF models. Similarly, if we convert the mean square errors to their root mean square errors (by taking square roots) we see that the average forecast error ranges from 22.5 percent to 29 percent. Hence, it appears that DCF estimates are reasonable

Table 9.1 Predictive Accuracy of Discounted Cash Flow Estimates of Market Prices

Measures of Forecast Accuracy	Firm Beta Forecast	Industry Beta Forecast	Market Beta Forecast
Percentage within ±15%	47.1%	62.7%	58.8%
Mean absolute error	21.1%	18.1%	16.7%
Mean square error	8.4%	6.7%	5.1%

Source: Kaplan and Ruback (1995). Used with permission.

(i.e., 60 percent of the forecasts are within 15 percent of the actual transaction value), but the DCF estimates differ from the transaction values by an average error of approximately 20 percent.

Valuing Bankrupt Firms

Gilson, Hotchkiss, and Ruback (2000) applied the Kaplan and Ruback (1995) CAPV model to the valuation of sixty-three publicly traded firms emerging from Chapter 11 and the values implied by the cash flow forecasts in their reorganization plans. The study indicates only limited success for the use of the CAPV model in this application.

Sample

With any empirical study it is always important to review the method used to select the sample firms so that we might assess the generality of the study's findings. In this study the authors began with a list of 1,342 Chapter 11 filings between 1979 and 1993. From this set they determined that 377 firms emerged from Chapter 11 by December 1993 as public companies. Of this group, 134 firms had their stock listed on the NYSE, AMEX, or Nasdaq, and the researchers were able to obtain disclosure statements for the final confirmed reorganization plans for 104 firms. The final sample of 63 firms contains all those firms for which at least two years of post-restructuring cash flow projections were available.

Valuation Methods and Forecast Accuracy

Firm value was estimated using Kaplan and Ruback's CAPV model as well as comparable company multiples based on the ratio of total capital to EBITDA in the first forecast year.[5] Table 9.2 indicates that the valuation errors the authors find for both methods are substantial

Table 9.2 Predictive Accuracy of Discounted Cash Flow vs. Multiple Valuation of Bankrupt Firms

	Discounted Capital Cash Flow Valuation	Comparable Company Multiple Valuation
Percentage within ±15%	25.4%	21.0%
Mean absolute error	37.7%	47.0%
Mean square error	23.3%	36.9%
Sample Size	63	62

Source: Gibson, Hotchkiss, and Ruback (2000). Used with permission.

and much larger than for the Kaplan and Ruback (1995) study of highly leveraged transactions. However, the study does offer some support for the use of discounted capital cash flow valuation in that the CAPV valuations provided smaller forecast errors than the comparable valuation methods.[6]

Unfortunately, the forecast errors for both methods were really quite large. For example, only 25.4 percent of the discounted capital cash flow model predictions fell in the ±15 percent band compared to 50–60 percent for the Kaplan and Ruback (1995) study of highly leveraged transactions. In addition, the mean absolute error and mean square error for the bankrupt firm predictions were substantially larger than for the highly leveraged transactions.

Testing the Edwards-Bell-Ohlson Residual Income Model

The accounting literature has recently contributed to the debate over how well DCF models predict stock prices. We comment on the Dechow et al. (1999) study while recognizing that there are many others. This literature makes use of a particular variant of the DCF model referred to as residual income for reasons that will become apparent.[7] The model hinges upon three basic assumptions. First, stock price at time t, P_t, is equal to the present value of expected future dividends,

$$P_t = \sum_{\tau=1}^{\infty} \frac{E_t(\text{dividend}_{t+\tau})}{(1 + r)^\tau} \tag{9.1}$$

where the numerator on the right-hand side represents the expected future dividends to the firm's stockholders over the indefinite future as of date t, and r is the risk-adjusted rate of return required by the firm's investors (assumed to be constant for all future periods). The second assumption is referred to as the "clean surplus accounting relation," which requires that all items of income and expense that affect a firm's book value of equity pass through the firm's income statement. That is,

$$b_t = b_{t-1} + x_t - d_t \tag{9.2}$$

where b is the book value of equity, x is the firm's earnings, and d is dividends. Substituting eq. (9.2) into eq. (9.1) and performing some algebraic manipulation yields

$$P_t = \sum_{\tau=1}^{\infty} \frac{E_t(x_{t+\tau} - rb_{t+\tau-1})}{(1 + r)^\tau} - \frac{E_t(b_{t+\infty})}{(1 + r)^\infty} \tag{9.3}$$

The final term in eq. (9.3) is so distant in the future that we assume it has a value of zero. Defining abnormal firm earnings as $x_t^a = x_t - rb_{t-1}$ and substituting into eq. (9.3) produces the residual income version of the dividend-discounting model found in eq. (9.1):

$$P_t = b_t + \sum_{\tau=1}^{\infty} \frac{E_t(x_{t+\tau}^a)}{(1 + r)^\tau}$$

(9.4)

The attraction of this formulation to the accounting literature relates to its explicit inclusion of earnings and the book value of equity.[8]

Dechow, Hutton, and Sloan (1999) evaluate the predictive power of several versions of eq. (9.4); they differ in terms of the way in which the time series of abnormal earnings, $x_{t+\tau}^a$, evolves over time. Table 9.3 contains the relative mean absolute forecast error for two variants of four models investigated by the authors. The four models vary in terms of the parameter values used to estimate the abnormal earnings process (related to persistence), and the first set of models ignores sources of information outside of that contained in the time series of abnormal earnings whereas the second set incorporates other sources of information.

The results of the tests indicate that on average the absolute value of the prediction errors is roughly 50 percent of the stock prices being forecast. The authors further state that their models tended to under-value equities relative to the stock market. Finally, they claim that their estimates provide only modest improvements in explanatory power over past empirical research using analysts' earnings forecasts in conjunction with the traditional dividend-discounting model.

Table 9.3 Predictive Accuracy of Residual Income Model of Equity Value

Relative Mean Absolute Forecast Error[a]		
	Price Estimates Ignoring Other Information	Price Estimates Incorporating Other Information
Model 1	46.1%	44.5%
Model 2	51.9%	40.2%
Model 3	46.1%	42.7%
Model 4	46.5%	41.9%

a. Relative absolute forecast error is calculated as the absolute value of the difference between the market price and the estimated value of the share divided by the market price.

Source: Dechow, Hutton, and Sloan (1999). Used with permission.

Analysts' Earnings Estimates and the Dividend-Discounting Model

Table 9.4 provides an example set of discounted future dividend valuations for a set of ten firms from the telecommunications industry. The analysis entails solving for the value of the shares of each of the sample firms using the following model:

$$P = \sum_{t=1}^{10} \frac{\text{Dividend}_0(1 + g)^t}{(1 + k)^t} + \frac{\text{Dividend}_{10}(1 + g_T)}{(k - g_T)(1 + k)^{10}} \qquad (9.5)$$

The calculations are based on year-end 1997 dividends, growth estimates, and rates of return. Specifically, ValueLine five-year earnings growth estimates are used for the ten-year planning period for each firm (g) and a 4 percent terminal growth rate (g_T) is used for all firms. The investors' required rate of return (k) is estimated for each firm using the Capital Asset Pricing Model based on the risk-free rate on long-term government bonds for year-end 1997 of 7.22 percent, a market risk premium of 7.5 percent, and ValueLine's beta coefficient for year-end 1997.

The prediction errors in table 9.4 show that this valuation exercise consistently underestimates the market prices of the shares (analogous to the Dechow et al. (1999) findings using the residual income model). However, the average absolute prediction error as a percent of share price is only 22 percent.[9] This result is very similar to the findings of Kaplan and Ruback (1995). A plot of the actual and predicted share values in figure 9.1 illustrates that the predicted values consistently fall short of the actual market prices but are highly correlated (R^2 equals 0.78).[10] The dashed line corresponds to a regression of actual share values regressed on estimated share values, and the arrow represents the line of perfect forecast that would prevail if the discounted dividend estimates were exactly equal to the observed market prices. The fact that the actual market prices generally plot above the line of perfect forecast reflects the fact that the estimated values are biased (i.e., too low).

Figure 9.2 contains the results of an analysis of discounted future dividend estimates for the entire S&P 500 stock universe as of year-end 1997 using the same methodology outlined earlier for telecommunications firms. These results indicate that although the discounted dividend model continues to provide reasonable estimates of share prices, the association is not as strong (the R^2 declines to 59 percent) as it was for the telecommunications industry. The average absolute prediction

Table 9.4 Discounted Dividend Valuation of a Sample of Firms from the Telecommunications Industry

| | Cost of Equity (%) | Present Value of | | DCF Value ($) | Stock Price ($) | Prediction Error ($) |
		Planning Period Dividends ($)	Terminal Value ($)			
AT&T	13.60	12.83	32.19	45.02	54.00	(8.98)
All Tell Corp	13.60	8.55	17.20	25.75	26.00	(0.25)
Ameritech	12.47	19.70	23.99	43.69	44.00	(0.31)
Bell Atlantic	13.22	27.11	24.84	51.94	57.00	(5.06)
BellSouth	12.47	28.33	29.96	58.29	64.00	(5.71)
Cincinnati Bell	13.60	7.77	20.88	28.65	25.00	3.65
GTE	13.22	18.60	13.89	32.49	35.00	(2.51)
HKTelecom—ADR	13.22	3.56	8.76	12.32	20.00	(7.68)
MCI	16.22	0.43	8.64	9.07	22.00	(12.93)
Vodafone ADR	16.97	4.32	8.32	12.64	38.00	(25.36)

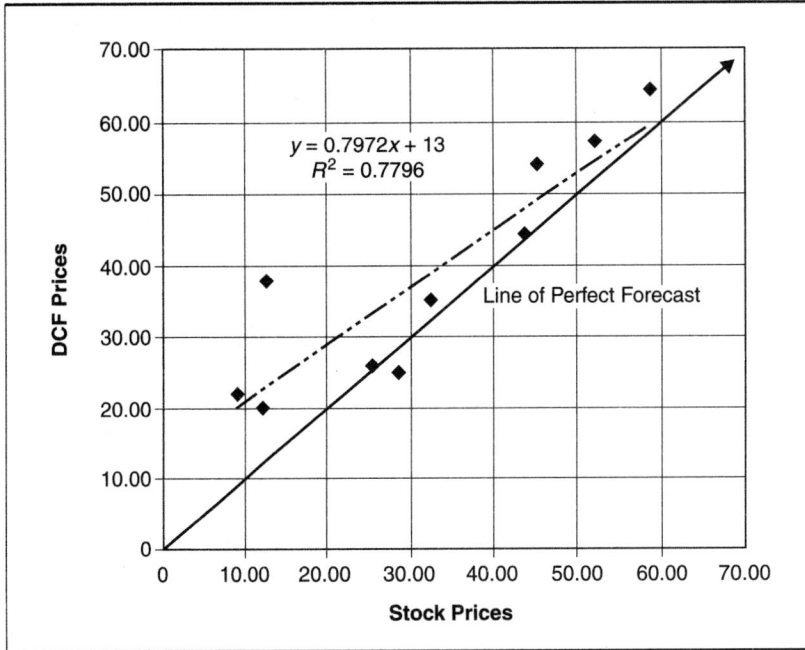

Figure 9.1 Market Prices and Discounted Dividend Estimates for Firms in the Telecommunications Industry

error relative to market price for the entire sample of S&P 500 firms is 35 percent, which is higher than we observed for the ten telecommunications firms but still substantially lower than the Dechow et al. (1999) study that used the residual income model.

Summary of the Evidence

The premises underlying all the value based management systems discussed in this book are as follows:

1. Firms implement VBM systems in an effort to increase shareholder value.
2. Share value is determined by investor expectations regarding future cash flows and required rates of return (the cost of capital).
3. Firms that focus their attention on the management of metrics that are linked to expected future cash flows and investor required rates of return can manage for value creation.

Figure 9.2 Discounted Dividend Valuations for S&P 500 Stocks

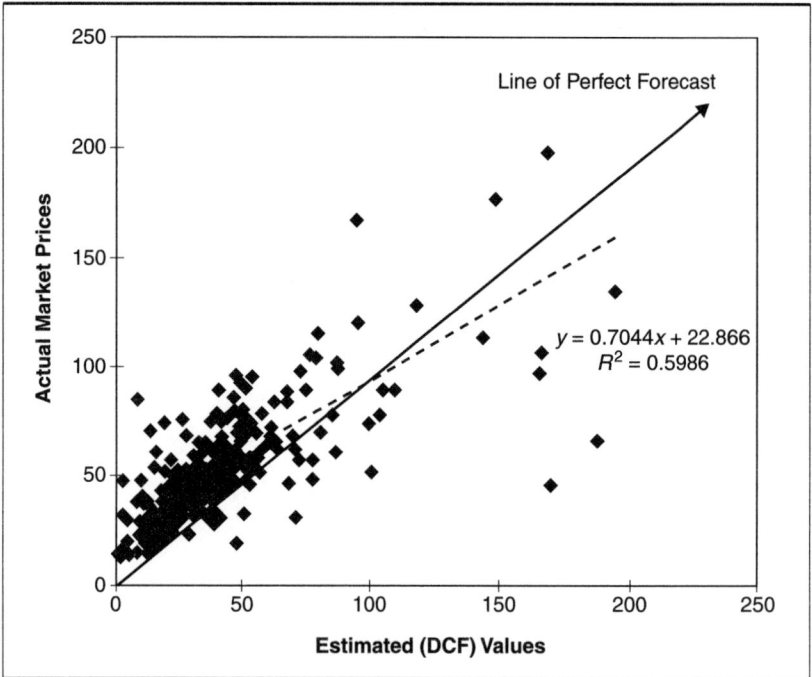

The whole point of our discussion of the empirical link between discounted future cash flows and firm value has been to evaluate the rea-
sonableness of the second premise. Obviously, if share prices are not
reliably linked to the discounted value of future firm cash flows, then
VBM systems that focus on the determinants of future cash flows and
capital costs cannot be relied upon to increase share value.

What have we learned from the studies reviewed here? It would
appear that the discounted value of future firm cash flows is indeed
related to observed stock prices. However, the connection involves a
high level of prediction error, that is, DCF predictions provide very
noisy estimates of market prices. This suggests that the development of
very finely tuned VBM systems based on the drivers of discounted
cash flow valuation models is only a distant possibility. Alternatively,
even crude predictions may be useful in turnaround situations where
firm performance has historically been very poor. In fact, when we
review corporate practice with regard to the application of VBM in
chapter 10 we see that many of the firms that are now held up as VBM

success stories are cases in which the firm suffered financial hard times just prior to the adoption of a VBM system. Although VBM may have worked for them, it could be that the VBM system simply nudged the firm in the direction of improvement (as a tug directs a supertanker into the harbor) rather than providing a tool for managing the details of precise shareholder value maximization. Hence, VBM systems may work better for some firms than for others.

VBM Metrics, Equity Values, and Stock Returns

GAAP accounting earnings and cash flow have recently come under criticism by consultants, members of the financial press, and even some members of the accounting profession. The basis for their criticism of reported earnings and cash flow numbers is the argument that these measures are insufficient for valuation analyses by common stock investors. For example, Stern Stewart & Co. has argued that the notion of accounting earnings should be abandoned (Stewart 1991, p. 2). This theme has also been picked up in the accounting profession. As noted in chapter 5, participants at an American Institute of Certified Public Accountants workshop on the future of financial management predicted that EVA would replace earnings per share in the *Wall Street Journal*'s regular stock and earnings reports.

Claims and Counterclaims

The empirical work that attempts to support one method as compared to another has largely come from the very same firms that are selling their proprietary methodology to clients. The potential conflict of interest is clear. For example, Stern Stewart (1995) claims that EVA drives stock prices, not earnings per share, return on equity, or return on investment. Stewart (1994) cites in-house research indicating that "EVA stands well out from the crowd as the single best measure of wealth creation on a contemporary basis" and "EVA is almost 50 percent better than its closest accounting-based competitor in explaining changes in shareholder wealth" (p. 75).

Furthermore, BCG claims that its valuation model exhibits 50–60 percent more explanatory power for total shareholder returns than an earnings per share momentum model, a cash flow model, and the Stern Stewart EVA perpetuity model.[11] Let's consider the evidence from the academic community.

The Academic Evidence

Recent academic studies have begun to investigate the claims of the consulting firms that use criticisms of competitors' methods to promote their particular brand of value based management. The potential problem with the research provided by the consulting firms is, of course, the natural desire of those firms not only to find support for their own metrics but to highlight the deficiencies in competitors' methods. Given the consulting firms' susceptibility to criticism, we will focus our survey of the empirical evidence on papers written by academic researchers or papers that have passed some form of peer review. The reader who would like to look at the professional research on the topic is referred to the Web sites of the individual consulting firms that offer value based management practices. Table 9.5 summarizes a portion of the academic evidence concerning the relation between various VBM performance measures and stock prices or returns. We focus our discussion on the Biddle, Bowen, and Wallace (1997) article as an example of this research and refer the reader who wants to gain a full appreciation for the evidence to the studies listed in table 9.5.

Biddle, Bowen, and Wallace (1997) compare the predictive powers of EVA with accounting earnings and residual income when used to predict contemporaneous stock returns. Specifically, they address the following questions:

- Does EVA or residual income dominate currently mandated performance measures, earnings, and cash flow from operations in explaining contemporaneous annual stock returns?

- Do components unique to EVA or residual income help explain contemporaneous stock returns beyond that explained by cash flow from operations and earnings?

The first question asks whether adjusting accounting earnings and cash flow measures for capital costs will improve the predictive power of the accounting-based performance metrics when estimating stock returns. Second, the authors question whether the adjustments to GAAP accounting recommended by Stern-Stewart add incrementally to the inclusion of capital costs with the use of residual income. Stated somewhat differently, does EVA or residual income complement currently mandated performance measures like earnings and cash flow from operations?

Using a sample of 6,174 firm-years of data representing both EVA adopters and nonadopters over the period 1984–1993, Biddle et al. found

Table 9.5 Correlation Between Performance Measures and
            Stock Returns

Author(s)	Correlation Between	Variance Explained (%)
Bacidore et al. (1997)	Current EVA and excess stock returns	1.14
	"Refined EVA" and market-adjusted stock returns	3.93
	Current and lagged EVA and market-adjusted returns	2.05
	Current and lagged "refined EVA" and market-adjusted returns	3.96
Biddle, Bowen, and Wallace (1997)	Earnings and market-adjusted returns	12.8
	Residual income and market-adjusted returns	7.3
	EVA and market-adjusted returns	6.5
	Cash flow from operations and market-adjusted returns	2.8
Chen and Dodd (1998)	Operating income and stock returns	6.2 and 9.4
	Residual income and stock returns	5.0 and 7.8
	EVA and stock returns	2.3 and 6.6
Dodd and Chen (1996)	EVA and stock returns	20.2
	Return on asset and stock returns	24.5
Mauboussin–CS First Boston (1995)	Market value/capital and (return on capital – cost of capital) for the packaged food industry	55–88
Stern, Stewart, and Chew (1995)	EVA and MVA for firm groupings	60
	Five-year change in EVA and five-year change in MVA	50
Thomas (1993)	EVA and MVA	4 and 27
Kramer and Pushner (1997)	EVA and MVA	9.9
	NOPAT and MVA	18
	Standardized EVA and standardized MVA	4.8
	EVA and changes in MVA	0.3

that accounting earnings are more closely related to market-adjusted annual stock returns ($R^2 = 12.8\%$) than residual income ($R^2 = 7.3\%$) or EVA ($R^2 = 6.5\%$).[12] Furthermore, they found that firm cash flow from operations displayed the lowest predictive power ($R^2 = 2.8$ percent).

Next, they tested whether the added adjustments required in moving from residual income to EVA add significant explanatory power when trying to predict contemporaneous stock returns. To perform this analysis they decomposed EVA into components representing cash flow from operations, operating accruals, capital charge, and accounting adjustments. The capital charge and accounting adjustment components are unique to EVA and provide an opportunity to test for their incremental value in predicting stock returns. The authors found that while each component is significantly associated with market-adjusted returns, the EVA components do not appear to be economically significant.

Combining all their results, the authors concluded that neither EVA nor residual income dominates earnings in explaining contemporaneous stock returns.[13] Thus, if the analyst wants to predict abnormal stock price changes (returns), then accounting earnings appear to work as well or better than either EVA or residual income with their added adjustments to reported earnings.

Is the Performance Metric-Stock Price Correlation Relevant?

So what is the manager to make of the low correlations reported in table 9.5? Not very much, according to Zimmerman (1997). He notes that the desire to select a performance measure that is closely aligned with year-to-year stock price changes is natural. Although this approach sounds appealing, Zimmerman argues, the logic is flawed in two respects. First, stock prices are forward-looking and the stock returns for any given period are likely to reflect not only the operating performance of the company over that period but also changes in the market's expectations about future performance as well as changes in macroeconomic variables. In essence he argues, quite correctly, that no single-year operating performance measure—whether it be EVA, CVA, or any other single-period performance metric—is likely to have a very strong correlation with same-year stock returns.[14] Furthermore, he notes that this failure of annual stock returns to line up well with delivered performance can create serious problems in using stock returns as the basis for incentive compensation. To illustrate the nature of the problem, he provides the following example:

> Consider the case of Amazon.com, which in May of 1997 had sales of $15.7 million in the trailing 12 months and no earnings. The company went public at $18 per share and raised $54 million. The shares closed at $23, giving the firm an initial market capitalization of $572 million. For sake of our example let's assume that the market is valuing the firm at 30 times expected earnings in two years, or $19 million. Management thus must produce earnings of $19 million in two years just

to maintain the stock price of $23. The point is that expectations of "extraordinary" operating performance are built into the current stock price. Thus, even if management is successful in delivering extraordinary performance the stock return that results will only be a normal return. Consequently, rewarding management for extraordinary stock returns is not the same thing as rewarding them for extraordinary operating performance. (pp. 105–106)

Does the Adoption of VBM Affect Managerial Behavior?

Throughout this book we have noted that a basic objective of adopting a VBM system is to alter managerial behavior by focusing managers' efforts more closely on increasing shareholder value. Thus, an important research question is whether the adoption of a VBM system actually changes managerial behavior in ways that might contribute to the creation of shareholder value.

Wallace (1998) studied the actions of a sample of forty firms that had adopted compensation plans based on residual income (defined as earnings before interest less a capital charge on total capital—debt and equity). The actions of these firms were then compared to those of a matched pair of control firms where incentive compensation continued to be based on traditional accounting earnings—earnings per share or operating profits. He found that the old adage "what you measure and reward gets done" was indeed true. When compared to the control sample, the VBM adopters (1) decreased their new investment and increased their dispositions of assets, (2) increased their payouts to shareholders through share repurchases, and (3) utilized their assets more intensively. All three of these responses are consistent with value creation where the adopters and the control firms each face similar investment opportunities. That is, other things remaining the same, disposing of nonproductive assets (assets that don't produce a return equal to or greater than the firm's cost of capital), returning cash flow to the firm's stockholders that is not needed to support the firm's wealth-creating investment opportunities (i.e., dispensing free cash flow), and getting greater use out of existing assets are all ways to increase shareholder value.

Does the Adoption of VBM Change Firm Performance?

The ultimate proof of the value of adopting a VBM system lies in whether firm performance improves after adoption. The evidence regarding the effect of VBM on the values of the shares of adopters is growing but has produced mixed results. Furthermore, the evidence to date has been focused on EVA to the exclusion of other VBM systems and is therefore far from complete.

Short-Term Price Reactions to the Adoption of a VBM System. If VBM leads to wealth creation, we would expect that the adoption of a VBM program would be recognized by investors and rewarded in the market place. Wallace (1998) studied the stock market's response to the adoption of a residual income–based compensation system by forty firms. He analyzed the monthly stock market returns of the adopters over the twelve months prior to the year of adoption and the twelve months of the adoption year. He looked at this wide span of months because of the uncertainty surrounding exactly when the investment community learned about the adoption of the VBM program. He found that the returns earned by the adopting firms throughout the twenty-four-month period averaged 4 percent higher than the market return but were not significantly higher.[15] This result calls into question the value that investors place on VBM programs; however, Wallace notes a number of limitations of his study that could explain the weak evidence in support of VBM. The primary one relates to ambiguity about the date on which the market learned about the adoption of the program. In many instances the first time that investors learn about VBM program adoption is in the proxy statement that comes out three months after fiscal year-end. In other instances a press release may announce the event. As a result of the announcement date uncertainty it is not surprising that the valuation consequences of the announcement are swamped by the noise of market stock price movements.

VBM and Long-Term Performance. Kleiman (1999) tested whether the adoption of an EVA program improves firm performance measured in terms of both operating performance and stock market performance. Over the three years following adoption of EVA, operating performance (measured using operating margin before depreciation and operating income before depreciation per employee) improves. Similarly, the abnormal returns (median adopter market return less the peer group return) increase over the three years following the adoption of EVA. He concludes that his findings "constitute strong evidence that the stock market performance of EVA companies is significantly better [than] that of their industry competitors" (p. 86).

Hogan and Lewis (2000) examined the performance of firms that adopted compensation plans based on economic profits or residual income type measures in an attempt to discern whether the claims made for these plans were confirmed in long-run performance. Specifically, proponents of VBM plans claim that their methods of measuring and rewarding performance overcome deficiencies in stock-based or earnings-based bonus plans and correspondingly better align managers' and shareholders' interests. The researchers examined the performance of a sample of fifty-one firms that adopted economic profit plans between 1986 and 1994.[16] They found that the new adopters did exhibit significant improvements in operating performance subsequent to adoption of the compensation plans. However, when the performance of a sample of nonadopting matched firms was examined, they found similar improvements. Furthermore there was no significant difference in the stock price performance of the two groups in the four-year period following adoption of the economic profit compensation plan.[17]

Hogan and Lewis also observed that in both adopting and nonadopting firms bonuses and equity compensation levels increased by a similar amount. They concluded that their findings are consistent with managers' making changes in both sets of firms to better align incentives but with different methods. However, their findings do not suggest that bonus plans based on economic profit are superior to more traditional plans that combine earnings bonuses and equity participation.

Is VBM a Useful Tool for Selecting Stocks?

Value based management is generally thought of as a tool for managing the internal operations of a business enterprise in ways that are thought to create shareholder value. It is not particularly surprising, then, that stock analysts have adopted the basic precepts of value based management, too. For example, Goldman Sachs organized a conference on May 6, 1997, entitled "EVA and Return on Capital: Roads to Shareholder Wealth," where they reported that EVA for the S&P industrials was higher than at any time in the last twenty-five years. This observation is supported by the observed increase in the spread between the return earned on invested capital and the cost of capital from 0 percent in 1986 to 4.1 percent in 1997.

CS First Boston published an *EVA Primer* by Jackson, Mauboussin, and Wolf (1996) that extols the insights into value creation and destruction that can be garnered using EVA as a foundation for analysis. They further suggest that the EVA methodology can explicitly address business and financial risks in a way that allows the investor to assess both the magnitude and sustainability of returns. They conclude by stating, "The CS First Boston Equity Research Department is increasingly using EVA in its analysis" (p. 2).

This interest in value based management from within the investment banking industry suggests that firms adopting these systems are viewed in a positive light by investors. The issue faced by an investor is whether following a stock selection strategy based on firms that utilize a VBM system will produce superior returns. By superior we mean returns greater than would be realized by selecting a portfolio of similar (nonadopting) firms. The evidence we reviewed suggests that the jury is still out as to whether such a strategy works. However, as we noted in our discussion, tests of this proposition are very difficult to carry out, so the ambiguity of the results reported thus far may be due to methodological problems.

Summary

The continuing growth in popularity of value based management systems suggests that VBM must work. The acceptance of industrial users and the countless pages in financial publications devoted to the subject are powerful supporting evidence. After all, some of the captains of industry are among the loudest proponents of VBM. However, we have pointed out that there are three fundamental questions that are relevant to the debate, to which the answers are not obvious. A brief summary of the evidence regarding each is found in the following list.

- Does the discounted cash flow theory of valuation provide reliable estimates of stock prices? All the VBM methodologies we have reviewed in this book rely on the belief that the answer to this question is yes, and there is evidence to support this response. However, the evidence suggests that the theory provides very noisy predictions. That is, the discounted cash flow model provides estimates of share values that are reasonably accurate but with large prediction errors. This raises a question as to whether our discounted cash flow models of equity value are sufficiently accurate. That is, are VBM methods based on value drivers derived from a discounted cash flow model of firm valuation useful in managing a firm for shareholder value?

- Do VBM metrics provide reasonable predictions of the market prices of common stock? Our review of the available evidence shows that much of the research provided by the consulting firms in this regard can be confusing. All too often, single-period measures of financial performance are used as the sole determinant of stock price even though this is inconsistent with the fundamental precepts of the discounted cash flow model. In fact, it would be surprising if a single-period's performance (however measured) were sufficient to predict firm value. The discounted cash flow theory upon which VBM methods are based postulates that firm value is equal to the present value of all expected future cash flows.

- Does VBM affect the performance of adopters? There is some evidence that suggests that firms that adopt a VBM system do indeed change the way they manage the firm's assets. Specifically, firms that adopt residual income or EVA-based systems tend to sell off or otherwise dispose of underutilized assets in an effort to boost EVA. This type of activity can, of course, have a beneficial effect on share value where the firm has made excessive investments. However, a question arises as to what the firm should do once these opportunities have been fully exhausted. There have also been some attempts to address the performance issue by studying the performance of firms that have adopted value based management. These studies have found that the act of adopting a residual income or EVA type of system does indeed lead to improved accounting- and market-based measures of performance.

However, recent studies of the long-term performance of firms that adopt VBM do not document significant differences in the performance of the adopting firms and similar nonadopters. As disappointing as this result may be to the proponents of VBM, this type of comparison cannot capture the performance of the VBM adopters had they not chosen to use VBM. In other words, things might have been worse if the firms had not adopted VBM.

References

Bernard, V. L. "Accounting-Based Valuation Methods, Determinants of Book-to-Market Ratios, and Implications for Financial Statement Analysis." Working paper, University of Michigan, Ann Arbor, January, 1994.

Biddle, Gary C., Robert M. Bowen, and James S. Wallace. "Does EVA Beat Earnings? Evidence on Associations with Stock Returns and Firm Value." *Journal of Accounting and Economics* 24, 3 (1997): 275–300.

Chen, Shimin, and James L. Dodd. "Usefulness of Accounting Earnings, Residual Income, and EVA: A Value-Relevance Perspective." Working paper, Drake University, Des Moines, Iowa, 1998.

Dechow, P. M., A. P. Hutton, and R. G. Sloan. "An Empirical Assessment of the Residual Income Valuation Model." *Journal of Accounting and Economics* 26 (1999): 1–34.

Easton, P., T. Harris, and J. Ohlson. "Aggregate Earnings Can Explain Most Security Returns." *Journal of Accounting and Earnings* 15 (June/September 1992): 119–142.

Edwards, E., and P. Bell. *The Theory and Measurement of Business Income.* Berkeley: University of California Press, 1961.

Gilson, Stuart, Edith S. Hotchkiss, and Richard S. Ruback. "Valuation of Bankrupt Firms." *Review of Financial Studies* 13, 1 (2000).

Hogan, Chris, and Craig Lewis. "The Long-Run Performance of Firms Adopting Compensation Plans Based on Economic Profits." Unpublished manuscript, Owen Graduate School of Management, Vanderbilt University, Nashville, Tennessee, 2000.

Jackson, Al, Michael J. Mauboussin, and Charles R. Wolf. *EVA Primer.* Rev. ed. Boston: CS First Boston, 1996.

Kaplan, Steven N., and Richard S. Ruback. "The Valuation of Cash Flow Forecasts: An Empirical Analysis." *Journal of Finance* 50 (September 1995): 1059–1093.

Kim, Moonchul, and Jay R. Ritter. "Valuing IPOs." *Journal of Financial Economics* 53 (1999): 409–437.

Kleiman, Robert T. "Some New Evidence on EVA Companies." *Journal of Applied Corporate Finance* 12 (1999): 80–91.

Modigliani, Franco, and Merton Miller. "Corporate Income Taxes and the Cost of Capital: A Correction." *American Economic Review* 53 (1963): 433–443.

O'Byrne, Stephen. "EVA and Market Value." *Journal of Applied Corporate Finance* 9 (1996): 116–125.

Ohlson, J. A. "A Synthesis of Security Valuation Theory and the Role of Dividends, Cash Flows, and Earnings." *Contemporary Accounting Research* 7 (1990): 1–19.

―――. "Earnings, Book Values, and Dividends in Security Valuation." *Contemporary Accounting Research* 7 (1995): 1–19.

Preinreich, G. "Annual Survey of Economic Theory: The Theory of Depreciation." *Econometrica* 6 (1938): 219–241.

Shiller, Robert. "Do Stock Prices Move Too Much to Be Justified by Subsequent Changes in Dividends?" *American Economic Review* (June 1981): 421–436.

Stern Stewart & Co. advertisement. *Harvard Business Review* (November–December 1995): 20.

Stewart G. Bennett III. *The Quest for Value.* New York: Harper, 1991.

―――. "EVA: Fact or Fantasy?" *Journal of Applied Corporate Finance* 7 (1994): 71–84.

Thomas, Rawley. *Total Shareholder Return Empirical Evidence: BCG/HOLT Valuation Model versus Cash Flow Model, E. P. S. Model, and Stern Stewart Perpetuity EVA Model.* Boston: Boston Consulting Group, 1993.

Wallace, James. "Adopting Residual Income–Based Compensation Plans: Do You Get What You Pay For?" *Journal of Accounting and Economics* 24 (1998).

Zimmerman, Jerold L. "EVA and Divisional Performance Measurement: Capturing Synergies and Other Issues." *Journal of Applied Corporate Finance* 10 (1997): 98–109.

What Do Adopters of Value Based Management Have to Say?

> We are never confused about why we exist. Although volume growth, earnings, returns and cash flow are critical priorities, our people understand those measurements are all simply the means to the long-term end of creating value for our share owners. . . . I wrestle over how to build shareholder value from the time I get up in the morning to the time I go to bed. I even think about it when I'm shaving.
>
> **—Roberto Goizueta, former Chairman and CEO,**
> **Coca-Cola (1997)**

When all is said and done, the usefulness of value based management should be judged by the experiences of the companies that have tried it. In this chapter, we share the wisdom and experiences of some high-profile VBM adopters. Most, *but not all*, of these experiences have been positive. Out of these experiences we glean important insights into making value based management work.

Two Companies Try VBM

Herman Miller, a nationally recognized manufacturer of office furniture, and AT&T provide noteworthy examples of firms adopting value based management with very different results.

For Herman Miller, VBM Was the Answer

In 1995, Herman Miller brought in a new management team. Michael Volkema, the firm's president and CEO, described the situation at the time:[1]

> When our leadership team was put in place, Herman Miller had a rich history and culture, great products and talented employees. The economy was strong, our industry was growing, and our sales were growing even faster. But something was missing. The results weren't showing up on the bottom line.

As a result, management decided to develop a value based management system within the firm, choosing EVA. Two years later, Volkema described the outcome of that decision.

> In two years, we've turned a corner. Employing the same amount of capital we did in 1995, our sales have moved from $1 billion to $1.5 billion. In 1997, our EVA was $40 million—an increase of nearly 300 percent over the $10 million generated in 1996. EVA analysis has enabled us to identify waste in both our costs and our use of capital. Inventories have been reduced by 24 percent or $17.2 million from two years ago. Outstanding accounts receivables have been reduced 22 percent from fifty-five days in 1995 to forty-three days at the end of 1997. Over the past two years, our sales have increased 38 percent. Our 13 percent operating margin is much improved from five years ago. At the same time, we have reduced our total square footage of building space by more than 15 percent.
>
> Using EVA, we've seen out business grow and we've seen our people grow in their commitment and contribution to Herman Miller. EVA is the backbone of our company-wide incentive and bonus system, and in the last two years, we've increased the wealth of our employee-owners by over $100 million. If you ask them, they would agree that EVA works at Herman Miller.

By 1999, Herman Miller's EVA had increased to over $90 million from the $40 million in 1997. The story continues, as reported in Herman Miller's 1999 annual report:

> Fiscal 1999 marked our third year of utilizing EVA as our business measurement tool. We believe there have been numerous benefits from this program, with the most significant being the business liter-

acy of our employee-owners. Nearly all of our 8,185 employees worldwide have received training in EVA. Our employee-owners know that capital is not free and that sustainable value is created through continuous improvement and growth. They also understand that their compensation is directly tied to EVA results.

Similar stories to Herman Miller's could be told by a number of other firms. However, not everyone has had positive results when implementing VBM.

AT&T and VBM: The Wrong Choice

In a popular 1993 *Fortune* article that sparked the business community's attention, AT&T was included in a list of the "highly regarded major firms" that were "flocking to the concept" of EVA (Tully 1993). The article quoted William H. Kurtz, an AT&T executive, as saying, "EVA played a significant role in the firm's decision to buy McCaw Cellular." Kurtz continued, "AT&T this year will make EVA the primary measure of business units' and managers' performance." In the firm's 1992 annual report, management was also in favor of EVA.

In 1992 we began measuring the performance of each of our units with an important new management tool called "Economic Value Added"—"EVA" for short. . . . EVA gives our managers a way to track the creation of shareowner value in individual AT&T units. . . . We have made it the centerpiece of our "value based planning" process. And we are linking a portion of our managers' incentive compensation to performance against EVA targets for 1993. . . . In summary, our performance planning, measurement, and reward programs are now fully aligned with the interest of the shareowners.

In the ensuing two years AT&T more than met the established EVA targets that had been set. Then, in 1995, the firm announced the spin-offs of Lucent Technologies and NCR. With the restructuring, the firm announced that the bonus plan would be

adjusted to provide 50% of the incentive on the EVA level of achievement and 50% based on successful accomplishment of the restructuring transition work, including the impact on PVA [people value added] and CVA [customer value added]. . . . Because of adjustments for the NCR write-down, the 1995 EVA target was not met and the portion of the Chairman's annual bonus that relates to this target was reduced accordingly. The 1995 results for the PVA, CVA, and restructuring transition measurements were met. (AT&T 1996 proxy)

In the same year, the AT&T compensation committee reported,

> The committee recognizes that the Company's impending restructure will render obsolete the performance criteria established for the long-term cycles 1994–96 and 1995–97. To address this transition period, and the difficulty of setting long-term financial targets while the restructure is in process, the Committee has recommended and approved that the criteria for performance periods 1994–96 and 1995–97 are deemed to have been met at the target level. (AT&T 1996 proxy)

By 1996 the company began to abandon EVA. Reading again from the compensation committee's remarks,

> The Company achieved its EVA target, but the committee noted that it did so, in part, by modifying spending plans, resulting in lower average capital deployed. The Committee therefore determined that, with respect to financial performance, the additional metric of Earnings Per Share results would be considered. . . . The company achieved its EVA target, but . . . shareholders experienced a 9% decrease in the value of their AT&T-related holdings during 1996, though the broad market rose 20%. In 1997, the Company will re-institute a performance share program tied to three-year relative total shareholder return ("TSR") as measured against a peer group of industry competitors. (AT&T 1996 proxy)

In 1997 the company discontinued using EVA completely and chose instead to use earnings per share and the expense-to-revenue ratio as its financial performance measures.

According to some reports, AT&T abandoned EVA as a performance measure because management was unable, or unwilling, to resolve two problems that can arise when using EVA: (1) inconsistencies between EVA and shareholder value creation that can occur from using GAAP depreciation accounting, especially when there is a "lumpiness" in the firm's investments, and (2) difficulties in establishing EVA incentive targets for management. The first problem was explained and demonstrated in chapter 7, where we discussed VBM models as applied to project evaluation; the second concern was considered in chapter 8. The underlying issue is the difficulty at times of making a value based management measurement consistent with shareholder value despite the claims that shareholder value is just a matter of "getting to cash." Some firms may be unprepared for the accounting complexity and effort required to make the computations consistent with shareholder value creation.

In distinguishing firms that continue to use EVA from those that discontinue its use, O'Byrne (1999) makes the following observation:

> It is my judgment, based in the case studies and my broader experience, that companies that take a contractual approach to management compensation, by making multi-year commitments to sharing percentages and performance targets, are much more willing to invest the time and effort required to address accounting issues that must be resolved to make economic profit consistent with shareholder value. For these companies, the accounting issues have important compensation consequences. The companies that provide the basis for the examples of accounting adjustments that reconcile acquisition economic profits with shareholder value all use the Stern Stewart EVA bonus plan design with multi-year commitments to sharing percentages and expected EVA improvement. Several of them also make multi-year commitments to fixed share stock option grant guidelines. The companies that have abandoned EVA, on the other hand, take a very discretionary approach to executive compensation.

Thus, O'Byrne suggests that companies had best be prepared to undertake the added accounting requirements and to take a strong contractual approach to executive compensation if value based management is to survive and prosper within a company.

Beginning to use value based management, only to later discontinue its use, suggests that even with the best of intentions reality may not match expectations. Certainly, no initiative of any significance, such as adopting VBM, can be accomplished without unanticipated problems. Integrating any value based management technique fits some companies better than others, so that success may be a function of the company itself, or it may be the result of mistakes made along the way in its implementation.

While the foregoing examples offer us some insights into two companies and their experiences with value based management, it is impossible to generalize from these examples. Thus, we now turn to a best-practices study of VBM, in which the authors were members of the investigating team.

The Views of Successful VBM Adopters

In 1996 we were members of a group sponsored by the American Productivity and Quality Center's International Benchmarking Clearinghouse to study firms that had successfully adopted and implemented VBM systems.[2] The objective of that study was to document industry best practices in the use of VBM. We, along with the corporate sponsors of the study, worked to identify companies that not only had adopted VBM but had done it successfully, and to document their stories.

We followed a four-stage process to document the case histories of VBM successes. First, we sent a mail questionnaire to over ninety potential candidates as a qualifying screen. We then phoned each of the respondents to confirm the extent of their experiences in using VBM and determine their willingness to participate in the subsequent phases of the study. With this information in hand, we selected five firms for continued study and on-site visits. The selected firms were also chosen to represent a sampling of the primary VBM methodologies then in use. The final list of firms included three EVA companies (Briggs & Stratton, CSX Transportation, and Harnischfeger Industries); one Boston Consulting Group company (National Semiconductor); and a firm that had designed its own program out of the components of a number of systems (Shell Oil). The fact that the selected firms are all very capital-intensive is no accident. We have observed that many firms that adopt VBM systems are manufacturers or companies that have sizable tangible assets to manage. (A company profile for each of the sample firms is found in appendix 10A.)

The managements of the site visit firms were asked to complete a comprehensive questionnaire before we made a site visit to the firm's home office. During our visit we spent a full day inquiring into the VBM adoption and implementation process and the related organizational issues that had arisen from the time of implementation up through the time of the visit. After we completed all the visits, we held a day-long session for the corporate sponsors of the study to meet with representatives of each of the five site visit firms. The results of this entire process are summarized in the next section.

Some of the key findings of the study are as follows:

- The adoption of VBM must have top management support.

- The decision to adopt VBM is frequently preceded by a mandate for change, such as erosion of economic value or a change in leadership.

- Not every firm benefits the same from using VBM.

- Organizations differ in the depth to which they push the VBM system.

- VBM is more than a finance exercise, if behavior is to be changed.

- Education is the place to begin when integrating a VBM system into the firm and is a never-ending process.

- Organizations tailor the VBM tool to their particular circumstances.

- Simplicity is preferred to complexity.

- A VBM system is not static. It is continually evolving. There are no "quick fixes."

A Sharing of Experiences

We believe the findings listed previously will prove beneficial to anyone wanting to implement a new VBM system. Thus, we provide clarification and expansion of these findings in this section.

Top Management Support Is Essential

The importance of management support cannot be overemphasized. Ideally, the CEO and the CFO are the champions of the VBM program. In the words of one manager, "If a VBM program does not have the support of senior management, it is doomed to fail." Another said, "If the CEO doesn't buy into VBM, you are wasting your time."

The organization's top management must not only approve of VBM but also be actively involved in promoting its use throughout the organization. All the companies interviewed demonstrated a commitment from top management. This commitment creates a chain reaction, causing the alignment of shareholder value with the corporate mission, vision and values, and the strategic plan.

There Must Be a Mandate for Change

Firms that adopt value based management do so as part of a strategy to provide a needed focus on what really matters in creating shareholder value. One executive used these words to capture the need for change when adopting VBM:

> Our firm was an income statement–driven company. Management of the company was focused on sales, and operating personnel were focused on their budgets. The company was run like a traditional manufacturing operation where incentive compensation was tied to the budget; consequently, the budgets were driven by negotiations. Lower budgets were prized and this lowered people's motivation to use budgets effectively. Capital management was also a problem. Capital investment was very high. Capital expenditures were allocated according to the size of the division, and money in the budget was usually spent in the last month of the year. Instead of being used for long-term strategic decision-making, capital expenditures were short-term fixes.

However, the decision was also frequently driven by some circumstance within the firm. There had to be a catalyst that brought management to the decision point. In the words of one manager, "We realized our return on equity was lower than our cost of capital; . . . it became clear that a change was needed."

Briggs & Stratton, for example, adopted its VBM program following a quarter in which it suffered a loss, the first in its long history. Similarly, National Semiconductor found itself suffering from excess capacity during a downturn in the semiconductor industry. CSX Transportation and Shell Oil had recruited new CEOs who mandated a focus on shareholder value. Furthermore, CSX Transportation was a firm focused on volume, where the goal was to have more locomotives to "maintain a competitive position." Capital was rationed but was used poorly. VBM offered these organizations an alternative performance metric that they believed was linked directly to the value of their companies' shares.

Benefits Aren't Uniform Across All Firms

It became clear to us that not all firms are equal when it comes to garnering benefit from a VBM system. While all the managers believe that they benefited from the use of VBM, some apparently benefited more than others. Most apparent was the benefit of VBM for companies that had room for significant improvements in the management of the firm's assets. Variety, the successor of Massey Ferguson, was experiencing large negative EVAs—$140 million to be exact. As a result of adopting a VBM system, it eliminated a large number of poorly performing assets in a single year. The improvement in return on invested capital, and in share price as well, was unmistakable.

In chapter 7 we argued that the benefits of VBM will be less in settings where the results of management actions are delayed. For example, when Boeing is successful at acquiring a large order for new aircraft, that success may not appear in any measurable way for as long as five or ten years. For that reason Boeing uses a metric that is forward-looking based on projected cash flows. However, as we noted in chapter 8, interjecting managerial projections into performance measures that drive incentive compensation is problematic.

Firms Differ in the Extent of VBM Application

Some firms extend VBM to the lowest-level employees, making them responsible for decisions that could affect shareholder value, while others use VBM only within corporate headquarters. One manager where VBM is driven down to the lower levels of the firm, described the use of VBM as follows:

> Our division has been very successful at driving VBM down into the organization. Through the compensation package, the value creation process affects almost every non-union person. VBM provides a definitive calculation used as a standard for performance. It links the impact of various investment decisions to business unit EVA. There is accountability for investment returns at all levels of the organization. We have teams that provide the backbone of the VBM system at our company. A large percentage of the employees has been involved, directly or indirectly, in these teams. Today, employees from various departments work on issues previously worked on only within the affected department. This new cross-functional approach has resulted in more team work throughout the company and a tremendous amount of cost savings and operational improvements.

But at another firm VBM was used only at corporate headquarters to evaluate alternative business strategies. The managers started off with the view that value based management would be used throughout the organization. However, after a while, they decided to use VBM only as a choice-making tool rather than as a performance measure.

VBM Is More Than a Finance Exercise

The most compelling reason for adopting VBM is to change behavior, primarily by encouraging managers and employees to think like owners. When firms consider adopting VBM, they usually are searching for more than a financial metric. Instead, they are looking for a way to motivate value-adding behavior throughout the company. Wallace (1998) put it this way. "The adoption of residual income incentives alters management decisions in ways that should contribute to shareholder wealth." But for this to happen, the VBM tool must be easily translated into terms that rank-and-file employees can understand and grow to trust. As one executive stated, "The employees must feel they're getting an honest shake out of the system."

The essential element of any VBM system is the link between performance and compensation. Without this connection VBM becomes just another accounting or finance exercise and will not change behavior. While company practice varied, all the firms interviewed tied their performance-based compensation to VBM metrics to some degree. One executive described his firm's commitment to basing compensation on VBM performance as follows:

> Our division is successfully driving compensation all the way down to the operational level. Almost every non-contract employee is tied to shareholder value in one way or the other. Managers see the result of linking employee compensation to the value creation process. Employees began to think and act like owners and thus employees' and shareholders' interests became aligned. In addition to their incentive compensation pay, the top 150 managers were required to buy stock equal to two years of salary as a way to align their interests more closely to the shareholders.

Another observed,

> At our firm, the incentive compensation plan is the same for the Chairman as it is for every salaried person in the office. Upon implementation of the compensation plan, there was an immediate behavioral/cultural change. For one thing, the quality of earnings improved; people were no longer trying to accomplish earnings by changing accruals. The budgets were no longer negotiated. There was a longer-term perspective on operations. Employees no longer make decisions on a quarter-to-quarter basis and they were held accountable for their decisions. The incentive plan encourages managers to think long-term.

Other managers, however, expressed skepticism about linking compensation directly to value creation throughout the entire company. In one executive's words:

> The top 150 executives of our company are compensated based on shareholder value. The compensation program is not a one-size-fits-all type of program. The rate of incentive compensation is decided at the appropriate unit level. Executives receive stock options or phantom stock options geared off the firm's cash flows generated. However, the company does not use VBM to compensate at the lowest levels of the organization. We are not totally convinced that shareholder value is the appropriate measure for compensation down deep in the organization. Performance against value drivers is a better measure for lower level compensation.

While there were certainly differences in how incentive pay is managed across firms, the perceived need for doing so was never in question at any of the firms. Everyone without exception believed that what a firm measures and rewards gets done. The only question is how. We also noticed that the effort to link pay to performance throughout the companies was more prevalent for companies that used EVA as their metric.

This finding is certainly not surprising in that Stern Stewart & Co. is so focused on linking performance and incentives in their consulting activities and in much of what they present. For instance, in their EVA seminar Stewart describes several qualities for a good incentive plan:

1. Objectivity, where managers are not allowed to negotiate the outcome.
2. Simplicity, to the point of being understood by employees who are not financially educated.
3. Variability, where a significant portion of an employee's compensation is linked to performance, as opposed to being fixed in amount.
4. Definitive, where there is no moving of the goal posts when the game gets under way.

Educate, Educate, Educate

To transform behavior, employees must understand their role in creating value, otherwise the value enhancement will be largely superficial. This requires a program of ongoing training for the employees so that they continually think about the effect of their actions on shareholder value. Training is also important to instill accountability and a "no more excuses" philosophy.

One executive explained that in his firm education included increasing awareness of each employee concerning the importance of capital and free cash flows. Each employee understood that he or she was responsible for increasing the utilization of assets as there are capital costs related to underutilized assets. Moreover, managers helped their employees strike a balance, telling them that "service is important, but not at any cost."

We found that training and education in the organizations we visited began prior to the implementation of the VBM system. This training continued throughout the deployment of the system within the organization and beyond.

One Size Doesn't Fit All

Most of the companies in our study had carefully reviewed the VBM tools of all the major vendors and customized their own application. Even those that had started with one particular vendor's methodology were aware of the alternative systems and were generally aware of their similarities. For the most part, the managers had specific reasons for preferring the method they adopted. However, in most cases, the choice was tied to a perception regarding the method's ability to help management focus both on capital efficiency and profitability. The following comment was typical:

> Our firm's use of EVA and free cash flow are very closely aligned and enable the organization to put more discipline in the capital area. We chose EVA rather than CFROI because we believed it was a comprehensive shareholder value based system and economically correct. However, we understood that both EVA and HOLT Value Associates' CFROI are premised on the belief that the value of the firm is the NPV (net present value) of expected cash receipts.

But another manager saw it differently:

> Our management examined all options carefully. We did have Stern Stewart in for a few sessions, but we did not think their program would work for us. We also looked at McKinsey's Free Cash Flow method and decided against it for our purposes—although we use it

for other purposes. But we adopted the BCG methodology through an independent consultant. For us, it pulled all the pieces together.

Finally, we found that many managers do not accept what the vendors say at face value. They learn from the consultants but then adapt the methods to fit their own situation. In fact, in most instances, firms develop their systems in-house rather than hiring a consulting firm. For instance, many of the firms that use EVA do not rely on Stern Stewart & Co. for designing or operating the system.

Simplicity Is Preferable

Virtually all the study participants agreed that a firm should keep a VBM system as simple as possible. The primary reason for simplicity relates to the fact that to be effective the program must be understood and trusted by employees. However, most felt that employees only need to understand the portion of the calculation for which they are responsible. Also, simplicity, according to some, requires consistency of measures across the firm; otherwise, there is only limited buy-in.

Two of the managers' opinions on the simplicity issue are as follows:

> Management believes that we should focus on three to four simple key concepts and apply them to the functional operations. We keep the training at a simple level to achieve a greater understanding of VBM. A great deal of time is spent ensuring that non-financial employees understand the concepts of VBM. Managers realize that not all details are relevant, that employees only need to know what is important to their situation.

> Managers simplified the financial measurement framework to communicate information necessary to identify value drivers. Employees now understand how these drivers affect stock prices.

Almost all the companies expressed the perceived need for keeping their use of VBM as simple as possible. Simplicity is thought to be a virtue when it comes to explaining VBM to their employees and preventing gamesmanship. They feel that if the tool is too complex, it will become known simply as another finance exercise and fail to accomplish the desired changes in operating decision making within the company. One manager said,

Our firm uses Value Discovery, a practical exercise to identify business drivers. In the discovery process, managers in each division learn how to maximize the choices they make to increase shareholder value over time. We also simplified the VBM tool for the purposes of explaining it to our employees. The simplification was essential so that the employees would not think the VBM system was simply another finance program that had little or nothing to do with operating performance.

In short, the sampled companies were successful in making VBM simple enough to be used as a tool for making a variety of decisions—rather than just a complex financial exercise that the finance department imposes on the operating managers.

Don't Expect Any Quick Fixes

As a concluding but important finding, we found that it is unlikely that the implementation of a VBM system will immediately meet all the needs of the organization. In fact, it has been estimated that for smaller firms, say with sales of $250 million or less, adopting a VBM system takes four to five months just to begin, compared to over a year for large companies. In every case, time is required for a plan to evolve and grow within the company. Moreover, implementing VBM will most likely require changing other systems, including such areas as the firm's compensation and information systems.

In other words, adopting a VBM system is not a quick fix to a firm's problems but more often requires change throughout the company. And the change will be ongoing.

They Would Do It Again

We asked each of the study participants, "If you could begin again, would you adopt VBM?" The uniform response was yes, if given the opportunity they would, and they had few regrets.

The managers did not say that adoption of a VBM system was accomplished without some trying experiences; each firm faced and overcame difficulties and barriers. They had become strong advocates of value based management, feeling that it had contributed positively to their company's effectiveness. The managers pointed to improved operational and financial efficiencies that had occurred. For some but not all there had been a corresponding increase in shareholder value, which was the primary motivation for adopting VBM. We would caution, however, that increased share price may not be a natural out-

A Success Story at CSX Transportation

VBM gave CSX Transportation an internal discipline. There were people in our business who wanted to aggressively grow the business and spend capital to support the growth. However, Wall Street was saying you are not a growth business, you are a mature business and you should be throwing off cash. We now know what Wall Street expectations are and are focused on the real drivers to increasing shareholder value. Before VBM there may have been a disconnect between our vision of the way to increase shareholder value and Wall Street's expectations.

Since 1991 car loadings were up 7 percent on a 20 percent drop in the equipment fleet. Total rail employment dropped from 39,675 in 1988 to 29,537 in 1995. Operating income was up 70 percent over the past five years, and capital spending decreased 10 percent over the same time frame. Performance Improvement Initiatives have improved efficiency and productivity to the tune of $500 million since 1992. Consequently, the operating ratio has improved dramatically since implementation of EVA.

When CSX's subsidiary, Sea-Land Service, wanted to enter different regions of the world, it did not purchase new ships but rather entered into vessel-sharing agreements which enabled it to avoid the capital costs associated with purchasing new vessels. The company increased the utilization of its existing fleet, extended its geographical reach, and met its strategic initiatives without spending additional capital.

come—certainly not in the short run. Thus, the motivation to adopt VBM should rest more on the need to motivate managers and employees to do what is consistent with increasing shareholder value. As Zimmerman (1997) aptly comments,

> The success of a given performance measure in tracking near-term changes in a company's stock price is unlikely to be the most important consideration in choosing a measure as a basis for managerial rewards. . . . The best performance measure is the one that without imposing excessive costs give managers the strongest incentives to take actions that increase firm value.

In other words, it is more important to change a firm's focus and direction than to work diligently to develop the "perfect" measure for value creation. It was certainly our impression that the firms visited were primarily focused on doing what made economic sense for the shareholders and only secondarily on what would happen to the near-term share price performance. To us, this perspective seems to be the right one.

A Success Story at Briggs & Stratton

Briggs & Stratton managers use EVA to evaluate new products. They also use EVA in the decision-making process that accompanies plant acquisitions. Further, they were also able to use EVA to justify in federal court the moving of 2,000 jobs from one area to another.

The VBM system is also a valuable tool to

- Provide employee empowerment
- Create superior value by developing mutually beneficial relationships with our customers, suppliers and communities
- Enhance our brand equity by concentrating on low-cost manufacturing and selling and servicing for a broad range of power equipment
- Provide opportunity for peoples throughout the world to develop their economies, improve the order and quality of their lives, and, in so doing, add value to our shareholders' investments

---

Summary

For the companies we interviewed, the adoption of VBM was a watershed event representing a turning away from doing "business as usual" toward a focus on shareholder value. In addition, we learned, the adoption of VBM is connected with a mandate for change that was often associated with an erosion of economic value or a change in leadership.

VBM, if used effectively, is more than a financial exercise; its objective is to change behavior so as to align the interests of a firm's management with that of its shareholders. We found that companies that successfully integrate VBM throughout their organization experience a dramatic change in culture. However, not everything worked perfectly. There were invariably trade-offs that had to be made between accuracy and simplicity, and no doubt there was significant resistance to change within the firm. However, based on the companies we interviewed, there are basic things that can be done to increase the chance of effectively implementing the system. Most noteworthy are the following:

- Top management support and involvement is essential.
- VBM without a linkage to incentive pay has no teeth and cannot be expected to generate lasting changes in behavior.
- Careful education and training throughout the firm is needed before linking pay to performance.
- Whenever possible, simplicity is a virtue worth pursuing.

Finally, we should note that the choice of the metric itself was not considered by any of the companies the primary key to success. While the selection process in each case no doubt considered finding the best fit between the metric and a company's characteristics, the ultimate key to success was effective implementation. Put in terms that can be understood by golfers and nongolfers alike (Myers 1997), "Much as hitting a good golf shot depends more on how you strike the ball than on what brand of club you use, achieving success through the use of any performance metric will depend more on how well you apply it than on which one you use."

Thus, there is no question that managing for shareholder value will always be a challenge, even in the best of circumstances. We should always be a bit suspect of anyone who tries to convince us that managing for value is easy if we will only do it their way. Also, we should never think that simply adopting a system is what counts; what matters is how well we do it. From what we observed, choosing a method that management can believe in and support and then being determined to be the best at implementing it will take us a long way down the road to success. And in listening to those managers who have been successful in this endeavor, the journey is well worth the effort for managers and shareholders alike.

Appendix 10A

Company Profiles of Site Visit Companies

Briggs & Stratton Corporation

Industry: Manufacturer, small gasoline engines and automotive locks

Headquarters: Milwaukee, Wisconsin

Employees: 7,950

Briggs & Stratton Corporation, a company with an eighty-six-year past, dedicates itself to a singular mission for the future—revolutionizing the outdoor power equipment industry as it applies to small combustion engines.[3]

For many years, Briggs & Stratton has led the industry in small air-cooled gasoline engines. In 1995 the Milwaukee-based corporation, known primarily for its four-cycle engines for outdoor equipment, continued as an industry leader. The gap widened between Briggs & Stratton and the competition in the areas of new product development, environmental research and development, and worldwide sales and servicing of its products.

Three corporate ideologies are advanced by Chairman of the Board and Chief Executive Officer Frederick P. Stratton, Jr. These were to reduce costs, improve product quality, and improve product performance. To reduce costs, the company seeks to find new and more efficient ways of manufacturing using the most sophisticated machinery with a highly skilled work force. Improved quality and product performance mean strict quality control, more funds for research and development, and aggressive programs to improve existing models.

Briggs & Stratton has a three-pronged business plan that is applied to every model and family grouping in the company's product line. These include aluminum alloy, single and twin cylinder gasoline engines, ranging from 3hp to 20hp, which cover a vast array of overhead and side valve configurations.

Backing all of the company's products is a strong support system. A worldwide network of over 32,000 authorized service centers exists to meet customers' needs and expectations. These centers are run by factory trained personnel and stocked with Briggs & Stratton parts.

VBM Cornerstones

In addition to stellar training programs and strong support from top management, Briggs & Stratton created divisional accounting management positions for each divisional level. These people communicated very well about the process and became the "internal priests of the religion."

In addition, Briggs & Stratton's program created performance compensation and measures that could be taken to decrease capital.

Finally, a consistent set of EVA calculations exists for each person, which is viewed as fair and honest.

CSX Transportation

Industry: Railroad: freight and distribution services
Headquarters: Richmond, Virginia
Employees: 146,747

CSX Transportation (CSXT) is a part of CSX Corporation which is a *Fortune* 500 transportation company providing rail, intermodal, and ocean container shipping, barging, trucking, and contract logistics services worldwide.[4] CSXT provides rail transportation and distribution services over some 32,000 miles of track in twenty states and Ontario, Canada. The company's rail network extends from Ontario to Florida; and from the Atlantic seaboard to the Mississippi River. CSXT delivers to more points than any other rail carrier on earth. CSXT is the largest hauler of coal in the United States and handles one third of all new domestic automobile shipments.

In 1995, CSXT accounted for 46 percent of CSX's operating revenue and 74 percent of its operating income. Formed in 1986, CSXT has significantly lowered its operating costs while improving reliability, performance, and efficiency. The company has created two specialized business units to manage key segments of the coal market. It has also established twenty-five specialized distribution centers to provide extensive new car transport services for both domestic and foreign manufacturers. Additionally, the company transports minerals, agricultural products, metals, forest products, food and consumer goods, chemicals, and fertilizer.

VBM Cornerstones

The company's VBM approach includes an innovative approach to incentive compensation. Top management gets direct compensation from return on invested capital (ROIC), and the employees get compensation from the operating ratio. Top executives are strongly encouraged to stay heavily invested in CSX stocks, and salaries, cash bonuses, and performance shares are all based on shareholder value. Incentive compensation for employees is divided into two parts. For the top 150 to 300 employees, there is a matrix that lays out the incentive calculation for percentage of ROIC achieved. The company also does a correlation analysis based on ROIC as it pertains to operating ratio. The return is correlated to the operating income required. Then the ratio is calculated. The employees not in the top 150–300 group are compensated on the operating ratio.

CSXT maintains a high level of commitment to VBM at the senior management level and drives that down through the organization: "We have done the math to get top management bonuses aligned with bonuses throughout CSXT. If top management gets a certain level of bonus, the employees get the same level of bonus." Individual "star performers" at all levels are awarded additional shares of stock. The company strives for a meritocracy, rewarding those who perform well.

Harnischfeger Industries

Industry:	Holding company for subsidiaries involved in papermaking, mining equipment, and material handling
Headquarters:	Milwaukee, Wisconsin
Employees:	16,250

Harnischfeger Industries was founded in 1884.[5] It is an international holding company with business segments involved in the manufacture and distribution of equipment for papermaking (Beloit Corporation); surface mining (P&H Mining Equipment); underground mining (Joy Mining Machinery); and material handling (P&H Material Handling). Global operations are located in Australia, Canada, Europe, South Africa, South America, Southeast Asia, and the United States.

The Papermaking Equipment Group (Beloit Corporation) produces papermaking machinery and systems for de-inking, recycled fiber/wood chip processing, pulp manufacturing, and stock preparation.

The Mining Equipment Group includes P&H Mining Equipment and Joy Mining Machinery. P&H is a world leader in the production of surface mining shovels, draglines, and drills. Joy Mining Machinery leads the industry in the manufacture of miners, shearers, face conveyors, mining systems, drills, loaders, and more.

The Material Handling Group is a leading supplier of cranes and hoists as well as modernization and engineering services. It is the industry's largest domestic installed equipment base, with over 40,000 overhead cranes and 100,000 hoists.

VBM Cornerstones

Harnischfeger's three core businesses have the following key characteristics:

- International scope
- Market leadership
- Strong aftermarket position
- Technological leader in field
- Positive economic value added potential

The company's focus and growth is driven by these core criteria.

Harnischfeger's common sense approach to VBM has been very successful. The components of their program include

- An aggressive training program
- A simple approach
- Incentive compensation tied to EVA
- A program that affects behavior

National Semiconductor Corporation

Industry: Semiconductor
Headquarters: Santa Clara, California
Employees: 22,300

National Semiconductor, a transistor company, was founded in 1959 in Danbury, Connecticut.[6] In 1967, Peter Sprague took over as chairman and hired manufacturing expert Charles Sporck away from Fairchild Semiconductor. Sporck transferred operations to Silicon Valley and invested heavily in the development of linear and digital logic chips. After pulling away from the memory chip business in 1985, Sporck transformed the company into a higher-margin supplier of niche products.

During a five-year restructuring plan initiated in 1991, CEO Gilbert Amelio narrowed the company's product focus to three high-margin, high-growth markets (analog, communications, and personal).

Analog-intensive products include automotive systems, audio equipment, and medical diagnostic equipment. Communication-intensive products include data communication hubs, voice/data systems, and networks. The personal systems market includes multimedia platforms and personal computing products.

The company is divided into two groups, Standard Products (commodity chips) and Communications and Computing (niche devices). Amelio has also established the Innovative Products Division, which serves as an incubator for new product ideas.

National Semiconductor is located in the heart of Silicon Valley and its manufacturing facilities are located in Malaysia, the Philippines, Scotland, and Singapore.

VBM Cornerstones

National Semiconductor began the Leading Change Program in the early 1990s, with thousands of managers attending a five-day seminar to understand the new vision of the company. During this time, the managers also collected information from the bottom up about what employees thought the direction of the company should be. The vision of the company was then established.

In 1991–1992, National Semiconductor did a corporate transformation in two phases. The first phase revisited their capital-intensive situation. The new CEO developed incentive compensation to facilitate the retrenchment. Initially, the incentive program was based on return on net assets (RONA). This was appropriate for phase 1 as they went from a loss company to positive numbers.

While this incentive program was appropriate for phase 1, the CEO and CFO realized it was necessary to move on to phase 2 and an incentive program based on changing managers' behaviors to drive shareholder value. Total shareholder return (TSR—the improvement of stock price over time) was the main focus. During the early 1990s, Boston Consulting Group was brought in and the National Semiconductor Value Model was initiated.

Shell Oil

Industry: Petroleum and petrochemical
Headquarters: Houston, Texas
Employees: 21,500

Shell made its first appearance in the United States in 1912. In 1985, Shell Oil Company became a wholly owned subsidiary of Royal Dutch-Shell Group, which has over 117,000 employees in more than 100 countries.[7]

Shell Oil's business has always extended beyond selling gasoline. In the 1930s, Shell scientists developed petrochemical fertilizer products. During the 1940s, Shell led the way in developing chemicals for synthetic rubber and explosives, invented a method for purifying penicillin, and supplied the Allies with aviation fuel.

Throughout the history of Shell, the company has met the needs of a changing world. From jet fuel to engine lubricants, to the investment of resources into processes and products that provide a safer environment, Shell has led the way.

Shell Oil has three principal businesses: exploration, production, and chemical products/oil products.

As President Philip J. Carroll states in his 1995 letter, Shell Oil's top priority continues to be achieving a return on investment of at least 12 percent. By setting the bar high, Shell intends to be the premier company in the United States.

VBM Cornerstones

A tremendously innovative structure at Shell has positive effects on VBM concepts. Shell has created an interesting dynamic from what used to be traditional center jobs. Four semiautonomous operating units have their own balance sheets. With this structure, Shell's principle businesses will be able to operate more independently while preserving a valued sense of unity.

In 1995, Shell Oil Company was split into four separate operating companies; a services company, an exploration and production company, an oil products (refining and marketing) company, and Shell Chemical. A board of directors was placed in each of these operating companies. The chairman of each of the boards is the CEO of Shell Oil Company. The boards include heads of the professional firms (tax, legal, planning, finance and investment services, and human resources) as well as CEOs from other operating companies. The company is moving toward having external directors on these boards.

Some of the effects are

- With shareholder value management in place, the capital decisions about the debt taken on are made at the operating level. They follow the debt down into these operating companies.

- The business heads are much more accountable now than they have been in the past.

- The professional firms within the company act as for-profit businesses even though all the profits are kept internally. The heads of each of these groups come together in council form to decide the policies to be established across the operating units.

References

Myers, Randy. "Measure for Measure." *CFO Magazine*, November 1997.

O'Byrne, Stephen F. "Does Value Based Management Discourage Investment in Intangibles?" Working paper, March 1, 1999.

Tully, Shawn. "The Real Key to Creating Wealth." *Fortune* (September 20, 1993): 38–50.

Wallace, James. "Adopting Residual Income–Based Compensation Plans." *Journal of Accounting and Economics* 24 (1998).

Zimmerman, Jerald L. "EVA and Divisional Performance Measurement." *Journal of Applied Corporate Finance* 10 (1997): 98–109.

Epilogue

Disney's overriding objective is to create shareholder value by continuing to be the world's premier entertainment company from a creative, strategic, and financial standpoint.

—**Disney, 1999 annual report**

Shareholder value has long been the focal theme of the financial economist, but the conversation has now moved from the classroom to the boardroom—where investors are no longer willing to remain passive and either suffer in silence or take the "Wall Street Walk" (i.e., sell their shares). They want access to the boardroom in an effort to stimulate the performance of their portfolio companies.

Managerial responses to the shareholder activism have been varied. Where there is a strong belief that the shareholder is but one of many constituents—and possibly no more important than others—the call to become shareholder-value driven is often ignored and in some cases publicly vilified as promoting myopic decision making. However, for the poorest performing firms the pressures of large institutional shareholders, and in some instances buyout firms, have forced a change in focus. The mandate is clear: create shareholder value or perish.

But, is this newfound enthusiasm for shareholder interests just a passing fad? Will continued full employment and the competition for human capital derail the shareholder value creation train? We are no better at gazing into the future than the Wall Street pundits, but if the intensity of the ongoing dialogue between shareholders and managements is any indication, the answer is, "Not anytime soon." However, even if the interest in shareholder value were to wane, the gains of the 1990s are undeniable.

Claiming the goal of maximizing shareholder value is easy. CEOs do it all the time in statements they make to the financial press and letters they write to stockholders in the annual report. However, translating the goal into practice is far from easy. Even where there is agreement that enhancing shareholder value is the *right* thing to do, there are often very divergent opinions about how best to implement the goal. Furthermore, value *creation* involves much more than merely monitoring firm performance. Value is created only where managers are actively engaged in the process of identifying good investment opportunities and taking steps to capture their value creating potential. Put simply, value creation requires management to be effective at identifying, growing, *and* harvesting investment opportunities.

If you want to manage for shareholder value, the first and foremost thing you have to do is identify just what drives shareholder value in the capital market. A key issue that frequently arises in this regard is the following: Does share value reflect a firm's quarterly earnings or does it encompass the firm's future cash flow generating potential? Many investors and corporate managers argue that Wall Street is far too concerned about current firm earnings to the exclusion of a firm's future prospects. On the other hand, financial economists generally argue that capital markets are far-sighted and do reflect the current value of the firm's future earnings potential. We would be remiss if we did not recognize the sincerity of the opinions on both sides of this issue. However, value based management models, without exception, are built upon the basic belief that capital markets look to a firm's future cash flows as the source of firm value. They reject the basic thesis that accounting-based measures, such as current quarterly earnings and earnings growth, are the key determinants of the value of a firm's shares. If you take the VBM road to managing for shareholder value, then you should be forewarned. You may find it necessary to defend your decisions to the analyst community when those actions increase future cash flows at the expense of current earnings.

In this study, we looked closely at the primary methods used by different companies to incentivize managers to focus on creating shareholder value. Here are our conclusions:

- The practices of the firms engaged in implementing VBM differ widely across firms. Some firms find themselves suffering from bloated investments that no longer earn a competitive return. Their immediate need is to implement a performance measurement and reward system that encourages managers to rationalize their investment in assets, determine what is necessary to carry on the firm's operations, and dispose of the excess. For other firms, the primary need may be strategic. In this case, VBM provides the tools for assessing the value of strategic alternatives. Thus, choosing the *right* VBM approach must focus on the firm's needs rather than the perceived superiority of one method over another. Having a clear understanding at the outset of what you want to accomplish is absolutely essential.

- Any student of financial economics knows that the process of value creation frequently takes many years and cannot be easily captured in a single-period measure, no matter how intuitive the metric. Unfortunately, firms do not have the luxury of being able to wait for their value creating efforts to run their full course before attempting to assess their success. The interim performance of the firm and its business units must be measured periodically so that management can recognize and reward those who are responsible. Thus, a very real need exists for a single-period performance metric that can measure historical performance in a way that appropriately reflects value creation for the period. We simply have no choice if we are to monitor the firm's operations over time. The tools of VBM represent improvements over traditional accounting metrics but still have their limitations. So do not fall prey to strong claims for VBM metrics—no matter how impressive their presentation—that a single-period measure will correlate highly with firm value year in and year out. You will be disappointed.

- Successful VBM programs have some common attributes: (1) they have top management support—genuine commitment not simply token involvement, (2) they are tied to compensation, (3) they entail a significant investment of time and money in educating the firm's workforce about the program and how it works, and (4) they value simplicity over complexity. Remember that the tools of VBM are not finely calibrated instruments. So you should view the use of your VBM system to create shareholder value more like using a tugboat to nudge a super tanker into port, rather than using a sophisticated laser guidance system to direct smart bombs down smokestacks!

- We have been surprised by the frequency with which we have encountered managers who could only describe their firm's incentive compensation program in very vague terms. Some went so far as to say that the determinants of their end-of-year bonus was a mystery. In these cases it is difficult to believe that the incentive system is leading to its intended results.

In closing, let's make it clear that no value-based system is perfect. Equally important, not all firms derive the same benefits from implementing VBM. For one thing, measuring performance is more difficult for firms that operate in rapidly changing markets. The value of these firms is tied closely to the firm's future growth opportunities, which are characteristically harder to assess than ongoing operations in a more stable environment. At the end of the day, there is no "Holy Grail" when it comes to selecting and implementing a value based management system.

Even with the above-noted limitations, there remains significant potential for unlocking shareholder value in many firms. Value based management involves transforming behavior in ways that encourage employees to think and act like owners. We believe the careful crafting of a capital market-focused measurement and reward system that measures employee performance using metrics tied to owner rewards will promote a continuous cycle of value creation that benefits everyone in the economy.

Notes

Chapter 1

1. In their book on value based management, McTaggart, Kontes, and Mankins (1994) go so far as to assert that "the great majority of large corporations throughout the world are not managed with the objective of maximizing wealth or shareholder value" (p. 41).
2. Although we do not report it here, a similar ranking, called the Shareholder Scoreboard, is prepared by L.E.K. Consulting LLC and published in the *Wall Street Journal*. This ranking, however, uses the total return to shareholders over one-, three-, five-, and ten-year holding periods to assess wealth creation/destruction. Total return includes price appreciation or depreciation, and any reinvestment from cash dividends, rights and warrant offerings, and cash equivalents, such as stock received in spinoffs. Returns are also adjusted for stock splits, stock dividends, and recapitalizations. See *Wall Street Journal*, interactive edition, February 24, 2000.
3. Although the 1990s produced the longest bull market for common stock in recorded history, many firms have struggled and even lost value for their shareholders. The manufacturing sector was particularly hard hit, with only one in eight manufacturers outperforming the S&P 500 since 1988 and one-third experiencing a decline in the value of their shares (Wise and Baumgartner 1999).
4. We use the term *value based management* to refer to performance metrics and reward systems that are designed to help managers enhance shareholder value.
5. If you are still unconvinced, consider the following example. In 1999 Intel Corporation spent $3,503 million on R&D, which equals $0.69 per share after taxes. In addition, the firm's 1999 earnings were $2.20 per share. The firm's stock sold for $135.00 on March 10, 2000, producing a price/earnings multiple of 61.36 times. Would Intel's stock price have been $42.13 ($0.69 in R&D per share × 61.36 times) higher if Intel had not spent anything on R&D? Of course it would not have been, for Intel's expenditures for R&D are its lifeblood, creating new products that drive its future profitability. Without R&D the firm's stream of new products would evaporate, as would future cash flows. Chan et al. (1990) provide evidence of the stock market's positive response to R&D expenditure announcements.
6. LEK/Alcar's model is based on the concept of shareholder value added.
7. The list of value based management vendors is much longer than suggested here. However, these tools (and vendors) were among the earliest to gain national prominence. For example, Marakon Associates, although not discussed directly in this book, has a prominent value based management consulting practice whose basic tenets are described in McTaggart, Kontes, and Mankins (1994).

8. To draw an analogy, VBM has more in common with steering supertankers than it does with laser-guided missiles. The idea is to point the firm in the direction that increases the likelihood that value will be created rather than trying to specify the exact details of value creation.

9. The American Productivity and Quality Center (APQC) was founded in 1977 as a nonprofit, 501-C3 organization. APQC's mission is to improve productivity and quality in the private and public sectors. The study was titled "Shareholder Value-based Management."

Chapter 2

1. Corporate governance refers to the methods used to control the activities of corporations. This generally refers to the oversight function of the board of directors, the discipline of product and capital markets, and compensation programs designed to provide incentives for managers to act in the best interest of stockholders. Monks and Minow (1995) define corporate governance in terms of the relationship among various participants in determining the direction and performance of corporations. The primary participants are (1) the shareholders, (2) the management (led by the chief executive officer), and (3) the board of directors.

2. ERISA's primary purpose was to protect workers who had worked for substantial periods of time under pension plans. ERISA is enforced by a myriad of labor and tax codes carried out under the supervision of the Department of Labor, the Internal Revenue Service, and the Pension Benefit Guaranty Corporation, as well as the actions of the courts. ERISA granted rights to workers in a number of areas related to coverage by a pension plan, vesting rights, distributions of pension benefits, fiduciary standards for persons administering pension plans or investing plan assets, and reporting of financial and actuarial data on the plan to the IRS, among other things.

3. These data are based on the *Institutional Investment Report: Turnovers, Investment Strategies, and Ownership Patterns,* The Conference Board 3, 2 (January 2000).

4. For example, under Rule 14a-1(1)(iii) "furnishing of a form of a proxy or other communication to security holders under circumstances reasonably calculated to result in the procurement, withholding or revocation of a proxy" is considered a proxy solicitation. See Choi (1997) for an extensive discussion of SEC proxy solicitation rules.

5. Jesse Unruh (California State Treasurer) and Harrison Goldin (New York City Controller) formed the CII in 1985. CII was initially formed in response to concerns about greenmail and antitakeover activities that flourished during the 1980s.

6. This section summarizes the results of a study by Kensinger and Martin (1996) that was published by the Financial Executives Research Foundation, which is the research arm of the Financial Executives Institute.

7. Judith Dobrzynski of *Business Week* uses this analogy.

8. Institutional activism is defined by how the institution chooses to deal with its poorly performing investments. The key distinction here is between

active and passive investment strategies. An active investor is one who takes an active role in encouraging performance improvements among portfolio companies, whereas a passive investor simply sells laggards.

9. CalPERS Approves $275 million Investment to Relational Investors, L. L. C., 1998 Business Wire, Inc. (May 19, 1998).

10. Steve Hemmerick, "Reform Effort: CalPERS and Hermes Share Focus on U.K. Governance," *Pensions and Investments* (May 3, 1999), p. 6.

11. Jane Martinson, "Insider's Outsider Sniffing Out the Corporate 'Rats,'" *The Financial Times* (February 4, 1999), p. 28.

12. Trustees control investment policies of public pension funds. They become trustees by political appointment (by governor), election by plan beneficiaries, or by virtue of their office.

13. For an in-depth study of the activist practices of financial institutions throughout the 1990s, see Kensinger and Martin (1996).

14. This description is drawn from Kensinger and Martin (1996).

Chapter 3

1. The idea of deducting a "return for the use of invested capital" from reported earnings is not a new one, as we later discuss. The basic concept is called "economic profit."

2. The Boston Consulting Group (BCG) refers to the problem we address here as the "old plant–new plant trap." We return to this issue again in chapter 6, where we discuss the use of BCG's VBM methodology

3. The shortcomings of the conventional accounting method for computing the RONA are discussed in Dearden (1969) and Seed (1983).

4. This and more detailed decompositions of the RONA metric are frequently referred to as the DuPont model of financial analysis. F. Donaldson Brown, an electrical engineer with E. I. DuPont's treasury department, dreamed up the methodology in 1919.

5. The $300 increase in pre-tax operating income resulted in a $210 increase in after-tax operating income due to a 30 percent tax rate.

6. In chapter 5, we discuss the use of economic value added, which is very closely related to the residual income concept.

Chapter 4

1. See the bible for explaining EVA and a lot more as advocated by Stewart (1991).

2. See Boston Consulting Group (1994).

3. Non-interest-bearing current liabilities (NIBCLs) are part of the firm's operating cycle as it purchases inventory on credit, sells on credit, pays its accounts payable and accruals, and eventually collects from its customers. Interest-bearing debt, on the other hand, is a source of financing provided by return-seeking investors, and as such is not part of the firm's recurring operating cycle.

4. To validate these numbers, refer to the financial statements for Johnson & Johnson in appendix 4A.

5. See Rappaport (1998) for an in-depth discussion on determining a firm's growth duration based on "market signals."

6. It is not apparent why this equation is the present value of a future cash flow stream continuing in perpetuity. But it is true and is demonstrated in most basic financial textbooks, so we leave the derivation to others and simply rely on their proofs.

7. For instance, the projected free cash flow in year 1 is $4.125 million; its present value is $3.619 million, computed as

$$\text{Present value of year 1 free cash flow} = \frac{\text{Free cash flow in year 1}}{(1 + \text{Cost of capital})^1} = \frac{\$4.125}{(1 + 0.14)^1} = \$3.619 \text{ million}$$

8. To learn the intricacies of computing a company's cost of capital, see Ehrhardt (1995).

9. The market risk premium is the rate of return above the risk-free rate that an investor would be expected to earn on a well-diversified portfolio of stocks. A source for this information is Ibbotson Associates (2000).

10. The ideas in this section originate from "Of Pigs and Pokes" (1998).

Chapter 5

1. EVA™ is a trademark name registered by Stern Stewart & Co.

2. We are assuming that the firm will continue to make *replacement* investments in the amount of the depreciation being taken. But there will be no need to increase the total invested capital after 2005.

3. If you have access to the computer software Lexis-Nexis, we would encourage you to search for the recent articles on Economic Value Added. You will find an ongoing discussion about the topic from a wide range of journals and magazines written by businesspeople as well as academicians. Also, the Bank of America *Journal of Applied Corporate Finance* dedicated its Summer 1999 issue to EVA and incentive compensation. For anyone wanting to gain a deeper understanding of EVA and its application, this issue is well worth reading.

4. *CFO Magazine*, October 1996.

5. Not everything the accountant does is bad. For Stern Stewart, depreciation is the accountant's one noncash charge that is acceptable. The rationale is that the assets consumed in the business must be replenished before investors achieve a return on their investment. Thus, depreciation is recognized as an economic cost, and accordingly capital should be charged, with the accumulated depreciation suffered by the assets.

6. For a more complete statement by Stern Stewart & Co. of what they believe to be the benefits of using EVA, go to their Web site at http://www.sternstewart.com.

7. Note that for simplicity's sake, this explanation of residual income valuation is based on an all-equity firm. That is, profits are after-tax net income (not net operating profit after tax) and the opportunity cost of capital is the cost of equity (not the weighted average cost of capital).

Chapter 6

1. We are indebted to Mike Kuldanek and Rawley Thomas of the Boston Consulting Group for their significant contributions to this chapter. BCG and HOLT Value Associates have a common heritage in that both groups came out of HOLT Planning Associates. HOLT stands for the four principals, Bob Hendricks, Eric Olsen, Marvin Lipson, and Rawley Thomas. Before forming HOLT Planning Associates in 1985, the principals worked at Callard Madden Associates. In 1991 the two entities were formed, with BCG/HOLT focusing its efforts on corporate applications within Boston Consulting Group and HOLT Value Associates developing investment advisory products for corporate money managers. In 1997, BCG/HOLT was fully integrated into BCG and the name BCG/HOLT was dropped.
2. While BCG works with all these metrics, HOLT Value Associates restricts its interest to TSR and CFROI.
3. Alternatively, we could employ the geometric mean of the annual returns, which assumes reinvestment of the annual free cash flows at the then value instead of the internal rate of return.
4. In many client assignments, BCG also suggests employing cash flow multiples (called "TBR-Lite") as a simplification for valuing operating business units. This multiples approach avoids the complexities of using a full valuation model like Time Fade while providing directionally correct answers to strategic value management issues.
5. The forty-year period reflects that fact that no firm survives into perpetuity; it represents a long enough time so that the residual value of winding down the existing assets beyond forty years is relatively insignificant to the valuation. BCG is working to enhance this approach by reflecting actual company dropouts and their release market value of capital.
6. The 300 company subset eliminates financials and other firms for which BCG feels the accounting numbers cannot be translated into economic returns accurately enough to be used for this important discount rate calculation.
7. One can argue with this underlying assumption. However, BCG believes that assuming a constant dollar level annuity is more reflective of most projects than the assumption inherent in the return on net assets (RONA) that cash flows decline with the increase in accumulated depreciation. Based on empirical tests, BCG says the correlation of value/cost versus CFROI in the 60%–70% range compared to price/book versus RONA in the 30%–40% range lends support to this empirical assumption.
8. We are obviously combining cash flows in different time periods in this example, which we would never do in a typical IRR analysis. We would instead be finding the IRR by computing the net cash flows in each period over the entire investment cycle. However, either approach gives identical results in terms of the IRR and the CFROI.
9. The problem with computing the IRR when a project is expected to incur negative cash flows after the initial investment is described in most finance textbooks. See for example, Ross, Westerfield, and Jaffe (1999, pp. 145–146).
10. One can argue whether the appropriate reinvestment rate is the cost of capital or the average CFROI level for the economy. BCG acknowledges

this controversy and accepts a client's preferences to use the cost of capital. However, BCG's research suggests most of the time the CFROI exceeds the market-derived cost of capital, because entrepreneurs in a dynamic economy continuously seek superior returns from investments in corporate assets over promised financial returns. The CFROI distribution is much wider than company costs of capital distributions, suggesting investors must be rewarded for the higher risk of loss in investing in corporate assets, which are less liquid than financial assets. Thus, BCG prefers to use the average CFROI as the reinvestment rate instead of the cost of capital or market-derived investor's discount rate.

11. We say more about this limitation in chapter 7.
12. BCG chooses to use its estimate of the CFROI for the economy as a whole as the reinvestment rate.
13. In actual consulting assignments, BCG emphasizes TBR more than CFROI.
14. BCG follows Ijiri (1980) here in saying that constant dollar adjustments are more appropriate than replacement cost. Ijiri suggests that investors care more about the cash flows they invest and the cash returns they receive, so the types of assets invested in or their replacement cost are irrelevant. What matters is the cash flows into the firm and out of the firm, all expressed in common units of purchasing power to the investor.

Chapter 7

1. Boston Consulting Group, "Shareholder Value Management (Book 2): Improved Measurement Drives Improved Value Creation" (July 29, 1994), p. 16.
2. Although BCG uses the term "economic depreciation" in evaluating a project's annual CVA, we will not. Instead we describe their depreciation calculation as sinking fund depreciation. Financial economists traditionally reserve the use of the term "economic depreciation" to refer to changes in the market value of an asset from one period to the next. As we learned earlier in chapter 6, BCG's depreciation calculation is equivalent to sinking fund estimation.
3. MCVA is not a BCG concept and is used here only to illustrate the connection between CVA and a project's NPV.
4. Note that the $ROIC_t$ are based on the use of present value depreciation in determining operating income and the invested capital for the period.
5. In chapter 6 we noted that BCG also calculate CFROI using the IRR method. This method recognizes cash flows generated by the project over multiple years and produces a multi-year measure as contrasted with the single-year measure discussed here.
6. SEC-10 refers to the estimated value of an E&P company's oil and gas reserves where the future production proceeds are discounted using a rate of 10 percent. Accounting standard SFAS-69 requires that E&P companies report SEC-10 figures in their annual report.
7. For a discussion of the value of managerial flexibility in the context of real options, see Dixit and Pindyck (1994) and Trigeorgis (1996).

Chapter 8

1. This quote was taken from the Stern Stewart Roundtables, *Discussing the Revolution in Corporate Finance,* ed. Joel Stern and Donald Chew (1998).

2. Reported in an interview by Martin (1996).

3. Simple examples of nonmonetary rewards that are important motivators to individual behavior within an organization include participation in the firm's activities, having a safer and easier work environment, public recognition, satisfying interactions with fellow employees, and promotions. All of these are important elements of the firm's overall compensation system.

4. For example, the Boise Cascade Corporation (annual proxy statement, April 15, 1999, p. 11) states that its executive compensation program is designed to

   - Attract, motivate, reward, and retain the broad-based management talent critical to achieving the company's business goals
   - Link a portion of each executive officer's compensation to the performance of both the company and the individual executive officer
   - Encourage ownership of company common stock by executive officers

5. Wruck (2000) suggests that effectively designed and implemented compensation systems create value for organizations by (1) improving the motivation and productivity of employees, (2) promoting productive turnover of personnel, (3) mobilizing valuable specific knowledge by allowing effective decentralization, and (4) helping overcome organizational inertia and opposition to change.

6. Our discussion of the components of compensation policy follows that of Baker, Jensen, and Murphy (1988).

7. We should recognize that pay for performance is not accepted in some quarters. Some psychologists and behaviorists have argued that pay for performance or merit-based compensation can create dysfunctional results. Kohn (1988), for example, argues that merit-pay systems are counterproductive for three reasons: "First, rewards encourage people to focus narrowly on a task, to do it as quickly as possible, and to take few risks. . . . Second, extrinsic rewards can erode intrinsic interest. . . . [Finally], people come to see themselves as being controlled by a reward." Similarly, Deci (1972) argues that money actually lowers employee motivation by reducing the "intrinsic rewards" that an employee receives from the job.

8. The discussion that follows is very basic because in most firms incentive pay is based on multiple performance metrics. For example, executives may receive 75 percent of their incentive pay based on financial results and 25 percent based on personal objectives. In other cases, incentive pay might be based on individual performance, financial performance, and strategic performance.

9. This incentive payout formula assumes that incentive pay will be equal to zero when actual performance is equal to zero. Many firms (e.g., Briggs and Stratton and Eli Lilly) use a bonus formula that allows them to either stop paying a bonus before the performance metric hits zero, or to pay out

a bonus even when the performance measure is negative. The modified incentive pay formula has the following general form:

$$\left(\begin{array}{c}\text{Incentive}\\\text{pay}\end{array}\right)_t = \left(\begin{array}{c}\text{Target}\\\text{bonus}\end{array}\right)_t \times \left[\frac{\left(\begin{array}{c}\text{Actual}\\\text{performance}\end{array}\right)_t - \left(\begin{array}{c}\text{Target}\\\text{performance}\end{array}\right)_t}{(\text{Leverage factor})_t}\right]$$

Note that where the (Leverage factor)$_t$ = (Target performance), this expression reduces to eq. (8.1).

10. For example, in 1999, Johnson & Johnson Medical used the following scheme to define its target percent of base pay for its incentive pool:

Base Salary	Target % of Base Pay
$64,000–$88,999	10
$89,000–$112,999	15
$113,000–$156,999	20

On the other hand, in 1999, Motel 6 set its incentive pay based on employee responsibilities and title. A manager had 10 percent of her base salary subject to incentive compensation, and a vice president had 25 percent subject to incentive compensation.

11. An alternative would have been to define the base pay as salary plus the target level of incentive compensation based upon the firm's achieving the target performance level. Using the latter approach, the base pay becomes the expected level of compensation (salary plus at-risk pay).

12. Incentive pay = $50,000 × 0.20 × 1.10 = $11,000, and total compensation = $50,000 + $11,000 = $61,000.

13. Implicit in our discussion is the assumption that the performance metric is bounded from below at zero.

14. Art Knight, CEO of Morgan Products, describes the problem as follows: "It used to be that our compensation plans for senior and divisional managers were tied, as so many plans are, to negotiated budgets—not to the enhancement of shareholder value. While meeting budget figures does enhance shareholder value, it may not give managers incentive to enhance value even more by going beyond budgeted numbers." (Edwards 1993)

15. The financial press concedes the practice by some managers of manipulating earnings to support their own gains (Bruns and Merchant 1990; Rich, Smith, and Mihalek 1990).

16. For a discussion of the calculation of sinking fund depreciation, see chapter 6.

17. We use the firm's 10 percent required rate of return to discount the managerial bonuses because the bonuses are contingent on the performance of the project. In addition, we set the pay-for-performance bonus equal to 1 percent of the chosen performance metric (EVA or CVA) for the period.

18. The manager does not have to leave the firm for the managerial horizon problem to arise. She may simply move to another operating unit or division where the performance of her current division does not affect her incentive compensation.

19. We use the term *decision horizon* to refer to the period of time over which the manager's compensation will be affected by a project (or firm). Gibbons and Murphy (1992) refer to this simply as the managerial horizon.

20. When asked whether there was a danger that managers would make short-sighted investment decisions to boost their EVA bonuses, CEO Tobias of Eli Lilly responded, "Yes. One of the things you never want to set up is a system where there's a great incentive to do something stupid in the short term. Theoretically you could lower your asset base and improve your EVA by depleting all your inventory. But then, come the first of next year, you'd have nothing to sell. . . . To make sure that kind of short-sighted decision making doesn't happen, we've set up something called a bonus bank that encourages managers to take a longer-term perspective." (Martin 1996)

21. Sometimes the bonus bank concept can be used in combination with another measure. For instance, if revenue growth is important (but secondary to the primary measure) a compensation system might be designed where a portion of the earned bonus (on a sliding scale) is banked if revenue growth goals are not attained.

22. Martin, Petty, and Rich (2000) show that by delaying the payout of bonuses a bonus bank system can actually exacerbate the problem associated with short managerial decision horizons.

23. We say "if managers believe" because there are many in the world of business who feel that stock prices are driven primarily by current earnings (as we discussed in chapter 3).

24. The proper use of stock options is a difficult task and a complete treatment of the topic is beyond the scope of this book. However, Rappaport (1999) provides an interesting overview of the problem. He argues that shareholder interests are best served when managers are rewarded for achieving superior returns (i.e., superior performance), such as returns that are better than the firm's industry peer group. Thus, if fixed exercise price options are used, managers are rewarded where their stock price rises because of superior performance or simply because of a rising market. Using premium-priced options, whereby the exercise price is set above the current stock price, does not eliminate this problem. Premium-priced options may serve as an incentive to push the price to higher levels, but the manager is rewarded if the stock price eventually rises above the exercise price even if her firm is a lagging performer whose share value simply follows a bull market. To resolve this problem a firm can tie the exercise price to an index reflecting "expected" return performance. For example, if the chosen index rises in value by 15 percent during the year, then the option exercise price is restruck 15 percent higher. Executives are likely to resist the use of index options because it makes it more difficult for them to realize a gain on their options.

25. To this point we have ignored stock- or equity-linked compensation payouts. For incentive systems based on these types of incentive payouts, the performance metric is stock price. We say more about this later.

26. Kole (1997) surveys the compensation contracts used in 371 of the 1980 *Fortune* 500 firms. She argues that the terms of stock option and restricted

stock plans, and the flexibility afforded the board of directors in negotiating with managers, varies systematically with the characteristics of the assets being managed. This variation, she argues, challenges researchers to incorporate the full richness of management contracts into their study of the incentive pay/performance relation.

Chapter 9

1. The formal arguments supporting this line of reasoning trace their roots back to the work of Robert Shiller (1981), who argued that stock prices were much too volatile to reflect changes in the fundamentals underlying a discounted cash flow model of equity prices. This article spawned a lengthy debate among financial economists.
2. See Kaplan and Ruback (1995) for the specifics of the research methodology.
3. The CAPV differs from the Modigliani and Miller (1963) valuation model only in that the interest tax savings in the former are discounted using the unlevered cost of equity, whereas in the latter the firm's borrowing rate is used.
4. Mean square error is defined as follows:

$$\frac{1}{n}\sum_{t=1}^{n} abs(Prediction_t - Realization_t)$$

and the mean absolute error is simply the average absolute difference in the predicted and realized values:

$$\frac{1}{n}\sum_{t=1}^{n} (Prediction_t - Realization_t)^2$$

Both these measures of forecast error avoid the problem of the canceling of positive and negative prediction errors that occurs where prediction errors are simply averaged.
5. EBITDA is earnings before interest, taxes, and depreciation and amortization expense. EBITDA serves as an approximation of firm cash flow for the period.
6. Kim and Ritter (1999) value IPOs using comparables and find very similar predictive accuracy.
7. Bernard (1994) is credited with coining the acronym EBO for the Edwards-Bell-Ohlson residual income valuation approach. Theoretical development of the model is found in Ohlson (1990; 1995) with earlier discussions found in Preinreich (1938) and Edwards and Bell (1961). We discussed the relation between this model and the standard DCF model in appendix 5A.
8. Dechow et al. (1999, p. 6) note that the residual income formulation of the dividend discounting model appeals to accountants because it focuses on accounting numbers; however, it provides no new empirical implications in and of itself. This equivalence suits our purposes because we are interested in whether discounted future cash flows can be used to predict observed stock prices.

9. $$\text{Average relative absolute prediction error} = \frac{1}{10}\sum_{j=1}^{10}\frac{|(\text{Market price})_j - (\text{DCF estimate})_j|}{(\text{Market price})_j}$$

10. R^2 represents the percent of the variance in actual stock prices that is explained by the predicted prices.

11. The EVA perpetuity model is uniquely defined for purposes of the analysis and is defined as follows, where c is the firm's weighted average cost of capital:

$$\text{Stern Stewart model price} = \frac{(\text{EVA}/c - \text{Debt})}{\text{Number of shares}}$$

The source for the BCG claims is Thomas (1993).

12. Market-adjusted returns are computed from CRSP data as a firm's twelve-month compounded stock return less the twelve-month compounded value-weighted marketwide return. To allow time for information contained in the firm's annual report to be fully reflected in market prices, a twelve-month nonoverlapping period ending three months after the firm's fiscal year-end is used.

13. Chen and Dodd (1998) reach similar conclusions. They find that accounting operating income exhibits a higher R^2 (0.062) with stock returns than residual income ($R^2 = 0.05$), which in turn has a higher R^2 (0.023) than EVA.

14. Over periods of ten years, accounting-based performance measures, including GAAP earnings, explain up to 60 percent or more of stock returns (see Easton, Harris, and Ohlson 1992).

15. Specifically, he calculated abnormal returns for each firm as the difference between monthly return and CRSP value-weighted market return.

16. The researchers identify their initial sample of economic profit plan adopters using a keyword search of the LEXIS/NEXIS database. The keywords used were economic value added, EVA, residual income, economic value management, economic profit, value based management, and market value added. They then eliminated regulated utilities and financial institutions and their holding companies. Further restricting the sample to firms on the Compustat Annual Research Database in the year of the plan adoption reduced the set of firms to fifty-one.

17. The matching nonadopting firms were selected so as to match the adopting firms based on industry affiliation, asset size, and normalized operating income similarities.

Chapter 10

1. As reported on the Stern Stewart & Co.'s home page (www.sternstewart.com).
2. The International Benchmarking Clearinghouse is a component of the American Productivity and Quality Center (APQC) and is located in Houston, Texas. The center was founded in 1977 as a nonprofit 501-C3 organization whose mission is to improve productivity and quality in the private and public sectors. The center has a staff of approximately 100, has

a governing board of directors, and has a budget of around $16 million. The Benchmarking Clearinghouse organizes and performs benchmarking studies whereby groups of independent corporations are brought together to share the costs and benefits of benchmarking efforts.

3. Excerpts and data in this profile are from Briggs & Stratton's corporate communications division and the site visit interview.

4. Excerpts and data in this profile are from *Hoover's Handbook of American Business 1995*, the CSX Corporation home page at http://www.csx.com, and the site visit interview.

5. Excerpts and data in this profile are from Harnischfeger's corporate communications 1996 fact sheet and the site visit interview.

6. Excerpts and data in this profile are from *Hoover's Handbook of American Business 1995*, National Semiconductor's publication *Inter National News*, and the site visit interview.

7. Excerpts and data in this profile are from Shell Oil's home page at http://www.shellus.com, and the site visit interview.

Index

accounting-based model
  adjusting data for CFROI and CVA, 113, 131–133
  vs. discounted cash flow, 7–8
  earnings measures, 36–40
  EVA proponent's view of, 87–88
  impact of EVA on, 86–87, 193
  and incentive compensation, 164, 174–175, 197
  limitations of, 8, 36–40, 50, 55, 193
  for predicting stock returns, 194–196
  residual income measures, 45–46
  RONA metric, 40–45
  straight-line depreciation, 135–138
  See also earnings measures
accounting profits, 80–81
activism. *See* institutional investor activism; private-sector activists
alignment, as compensation objective, 159
Amelio, Gilbert, 224
American Productivity and Quality Center (APQC), 10, 208
assets
  depreciating, 124–125, 131–132 (*see also* depreciation)
  inflation adjustments to gross, 132
  nondepreciating, 124
  value of nonoperating, 57
assets-to-sales relations, 59, 61, 72
AT&T, 190
  VBM experience of, 205–208

Baker, George P., 172, 173, 175
Bausch & Lomb, 86
Befumo, Randy, 55
Berkshire Hathaway, 100
Berle, Adolph, 5, 11
Biddle, Gary C., 194
Bierman, Harold, 42, 140, 141, 144, 146, 152, 153
board of directors
  insider-dominated, 22–23
  lopsided, 22
Boeing, 211
Boldt, Robert, 86
bonus plans, 159
  based on percent of EVA, 170–172
  bonus bank system, 168–170
  See also compensation programs
Boston Consulting Group (BCG), 9, 51, 111, 112, 113, 114, 115, 116, 117, 118,

121, 123, 125, 128, 129, 130, 131, 133, 140, 141, 144, 193, 215
Bowen, Robert M., 194
Briggs & Stratton, 86, 90, 208, 210, 218
  company profile, 220–221
budget-based performance standard, 174
Buffet, Warren, 49, 100
business unit performance, evaluating with RONA and ROS, 43–45

California Pension Protection Act, 26
California Public Employees Retirement System (CalPERS), 13, 17, 26
  effectiveness of activism of, 24–25
  and EVA, 86
  partnership with Enron, 23
  relationship investing of, 18, 19
  strategies of, 22
  targeting procedures of, 31–32
CAPITAL
  calculating, 89–98
  financing perspective for computing, 97–98
  in measuring EVA, 88–89
  operating perspective for computing, 98
Capital Asset Pricing Model, 65–66, 117, 185, 189
capital market focus, of measurement and reward, 6–7. *See also* compensation programs
CAPV. *See* Compressed Adjusted Present Value model
Carroll, Philip J., 225
cash flow return on investment (CFROI), 111, 113, 214
  adjusting data in, 131–133
  and asset life, 124–125
  computing Motorola's, 125–128
  and current dollar gross cash flow, 123
  and current dollar gross investment, 122–123
  defined, 116–117, 129–130, 144
  to evaluate project value, 144–146
  multi-period approach to measuring, 117–118, 127–128
  and nondepreciating assets, 124
  single-period approach to measuring, 118–121, 126–127
  and TBR metric, 113, 116
  and uneven cash flow projects, 149

243